■ The Alaska State Constitution

The Oxford Commentaries on the State Constitutions of the United States
G. Alan Tarr, Series Editor

Professor G. Alan Tarr, Director of the Center on State Constitutional Studies at Rutgers University, serves as General Editor for this important new series which in its entirety will cover each of the 50 states. Each volume of The Oxford Commentaries on the State Constitutions of the United States contains a historical overview of the state's constitutional development, plus a section-by-section analysis of the state's current constitution. Other features included in the volumes are the text of the state's constitution, a bibliographic essay, table of cases, and index. This series provides essential reference tools for those investigating state constitutional development and constitutional law.

The Alaska State Constitution

Gerald A. McBeath

Foreword by Tony Knowles

THE OXFORD COMMENTARIES ON THE STATE CONSTITUTIONS OF THE UNITED STATES

G. Alan Tarr, Series Editor

OXFORD
UNIVERSITY PRESS

OXFORD
UNIVERSITY PRESS

Oxford University Press, Inc., publishes works that further Oxford University's objective of excellence in research, scholarship, and education.

Oxford New York
Auckland Cape Town Dar es Salaam Hong Kong Karachi Kuala Lumpur Madrid Melbourne
Mexico City Nairobi New Delhi Shanghai Taipei Toronto

With offices in
Argentina Austria Brazil Chile Czech Republic France Greece Guatemala Hungary Italy
Japan Poland Portugal Singapore South Korea Switzerland Thailand Turkey Ukraine
Vietnam

Published by Oxford University Press, Inc.
198 Madison Avenue, New York, New York 10016

Library of Congress Cataloging-in-Publication Data

McBeath, Gerald A.
The Alaska State Constitution / Gerald A. McBeath; foreword by Tony Knowles.
p. cm. — (The Oxford commentaries on the state constitutions of the United States)
Includes bibliographical references and index.
ISBN 978-0-19-977829-4 (hardback)
1. Constitutions—Alaska. 2. Constitutional law—Alaska. 3.
Constitutional history—Alaska. I. Alaska. Constitution. II. Title.
KFA16011956.A6 M327 2011
342.79802—dc22 2011002404

Note to Readers
This publication is designed to provide accurate and authoritative information in regard to the subject matter covered. It is based upon sources believed to be accurate and reliable and is intended to be current as of the time it was written. It is sold with the understanding that the publisher is not engaged in rendering legal, accounting, or other professional services. If legal advice or other expert assistance is required, the services of a competent professional person should be sought. Also, to confirm that the information has not been affected or changed by recent developments, traditional legal research techniques should be used, including checking primary sources where appropriate.

(Based on the Declaration of Principles jointly adopted by a Committee of the American Bar Association and a Committee of Publishers and Associations.)

To my mother,
Astrid Hjelmeir McBeath,
and to the memory of my father,
Gordon Stanley McBeath

CONTENTS

■ SERIES FOREWORD

In 1776, following the declaration of independence from England, the former colonies began to draft their own constitutions. Their handiwork attracted widespread interest, and draft constitutions circulated up and down the Atlantic seaboard, as constitution-makers sought to benefit from the insights of their counterparts in sister states. In Europe, the new constitutions found a ready audience seeking enlightenment from the American experiments in self-government. Even the delegates to the Constitutional Convention of 1787, despite their reservations about the course of political developments in the states during the decade after independence, found much that was useful in the newly adopted constitutions. And when James Madison, fulfilling a pledge given during the ratification debates, drafted the federal Bill of Rights, he found his model in the famous Declaration of Rights of the Virginia Constitution.

By the 1900s, however, few people would have looked to state constitutions for enlightenment. Instead, a familiar litany of complaints was heard whenever state constitutions were mentioned. State constitutions were too long and too detailed, combining basic principles with policy prescriptions and prohibitions that had no place in the fundamental law of a state. By including such provisions, it was argued, state constitutions deprived state governments of the flexibility they needed to respond effectively to changing circumstances. This—among other factors—encouraged political reformers to look to the federal government, which was not plagued by such constitutional constraints, thereby shifting the locus of political initiative away from the states. Meanwhile, civil libertarians concluded that state bills of rights, at least as interpreted by state courts, did not adequately protect rights and therefore looked to the federal courts and the federal Bill of Rights for redress. As power and responsibility shifted from the states to Washington, so too did the attention of scholars, the legal community, and the general public.

During the early 1970s, however, state constitutions were "rediscovered." The immediate impetus for this discovery was former President Richard Nixon's appointment of Warren Burger to succeed Earl Warren as Chief Justice of the United States Supreme Court. To civil libertarians, this appointment seemed to signal a decisive shift in the Supreme Court's jurisprudence, because Burger was expected to lead the Court away from the liberal activism that had characterized the Warren Court. They therefore sought ways to safeguard the gains they had achieved for defendants, racial minorities, and the poor during Warren's tenure from erosion by the Burger Court. In particular, they began to look to state bills of rights to secure the rights of defendants and to support other civil-liberties claims that they advanced in state courts.

The "new judicial federalism," as it came to be called, quite quickly advanced beyond its initial concern to evade the mandates of the Burger Court. Indeed, less than two decades after it originated, it has become a nationwide phenomenon. For when judges and scholars turned their attention to state constitutions, they discovered an unsuspected richness. They found not only provisions that paralleled the federal Bill of Rights but also constitutional guarantees of the right to privacy and of gender equality, for example, that had no analogue in the U.S. Constitution. Careful examination of the text and history of state guarantees revealed important differences between even those provisions that most resembled federal guarantees and their federal counterparts. Looking beyond state declarations of rights, jurists and scholars discovered affirmative constitutional mandates to state governments to address such important policy concerns as education and housing. Taken altogether, these discoveries underlined the importance for the legal community of developing a better understanding of state constitutions.

Yet the renewed interest in state constitutions has not been limited to judges and lawyers. State constitutional reformers have renewed their efforts with notable success: since 1960, ten states have adopted new constitutions and several others have undertaken major constitutional revisions. These changes have usually resulted in more streamlined constitutions and more effective state governments. Also, in recent years political activists on both the left and the right have pursued their goals through state constitutional amendments, often enacted through the initiative process, under which policy proposals can be placed directly on the ballot for voters to endorse or reject. Scholars too have begun to rediscover how state constitutional history can illuminate changes in political thought and practice, providing a basis for theories about the dynamics of political change in America.

Gerald A. McBeath's fine study of the Alaska Constitution is the latest volume in the series, The Oxford Commentaries on the State Constitutions of the United States, which reflects this renewed interest in state constitutions and will contribute to our knowledge about them. Because the constitutional tradition of each state is distinctive, the volume begins with the history and development of the Alaska Constitution. It then provides the complete text of Alaska's current constitution, with each section accompanied by commentary that explains the provision and traces its origins and its interpretation by the courts and by other governmental bodies. For readers with a particular interest in a specific aspect of Alaska's constitutional experience, the book offers a bibliography of the most important sources dealing with the constitutional history and constitutional law of the state. Finally, the book concludes with a table of cases cited in the history and the constitutional commentary, as well as a subject index.

G. Alan Tarr

FOREWORD

The creation of a government is most often relegated to the history books and viewed across many generations. Alaskans have the good fortune that many of those who authored Alaska's state constitution are still living. We personally know many of those who took part. For all of us, however, Jerry McBeath's book allows us to see, feel, and understand an important event taking place so close to our lifetime.

"We the people of Alaska. . . ." These are simple words. Could the original framers of our state constitution have known they were embarking on a path that would culminate in the signing of the preeminent state constitution? Perhaps they did, because the 55 delegates to the constitutional convention, held at the University of Alaska during the chilly winter of 1955–1956, knew they had a momentous task before them: not just to write a constitution, but to prove to the reluctant U.S. Congress that Alaskans were ready for statehood. They did both.

Tolling tirelessly, these men and women—who should all be considered Alaskan heroes and heroines—were of diverse backgrounds. This diversity and sense of purpose are clearly reflected in the constitution itself. Professor Jerry McBeath's scholarly tracing of discussions at the Alaska Constitutional Convention brings to life the crucial moments in the territory's constitutional development and subsequent state history.

Today, 40 years after the signing, on February 5, 1956, Alaska's constitution stands as a shining example of simplicity, modernity, coherence, vision, and most important, accessibility. Delegates brought with them a wealth of experience in government and an understanding of how government affects the governed. Moreover, they wanted "good government," just as we all want the same today. Drawing on that drive and determination, the framers wrote a document that earned this headline in the local Fairbanks newspaper: "Convention's work hailed as 'model' by experts."

Historians note that the 1950s were a time of progressive reform in state governments and their constitutions. Our constitution is also a product of that reform, coupled with a healthy dose of the Alaskan pioneer spirit. Thus, our constitution is a model in many respects. As the 49th state, we were able to learn a great deal from the experience of the other 48.

By being among the last states to write a constitution, we now have the advantages of correcting the mistakes of others, simplicity, and the delegation of responsibility, which can be clearly seen by our citizens. Rather than expressing details, as did the constitutions of many states, ours set broad goals for the new state of Alaska. Details would come later during the legislative process.

The language of the constitution is highly readable, and therefore accessible to the reader—with no flowery words like whereas and wherefore to add heft without weight to the fifteen articles. Most important, the Alaska Constitution establishes a resilient framework for government authority based on strong, independent branches.

Relative to those in other states, Alaska's three branches have a distinct centralization of authority, each granting great potential power, within basic inherent limits, to those leaders wise and willing enough to assert it. The constitution bestows extensive powers to the chief executive. For example, Alaska is one of only three states in which the governor is the only elected official in the executive branch. Powers of reapportionment are vested solely with the executive branch—just to name a few.

However, as Alaska's eighth governor, I'm sure it is safe to say that the powers of the executive never seem quite strong enough when measured against a highly independent judicial branch and a legislature that is assertive and highly responsive to public opinion. Our framers were full of foresight in creating dynamic interbranch competition. Take my word for it—we have it. However, a basic American belief is that from competition comes the best products. It is just as true for public policy.

As mayor of Anchorage for two terms, I fully appreciated Article X, pertaining to local government. Our framers desired to move away from the antiquated county system that pervaded the Lower 48, which they replaced by a smaller number of local government units with broad powers. Few state constitutions even mention local governments, much less define "maximum local self-government." One example of what that means is that municipalities "may exercise all legislative powers not prohibited by law." Another purpose of this article, which was written to give municipalities wide opportunities to raise funds locally, is to "prevent duplication of tax-levying jurisdictions." As governor, I still see the wisdom of the adage that the best government is that which is closest to the people.

While a model, is Alaska's constitution perfect? Of course not. It swells and shrinks to reflect the times, already having evolved by amendment 24 times. Our framers could not have imagined the modern telecommunications tools now readily available to better inform the citizenry. We Alaskans are proud of the pioneer ideals embodied within our constitution and resolute in accomplishing precisely what the preamble states: "secure and transmit to succeeding generations our heritage of political, civil and religious liberty." I have sworn to support and defend these words, and I endeavor to ensure Alaskan families that they have safe, healthy communities, educational and economic opportunities, and a fair, fiscally disciplined state government.

Professor McBeath's commentary, which examines the interpretation of each article, section, and amendment, will enlighten those who seek to understand the Alaska Constitution.

Tony Knowles, Governor

■ ACKNOWLEDGMENTS

Three research assistants provided indispensable assistance to this project. Jennifer Brice and Martha Bristow pored over the minutes of the proceedings of the Alaska Constitutional Convention and sifted through mountains of newspaper records. Jake Ketscher searched methodically through hundreds of cases and statutes to ensure that our coverage was complete. For support of their work, I gratefully thank the Office of Faculty Development and the Dean's Office of the College of Liberal Arts, both at the University of Alaska Fairbanks. Finally, Linda Ilgenfritz, administrative assistant in the Department of Political Science, assisted in the production of the manuscript in ways too numerous to mention; meeting deadlines without her help would have been impossible.

A number of colleagues and friends have provided immeasurable assistance to my developing understanding of the Alaska Constitution: Thomas A. Morehouse, Professor Emeritus, University of Alaska Anchorage; Gordon S. Harrison, Director, Alaska Legislative Research Agency; Claus-M. Naske and Terrence Cole, Professors of History, and Fae Korsmo, Associate Professor of Political Science, University of Alaska Fairbanks; Niilo Koponen, Alaska State Legislature (retired); and Andrew Kleinfeld, U.S. Circuit Court Judge. I also gratefully thank G. Alan Tarr, Professor of Political Science, Rutgers University, Camden, and series editor for Reference Guides to the State Constitutions of the United States, who has patiently shepherded my work on this project, and Nita Romer of Greenwood Press. Any remaining mistakes and omissions are my responsibility.

The Alaska Humanities Forum provided a research grant to support the project in its final year, for which I am deeply appreciative.

PART ONE

The History of the Alaska Constitution

Alaska's model constitution is a political response to the weakness of territorial government institutions, which was crafted at a time of progressive reform in basic state laws. It is a powerful outline of government powers expressed in simple, spare terms.

This part chronicles constitutional development in Alaska, examining in detail the political, structural, and legal processes through which that development occurred. It also assesses the results of constitutional engineering in Alaska.

THE COLONIAL AND TERRITORIAL EXPERIENCE

When the framers of the Alaska Constitution met in 1955, they were strongly influenced by Alaska's 88 years as an American colony and territory. Many residents perceived these as years of neglect by the U.S. government and exploitation and abuse by powerful interests outside Alaska.

Colonial Rule (1867–1912)

Few settlements existed for the United States to occupy when it purchased Alaska in 1867. In the first fifteen years of American rule, fewer than 3,000 non-Natives lived in Alaska. As far as the rest of the country was concerned, no compelling reason existed to defend the area and provide it with law. A few hundred soldiers guarded the colony of Alaska for the first ten years.[1] The army departed in 1877 because of jurisdictional problems, matters of economy, and the need to redistribute manpower strength for the Sioux campaigns in the Dakota Territory. In place of the army, a customs collector was left in charge. The only U.S. laws extended to Alaska concerned commerce, navigation, and the prohibition of liquor sales and imports.[2]

In 1879, settlers in the town of Sitka called on the U.S. government for help in their defense against the Tlingit Indians. They feared another uprising such as the one that occurred in 1802, when Tlingit warriors killed over 100 Russian and Aleut men, stole 3,000 pelts, and left the settlement in ashes.[3] When the navy dallied over sending a vessel, Sitka residents appealed to the British for protection. As a result, the U.S. Navy arrived several months after a British warship. This event is representative of the federal government's neglect of Alaska in the early years.

Gradually, the Caucasian population increased as new settlers exploited the salmon runs and gold mines of southeast Alaska. The increase of the settler population without a corresponding network of government services created tension and conflict. Settlers, organized in self-governing "miner's meetings" on the New England model, developed local ordinances and elected a recorder of claims. They employed "miners' law" to protect claim staking and mete out rough, frontier justice. Miners petitioned Congress, sending a delegation to Washington, D.C., in 1881. Congress responded by passing the Organic Act of 1884, which was a simple and cheap—but only temporary—way to end military rule and institute civil government.[4]

The legislation made Alaska a judicial district, which was a limbo between colonial and territorial status. As a judicial district, Alaska would have a governor appointed by the president, a district court judge, and a tiny law enforcement staff. It had no legislature and no representative in Congress. The act also extended where applicable the laws of Oregon, then the closest state (Washington was still a territory) to the new district.[5] Like the Treaty of Cession, the First

[1] Citations to the *Minutes of the Daily Proceedings of the Alaska Constitutional Convention* (Juneau: Alaska Legislative Council, 1965), abbreviated as *PACC*, appear throughout the text.

[2] Ernest Gruening, *The State of Alaska*, 2d ed. (New York: Random House, 1968), 36.

[3] A. I. Alekseev, *The Destiny of Russia-America, 1774–1867* (Fairbanks: Limestone Press, 1990), 124. Then, British captain Henry Barber, in the *Unicorn*, saved a handful of Russians and Aleuts, but demanded 50,000 rubles in ransom (and received 10,000 in furs from company leader Alexander Baranov).

[4] Ted Hinckley, *The Americanization of Alaska* (Palo Alto, CA: Pacific Books, 1972), 153–156.

[5] The Oregon Code was based on the New York Code, which in turn reflected Dutch (i.e., Roman) law, and which contrasted with English common law, familiar to most Americans.

Organic Act recognized Native rights to land they occupied "from time immemorial," but left the disposition of these rights to a future Congress.[6]

With the discovery of vast riches of placer gold in the Klondike in 1896, a massive gold rush took place, which overwhelmed Alaska's bare-bones governmental structure. Congress responded with a variety of actions, most notably, legislation modifying the First Organic Act. In 1898, Congress extended the Homestead Act to Alaska, providing an incentive for more stable settlement. The following year, lawmakers revised the Oregon Code on criminal procedure to better fit Alaska conditions. In addition, they levied taxes on businesses to support education. In 1900, Congress adopted a civil code and added two judicial districts to accommodate the doubling of the population that followed the gold rush.[7] Congress also moved the capital from Sitka to Juneau in 1906. Finally, it provided for the incorporation of towns and permitted property taxes; it did, however, limit the rate to 1 percent and forbade borrowing.[8] Five years later, the Nelson Act established schools for Native Alaskans while directing license fees collected outside towns to go to road building, care of the insane, and education. Then, in direct response to pressures from Alaskans who demanded representation along with their taxation, Congress in 1906 granted Alaska a nonvoting delegate in Congress.

The delegate's post proved critical to the development of home rule for Alaska. The third elected delegate, James Wickersham (a former Alaska district court judge), lobbied for Alaska interests and fought tirelessly for an elected territorial legislature and mine inspection laws. Wickersham eventually won home rule for Alaska with the passage of the Organic Act of 1912, which was known as the Second Organic Act. However, Wickersham's role was ambiguous, for the restrictions of this act—drafted largely by Wickersham—were later blamed for withholding full territorial government from Alaska.

Territorial Era (1912–1958)

Alaskans expected that the establishment of territorial government would enable them to rule themselves independently and proceed with fast and orderly resource development. They gained some rights of citizenship, but could not vote in federal elections. Alaskans could elect their own legislators, who met in

---

[6] See Claus-M. Naske, "The Shaky Beginnings of Alaska's Judicial System," *Western Legal History* 1, no. 2 (Summer/Fall 1988): 163–210; and also his "The First Organic Act of 1884 Creates a Judicial System," in *A History of the Alaska Federal District Court System, 1884–1959, and the Creation of the State Court System* (Juneau: Alaska Court System, July 1995).

[7] The 1899 Criminal Code and 1990 Civil Code were the first codes that Congress ever enacted for a territory.

[8] Claus-M. Naske and Herman Slotnick, *Alaska, A History of the Forty-Ninth State*, 2d ed. (Norman: University of Oklahoma Press, 1987), 86–87.

biennial sessions in the new capital of Juneau; however, the legislature's powers and fiscal authority were strictly limited.

In a flurry of activity at the first session in 1913, the territorial legislature proclaimed its autonomy. It gave women the right to vote; developed labor legislation establishing the eight-hour work day and regulating mining conditions; granted aid to schools and set up a territorial board of education; and gave some self-government rights to Native villages in southeast Alaska.

In the opinion of critics, such as territorial governor Ernest Gruening (1939–1953), however, territorial status did not significantly enhance the self-governing abilities of Alaskans. Gruening and others were correct in that the federal government had a history of treating territories shabbily. Like other former colonies, Alaska's law-making powers were circumscribed by Congress, which could veto any legislative act. America's expanded involvement in world affairs during the early twentieth century limited federal scrutiny of Alaska.

The critics proved right in their assessment of the obstacles erected to self-rule in Alaska. The people lacked the right to elect their territorial governor. Alaska had no judiciary of its own to handle conflict in the territory or its localities. All courts were federal. The congressional "Alaska lobby" of mining and fishing interests, most of which were controlled by Outside corporations, added a clause to the Second Organic Act forbidding the territorial legislature any jurisdiction over fish and game or over the settlement and management of Alaska lands. Moreover, the territory was denied the power to set up county governments, borrow money, or raise taxes on property. The legislature did have the authority to enact a tax code, but it did not elect to do so until 1949.

Overall, during the three decades of territorial rule leading up to World War II, Alaskans' expectations for economic development and government services were not met. However, the federal government probably did much more for Alaska than its small population warranted. For example, from 1915 to 1923, the federal government constructed the Alaska Railroad to support coal and other mining; it also established Anchorage as a center for development and linked the interior and south-central regions of the territory.[9]

With the onset of the air age and Japan's increasingly aggressive behavior in Asia, Alaska's strategic significance became key, and as a result, the role of the federal government in the territory became pronounced. As world hostilities developed, Alaska became the geopolitical prize of the United States. By the early 1940s, military planners for America's Pacific campaign had sketched a large role for Alaska, one result of which was another population boom.

Through wartime planning, mobilization, and action, Alaska's military population peaked at 152,000 in 1943. The territory's civilian population increased

[9] See Claus-M. Naske, "Some Attention, Little Action: Vacillating Federal Efforts to Provide Territorial Alaska with an Economic Base," *Western Historical Quarterly* 26, no. 1 (Spring 1995): 37–68.

by 50 percent, reaching 112,000 in 1950. From 1941 through 1945, the federal government spent over $1 billion in Alaska, and the onset of the Cold War in 1947 brought new growth in the military presence. Not until the mid-1950s did military spending begin to decline from its peak of $513 million in 1953.

THE ALASKA STATEHOOD MOVEMENT

Historians point to several dates as the beginning of the Alaska statehood movement. As early as 1916, Delegate Wickersham submitted the first statehood bill to Congress; while on his visit to Alaska in 1923, President Warren Harding said that Alaska was destined for ultimate statehood. For two decades, however, the call met only indifference from federal bureaucrats and members of Congress.

Anthony J. Dimond, Alaska's delegate to Congress from 1933 to 1944, introduced the first serious statehood bill in 1943. One year later, Dimond turned over his post to a son of Alaska pioneers, E. L. (Bob) Bartlett, who proved an even stronger advocate in Washington. Before the delegates could make significant progress in the nation's capital, however, statehood advocates had to coalesce support at home. Territorial governor Ernest Gruening proposed an information campaign and a territorial referendum. A private group commissioned Juneau journalist George Sundborg to write a pamphlet, "Statehood for Alaska," which presented a persuasive case. In 1946, by a 3-to-2 margin in a territorial referendum, Alaskans supported the concept.[10] From 1946 until 1959, when Alaska won statehood, the territorial legislature consistently called on Congress to grant first-class status.

The relevant federal department, Interior, expressed support for statehood in 1945. Public opinion nationwide supported it as well, as a 1946 Gallup poll indicated. Hearings in the U.S. House of Representatives in 1948 also reflected favorably on statehood. A year later, the territorial legislature reformed Alaska's tax laws, instituting an income tax that later proved influential in the campaign.[11]

Also in 1949, the legislature formed the Alaska Statehood Committee, which was headed by Robert Atwood, publisher of the territory's largest newspaper, the *Anchorage Times*. The committee's objective was to ignite both territorial and national support for the idea of Alaska statehood. It made preparations for the constitutional convention, planned for the transition from territorial to state government, and lobbied the Congress for a reenactment of enabling legislation. In March 1950, the U.S. House of Representatives passed an Alaska statehood

[10] Naske and Slotnick, *Alaska, A History of the Forty-Ninth State*, 145–147.

[11] Ibid., 147.

bill, but movement stalled at that point as the Korean War pushed Alaska's statehood campaign to the back burner.

The war was not the only complication, however. There were at least three other major issues hobbling statehood efforts, the first of which was a disagreement about the statehood land grant. Bills in Congress up to mid-1950 specified that the traditional land-grant method be used (which gave new states small land grants and had specific township-section requirements), and that grants be limited to a total of 20 to 45 million acres. This scheme would have scattered state holdings throughout Alaska in a patchwork pattern. Winston C. Arnold testified in congressional hearings that the land transfer and natural resource provisions, among others, "would doom the new state to perpetual pauperism and bureaucratic control."[12] The second issue involved the composition of the U.S. Senate. With Democrats and Republicans nearly evenly divided, the admission of a new state would have political ramifications. Because Alaska had voted Democratic since the 1932 presidential election, Republicans and conservative Democrats, who saw the 1950s as pivotal years for civil rights legislation, felt threatened. Reporter John Morley had this to say in the June 24, 1953, edition of the *Pacific Palisades Post* of Santa Monica, California:

> This reporter discovered in Washington (what informed Alaskans already know) that statehood does not entirely hinge on Alaska's "right to be a state[[,"]] . . . on its "peoples' preference" . . . or in "the ability to finance state government," but also on important political implications. Right now the "word" I heard going around Washington's "cloak rooms" on Alaska statehood can be summed up in one sentence: The Republicans fear that statehood may bring Washington two Democratic senators and one Democratic representative. On the determination of that question, probably more than any other, it seems to this reporter, the fate of Alaska's statehood rests today.[13]

The third issue was momentum. The last territory admitted to statehood was Arizona in 1912, and a special push seemed necessary to overcome congressional inertia.

Events over the next few years brought closure to the statehood issues. By 1954, the size and nature of the Alaska statehood land grant had been resolved. Alaska was to use a new formula, which recognized the need for land dispersal without a rigid observance of section lines in order to spur development, and both the House and Senate versions of the statehood bill proposed grants of some 100 million acres. The linkage of the Alaska and Hawaii statehood campaigns settled the political issue. Unlike Alaska, Hawaii had voted Republican in

---

[12] Quoted in ibid., 152.

[13] Carroll V. Glines, "America's Press and the Battle for Statehood" (Master's thesis, American University, Washington, DC, 1969), 74.

previous elections. The entry of two new states, of which one was Republican and one Democratic, would not alter the Senate's partisan balance. The issue of political momentum was completely resolved, largely through the calling of a constitutional convention in 1955, which helped demonstrate Alaska's ability to manage its own affairs and accelerated the campaign for statehood.

By the time the U.S. House of Representatives voted in 1958, the margin of support for Alaska statehood had widened. Within a month, the Senate assented. Editorials in the *New York Times, Washington Post, Chicago Sun-Times,* and other newspapers endorsed statehood, as did many groups such as the American Political Science Association, labor unions, chambers of commerce, Jaycees, Kiwanis Clubs, Veterans of Foreign Wars (VFW) posts, and the legislatures of several western states.[14]

Ultimately, few interests opposed statehood. Mining and fishing groups feared that state government would increase the regulation of economic development activity, but their arguments failed to sway either the Senate or President Dwight D. Eisenhower, although initially, he had seen no reason to create a state from a vast and largely unpopulated area whose greatest value, it seemed, was in national defense. Reservations aside, however, Eisenhower signed the statehood bill in July 1958, and Alaska entered the union on January 3, 1959.

ROLE OF THE CONSTITUTIONAL CONVENTION

As the statehood movement stalled in Washington in the early 1950s, its leaders looked for ways to reignite the cause. One strategy that surfaced was to hold a constitutional convention as a reasoned and deliberate action of responsible citizens who were worthy of self-government.[15] At least part of the impetus for the convention came from halfway across the Pacific Ocean, as noted by Victor Fischer, who served as a convention delegate:

> The fact that Hawaii had held a state constitutional convention in 1950 was a consideration in this decision. Since the issues of Alaska and Hawaii statehood were repeatedly being intertwined, there appeared to be some logic in Alaska also writing its constitution and thus being on a par with Hawaii. Even though its constitution had not brought Hawaii statehood, Alaskans believed they had nothing to lose by making a move on their own.[16]

---

[14] Ernest Gruening, *The Battle for Alaska Statehood* (College: University of Alaska Press, 1967), 74.

[15] One of the early proponents of holding a constitutional convention before statehood was the "All-Alaska League for a State Constitution," which developed in Fairbanks under the chairmanship of Dr. James T. Ryan, Fairbanks Superintendent of Schools and former territorial commissioner of education in the Gruening administration. I am indebted to Niilo Koponen for this observation.

[16] Victor Fischer, *Alaska's Constitutional Convention* (Fairbanks: University of Alaska Press, 1975), 11–12.

The concept of writing a constitution before statehood received a well-timed and unintended endorsement when a high-ranking federal official visited the territory in 1954. Secretary of the Interior Douglas McKay, who was a known opponent of statehood, criticized Alaskans in a visit to Anchorage, "telling them to 'start acting like ladies and gentlemen' and to come to Washington with 'hat in hand' rather than demand statehood as a right."[17]

In addition to the convention, statehood leaders found another strategy to win the support of Congress—the Tennessee Plan. Under this plan, Alaskans would elect a congressional delegation and send it to Washington to lobby for statehood. Tennessee had become a state in just over two months by employing this method in 1796, and other states had successfully followed suit. However, support for the Tennessee Plan was not widespread until the constitutional convention. A New Orleans businessman named George Lehleitner came to Alaska before the convention to give a sales pitch for the Tennessee Plan. In his presentation to convention delegates, he congratulated them for their dedication but urged them to look beyond the drafting of a constitution: "'Hawaii,' he pointed out, 'had drafted a fine constitution' but that document 'has been collecting dust in the Hawaiian archives building for almost six years.'"[18] After Bob Bartlett, Alaska's delegate to Congress, telegrammed his support of the Tennessee Plan, the convention delegates set to adapting it to Alaska's situation.

THE STATE CONSTITUTIONAL REFORM MOVEMENT

Two trends influenced the environment in which the Alaska Constitution was written. The first was a strengthening of federalism in reaction to the New Deal centralization of government authority and services. President Eisenhower in 1953 called for an investigation of state-federal relations, and appointed Chicago businessman Meyer Kestenbaum to head a commission on intergovernmental relations. It conducted the first broad-ranging review of national, state, and local relations since the adoption of the U.S. Constitution. One of the commission's recommendations was a call for state constitutional renewal in order to give greater energy to states in the federal system.[19]

The second trend, which emerged in the early 1930s, was a focus on the reform of state constitutions. Many state governments were hobbled by excessively detailed constitutions that inhibited their ability to address popular needs. The reform movement emphasized shortening and simplifying state

[17] Ibid., 12.

[18] Quoted in Gerald Bowkett, *Reaching for a Star* (Fairbanks and Seattle: Epicenter Press, 1989), 79.

[19] Gerald A. McBeath and Thomas A. Morehouse, *Alaska Politics and Government* (Lincoln: University of Nebraska Press, 1994), 117.

constitutions, as well as clarifying the powers of executives and legislatures to enable them to direct state policy making more effectively.[20]

The National Municipal League, whose offices were in *New York City*, took the lead in championing reform. It published a *Model State Constitution*, which was developed by lawyers, political scientists, and legislators and executives who were experienced in state government.[21] This document was a major source of ideas in the development of Alaska's constitution.

PRELIMINARIES TO THE CONSTITUTIONAL CONVENTION

The 1954 territorial elections brought Democrats into control of the House and Senate, and their first action during the 1955 legislative session was to issue a call for a constitutional convention. Before the session began, Juneau attorney and Alaska House member Thomas Stewart traveled to the contiguous 48 states to interview political scientists and lawmakers on enabling legislation and on procedural aspects of the Tennessee Plan. As chair of the House Constitutional Convention Committee, Stewart wrote and filed an enabling House bill (HB 1), as did the chair of the Senate committee, William Egan (SB 1).

Discussion of this legislation focused on the site of the convention, when it should be held, and how delegates should be elected. Initially, territorial legislators were disposed to hold the convention in the territorial capital, Juneau. Adequate facilities for holding the convention were available in Juneau, and as the center of territorial government, the site seemed most convenient. Stewart and other legislators, however, proposed that the convention be held on the University of Alaska campus outside Fairbanks, in Interior Alaska. They argued that this site would be removed from the influence of lobbyists and the normal pattern of government (including Juneau's bar scene). Additionally, they referred to the successful New Jersey constitutional convention of 1948, which was held in New Brunswick, at the site of Rutgers University. Conducting a constitutional convention in a university setting, they argued, would lend an academic air to the proceedings, thus removing the event from the arena of politics as usual. The Fairbanks site won out.

Initially, convention backers suggested that the meeting should run 60 days during the winter. Legislators modified this proposal by extending the schedule to 75 days, starting in November 1955 and ending in February 1956. The new schedule also included a two-week intercession break over the holidays so delegates could hold hearings on convention progress in their home communities.

---

[20] Gordon S. Harrison, *Alaska's Constitution: A Citizen's Guide*, 3d ed. (Juneau: Alaska Legislative Research Agency, 1992), 7.

[21] National Municipal League, *Model State Constitution*, 5th ed. (New York, 1954).

Considerable attention was devoted to selecting delegates. At the time, territorial legislators were selected from within Alaska's four judicial districts, which had been reapportioned just after the 1950 census. Elections were held at-large, and residents of the territory's population centers (Anchorage, Fairbanks, and Juneau) were overrepresented in the legislature, at the expense of residents of small towns and villages.

Convention proponents recommended having 55 delegates, the same number that had crafted the U.S. Constitution. Not only did this lend historical legitimacy to the process, proponents said, but such a small number of delegates would allow more open, face-to-face discussion during proceedings. Having settled on a 55-member body, organizers developed an election proposal that won support from the territorial legislature. The plan provided that seven of the delegates would be selected at-large from the territory, a facet designed to advance the selection of notables (including participants in the Alaska statehood movement) and those with less parochial interests. Fifteen delegates would be selected from newly created single-member districts, while the rest of the delegates (33) would be chosen by election districts carved within the judicial districts.[22] This scheme was hailed as more representative than any that had previously been used in the territory for the selection of government officials.

The territorial legislature provided a generous grant of $300,000 to pay for the constitutional convention. This covered per diem expenses and travel for the delegates and provided $75,000 for technical assistance from the Public Administration Service (PAS), an organization that supplied consultation services to state and local governments.[23] PAS provided detailed reports to each of the convention's committees, where influential drafts were prepared.

CAMPAIGNS FOR DELEGATE SEATS

The territory scheduled a special election for convention delegates for September 13, 1955. The races were nonpartisan, and 171 candidates filed for the election. Among the candidates were some of the strongest advocates for Alaska statehood, including Mildred Hermann, one of the territory's two female lawyers and the secretary of the Alaska Statehood Committee. Other committee members running for convention seats included Frank Peratrovich, Victor Rivers, and Warren Taylor.

The low-key campaigns emphasized where candidates stood on statehood. The turnout for this special election was low. Most races were not close, and tended

---

[22] The idea was developed by Niilo Koponen and passed at an All-Alaska League meeting in Fairbanks.

[23] Fischer, *Alaska's Constitutional Convention*, 49.

to reflect the "friends-and-neighbors" flavor of territorial politics. One legal issue that temporarily clouded campaigns was whether members of the territorial legislature could hold seats as delegates as the territorial charter forbade members of the territorial government from holding another "position of profit" within the territory. The question was resolved in federal court, allowing legislators to serve as delegates. At the 35th reunion of the Alaska Constitutional Convention, delegate George Sundborg gave this inventory of the people who had served in the convention:

> We were 49 men and six women. Eight had been born in Alaska and one in the Yukon Territory. Cumulatively, we had spent 1,512 years in Alaska, an average of about 27½ years per delegate. And talk about the practical experience! Among our numbers were 15 businessmen, 12 lawyers, three commercial fishermen, two miners, two bush pilots, two preachers, a banker, transferman, grocer, town planner, wildlife agent, public relations man, policeman, architect, geologist, newspaperman and, surprisingly, five druggists. We also had five otherwise unclassified ladies who resented being called housewives. At the insistence of ½delegate] Ada Wien, we will call them homemakers.[24]

Most of the delegates had political experience in Alaska, including sixteen as legislators, nine as mayors, and ten on city councils. In addition, three delegates had served as U.S. commissioners, and four had been elected to local school boards. Ralph Rivers, an attorney and former mayor of Fairbanks, also was a former elected attorney general of Alaska.[25] The delegates' collective experience in territorial government helped expedite convention deliberations.

ORGANIZATION AND LEADERSHIP OF THE CONVENTION

Delegates converged at the University of Alaska on November 8, 1955. Former territorial governor Ernest Gruening made an opening address, decrying Alaska's colonial status:

> If there has been one important ingredient missing in our 88 years as a district, as a territory, it is that little preposition "by." Many things have been done for us; even more things have been done to us, but very little have we been permitted to do by us. (*Minutes of the Daily Proceedings of the Alaska Constitutional Convention* [hereafter PACC], 1839–1840)

---

[24] George Sundborg, "Who We Were: A Tribute to My Fellow Delegates" (Speech given at the 35th Reunion of the Alaska Constitutional Convention, April 26, 1991, Juneau).

[25] Fischer, *Alaska's Constitutional Convention*, 23.

These comments were followed by a sales pitch by *Anchorage Times* publisher Robert Atwood, who was an active member of the Alaska Statehood Committee:

> You are about to write a document that will be much more than a framework for the state government of Alaska. The document you write will be, can and should be a compelling new argument for statehood itself. The first use your product will be put to will be the nature of salesmanship. It must be presented to the people of Alaska, sort of as a list of specifications of a thing they have already decided they want to buy. They will scrutinize it as they would a warranty deed if they were purchasing a piece of property or a guarantee if it's a manufactured item. If they like it they will buy it. They are not obligated that way. This is a custom job you have on your hands. It's to be built and it must please the customer. (*PACC*, 8)

Preliminary work by the Public Administration Service included the preparation of detailed analyses on sections of the model constitution, as well as analyses of the process of conducting a convention. The first critical action was the selection of the convention's presiding officer and secretary. The delegates chose Mildred Hermann as the temporary presiding officer. Four delegates ran for the permanent position, and on the third ballot, William Egan, a former Valdez shopkeeper and a member of the territorial senate, was elected. Egan proved an excellent choice, as he was liked by all the delegates, was assertive without being perceived as aggressive, and was persistent to a fault. He also had an impeccable sense of timing, which proved of great value in reaching closure on the major issues before the convention.

With the exception of two areas, the delegates followed the PAS proposal on committee organization. Egan selected experienced political leaders to chair the committees. Each committee also had a consultant available during its deliberations. The Rules Committee and Style and Drafting Committee kept a tight rein over the process and products of committee work.

ISSUES OF GOVERNMENT AND POLICY AT THE CONSTITUTIONAL CONVENTION

Discussion and debate at the Alaska Constitutional Convention focused on three major areas: citizen rights and liberties, the design and powers of government institutions, and special issues of Alaska statehood. In most instances, these issues were either resolved with language in the constitution itself or clearly assigned to the legislature.

Citizen Rights and Liberties

Two issues of voting qualifications occupied several days of the convention delegates' time and generated some heated discussion. The initial article proposed by the judiciary committee required voters to be able to read and speak English. Delegates considered strengthening this statement by requiring that voters should also be able to write English—a suggestion that was not accepted. The only Native Alaskan delegate, Frank Peratrovich of Klawock, was instrumental in changing the article's original language from "reading *and* speaking" to "reading *or* speaking." (This prerequisite was eliminated by a constitutional amendment in 1970.)

The second voting qualification issue concerned the age of suffrage. The original proposal called for the voting age of 20. Discussion and debate focused on lowering the age to 18, with arguments stressing that by that age, youth were finished with high school and men were available for military conscription. Because all states then gave suffrage to youth at age 21 and delegates did not want to upset Congress by being too innovative, there was insufficient support for this proposal. However, delegates reached a compromise, setting the voting age at 19.

The role of direct citizen involvement in government generated one of the most intense debates of the convention. One camp, whose members possessed a healthy distrust of the legislature and lobbyists, strongly supported the right of citizens to use the initiative, referendum, and recall. The other camp included those who wanted to limit these rights in the interest of preserving the republican form of government and to avoid hobbling the executive and legislative branches with excessive restrictions. The cost of special elections generated by initiative, referendum, and recall raised concern also, but delegates circumvented this concern by voting to place initiative and referendum questions on the general election ballot. Toward the end of the discussion, debate focused on the percentage of electoral signatures needed to put an initiative, referendum, or recall matter before the public. Delegates agreed to require signatures "equal in number to ten percent of those who voted in the preceding general election" (*PACC*, 36).

The final issues of citizen rights reflected two concerns—sexual equality and personal liberties (particularly privacy). When delegates were discussing the provisions against discrimination in the Declaration of Rights, a few proposed that women's rights be spelled out. Most of the female delegates were against the idea, however. Mildred Hermann said that the neutral noun "person" used throughout the constitution gave adequate protection for women's rights. She noted that Alaska, as one of the first political subdivisions under the American flag to grant suffrage to women, had a good record on this matter: "I think Alaska as a territory and even before it had a legislature amply provided for the political and civil rights of its women and we have nothing at all to complain about in those respects" (*PACC*, 1292). Delegates agreed and left the specific protection of sexual equality out of the constitution (until it was amended by the voters in 1972 to prohibit discrimination based on sex).

A related discussion concerned the right of privacy of Alaskans. Two of the delegates introduced proposals specifically prohibiting the use in court of evidence obtained through wiretapping, and they were supported by a number of delegates who made reference to the wiretapping provisions of several states in the Joseph McCarthy era. This debate raised two issues: Was it necessary to make legislative-type recommendations in the state's basic law? Moreover, was the record of civil liberties in Alaska such that specific constitutional prohibitions were essential? Most delegates believed that this language was not needed for either reason. (In 1972, however, voters amended the constitution to add an explicit right to privacy.) The discussion and debate in the area of citizen rights reflected the delegates'support for self-government and independence, as moderated by their realism.

A significant omission in the citizen rights article was any mention of Alaska Native rights. A few delegates did want to grant constitutional land rights to Natives. However, the majority sense was that the issue was too complex to resolve quickly, and that it was primarily a federal responsibility. Therefore, the general provisions section of the Constitution (Article XII) disclaimed rights to lands "held by or for" Natives and recognized that Congress ultimately held the power to dispose of these lands.[26]

Institutional Design

Delegates considered at some length the design and construction of each of the three branches of government. They tended to rely on committee recommendations, but issues emerged concerning the recruitment of officials to Alaska government positions, the administrative arrangement of the institution, and the powers and interrelationships of institutions.

The initial issue before the legislature was innovative: should the state legislature be unicameral or bicameral? Alaska's sparse population suggested the practicality of a unicameral legislative body, and the delegates addressed the subject in prolonged debate on the convention floor. It quickly became clear, however, that a majority of the delegates supported the bicameral system then prevailing in the territory and all states except Nebraska. Delegate Dora Sweeney pointed out that resolutions to develop a unicameral legislature for the territory of Alaska had failed. Stating the argument that tipped the scales in favor of a bicameral legislature, she said:

> I think we have to reckon with the fact that we must get approval of a unicameral legislature if that is what we put in the constitution and there is a question in my mind whether you can get that and whether you can get it from the people of Alaska and Congress too. (*PACC*, 437)

[26] McBeath and Morehouse, *Alaska Politics and Government*, 130.

Another area of discussion concerned legislative salaries and length of legislative sessions. Delegates debated whether legislators should get a high rate of pay for per diem and stipends, reflecting the interest of some delegates in legislative professionalism, or whether legislators should remain "amateurs," receiving limited support for their public duties. A related issue was whether the sessions of the legislature should be biennial or annual, and if annual, whether they should be limited in length. Although there were scattered comments endorsing limited legislative pay and session length, the consensus of the delegates was that these areas should not be specified in the constitution. This expressed the belief that Alaska should have a professional legislature, and that it should be able to determine the compensation and activity period of its members without specific constitutional restrictions.

Finally, delegates devoted a good deal of attention to issues of legislative apportionment. The most novel feature of the reapportionment system advanced by the committee—that the governor should reapportion the legislature, based on the recommendation of a reapportionment board selected by him or her—received almost no discussion or debate. This may have resulted from agreement with PAS reports pointing out the problems in having legislatures reapportion themselves. The debate on reapportionment focused on what criteria should be considered in creating legislative districts, and how these criteria should be weighted. Among the competing interests were highly populated urban areas, sparsely populated regions, and distinctive aboriginal cultures. The reapportionment article to the constitution reflects a compromise of these interests by apportioning the House based on population, and the Senate based on geography. The compromise briefly protected Alaska Native interests, as most Natives then resided in rural areas. (In 1965, Alaska reconfigured its electoral districts to conform to the U.S. Supreme Court's "one-person, one-vote" stricture.) This delicate balance was maintained largely through the careful efforts of the convention's Committee on Suffrage, Elections and Apportionment. Committee chair John Hellenthal explained the committee's rationale to fellow delegates this way:

> Now an analysis was made of the present judicial divisions which . . . have guided Alaskans in their history in [their] senate, and the Committee, after that analysis and studying it, believed that the major criticism, among others of the judicial divisions, was that it permitted a situation to develop . . . where frequently . . . those hinterland countries were left to the voting strength of the urban areas, and frequently a definite tendency, the senators were chosen from the urban areas of Alaska, and the committee felt definitely that that situation should be avoided. (*PACC*, 1839–1840)

Much of the discussion on the Alaska executive related to succession to the governorship in the case of death or disability. Delegates wondered whether the successor should be elected or appointed, and if elected, whether the position should be linked with that of the governor. The territory's negative experience with appointed officials, who had little allegiance to the people they supposedly served, made many delegates wary. Some went so far as to suggest that Alaska did not need a lieutenant governor or secretary of state at all. Bush pilot Frank Barr of Fairbanks thought it wiser to avoid "a figurehead who receives a high salary and does nothing" (*PACC*, 2069). Delegate Seaborn Buckalew, an Anchorage lawyer, said that if the governor died or fell ill, the president of the Senate could move into the office; there was no need for a full-time second-in-command:

> Now, this particular job, I don't care what you say about it here in the further articles, is going to be an unimportant job, and you are not going to get anybody with any ability to take that job, and I just think that the whole idea of succession falling on this individual is ill-advised. (*PACC*, 2068)

In the end, delegates agreed on an elected secretary of state (the constitution was later amended to rename the second-in-command lieutenant governor). Candidates would run on the same general election ticket with gubernatorial candidates, presenting voters with an executive team from each party.

Whether other high administrative officials of the state should be elected or appointed was also at issue. Discussion centered on two questions: First, should the attorney general be elected? Second, should commissioners of all departments be appointed directly by the governor, or should provision be made for the use of boards in their selection? The experience of other states, most of which had elected attorneys general, entered debate; against their experience was opposed the concept of the unified executive, a proposition that was central to the model constitution. Delegates opted for the latter interpretation and designated the governor and lieutenant governor as the only elected officials, greatly strengthening the executive.

The constitutional convention was, in general, free from the pressure of interest groups.[27] However, most of the delegates had some experience with resource issues, including fish and game matters, and with education. Thus, even though the interests of education and of fish and game were not present in the form of lobbyists, the delegates themselves raised issues relating to the creation of special provisions for selecting the commissioners of education and of fish and game.

The last issue concerning construction of the Alaska executive was gubernatorial veto powers—in particular, their extent and ease of nullification. Some delegates raised objections to the proposed line-item veto power of the governor, but most thought that this would contribute to strength in

---

[27] Former state legislator Niilo Koponen, an observer of the constitutional convention, remarked that "Doc" Robinson "unsuccessfully represented fishing interests" and that the "mining lease provision was written by the Vice President of USS Refining & Mining Co." (personal communication, February 12, 1996).

government administration. A larger number of delegates objected to the unique proposal that gubernatorial vetoes would need to be overridden in a joint session of the legislature. The debate on this issue was limited and not directly relevant to the issue, given the absence of information and practice from the other American states.

The final issue of institutional design concerned the judiciary. No objection was raised to the committee proposal on the structure of the court system. However, delegates were divided on the issue of the appointment versus election of justices. The practice of the state of Missouri was extremely influential in this area, as it was in the other areas of convention discussion. The Missouri Plan system of gubernatorial appointment on the recommendation of a judicial council, followed by retention elections, was supported by the majority of delegates.

Delegates to the Alaska Constitutional Convention considered local government issues when they proceeded to Article X of the constitution. This was the most novel area of constitutional discussion, as Alaska had few local governments under territorial rule. Although few delegates raised an objection to the concept of this unit (which was strongly supported by Anchorage town planner Vic Fischer), the label *borough* generated much discussion. Delegate Frank Barr of Fairbanks was among several delegates who vehemently opposed the concept: "I don't particularly like the word borough; I don't like the sound of it and I think it's confusing to some people; as a matter of fact, if they don't know how to spell it, they might confuse it with another kind of burro, which is a donkey" (*PACC*, 2618).

Although convention minutes indicate that few delegates had a clear grasp of how this new governmental unit would operate, the borough was approved without modification, much to Frank Barr's discouragement. Significantly, the new boroughs were to encompass cities and school districts and yet present a unified system of local government, unlike any in the American states at that time or since.

Policy Issues

Three issues do not conveniently fit into the previously mentioned categories of analysis: unified finance, natural resource management, and fish traps. In the finance and taxation article of the constitution, delegates followed the pattern of the model constitution in avoiding any earmarked or dedicated funds. Reflecting on their frustrations with territorial government, delegates accepted the advice of consultants who advised giving the legislature broad latitude in determining how public money should be raised and spent.[28]

[28] McBeath and Morehouse, *Alaska Politics and Government*, 127.

Alaska is the only state that has a clear and explicit article in its basic law on natural resources. (In Alaska parlance, natural resources include those that are nonrenewable—such as oil, gas, coal, gold and other minerals—as well as those that are renewable, such as fish, game, forests, and agriculture.) This article occasioned spirited debate over both the management and principles of natural resource use. The territorial practice of resource administration was through commissions, which were virtually autonomous from the governor. Additionally, congressional control and the intervention of resource interests reduced the ability of Alaska commissions to make decisions on fish and game management. Delegates debated briefly as to whether the control and management of natural resources should be centralized in a single commission, left in two (a board of fisheries and board of game) as was the territorial practice, or given to the state legislature. The decision that was reached was to continue the territorial practice while acknowledging that the new system of state government would give far greater power to the commissions than they had previously held.

The second area of discussion concerned the principles under which Alaska's natural resources should be managed. The delegates were of one mind with respect to the exploitation of Alaska's mineral and other natural resource bounty: they believed that there should be sustained development directed to the maximum beneficial use of the state.

The other special issue concerned fish traps. These log-pole and net devices, which were set up on the salmon-spawning streams and rivers, were hugely efficient in capturing fish. They also were quite controversial in territorial days because Outside fisheries interests established and maintained them, depriving Alaska residents of the benefit of the fisheries resources. If there was a symbol of the tyranny of colonialism in Alaska, it was the fish trap, as Ernest Gruening illustrated in a speech on the second day of the convention. He pointed out that the salmon pack (total amount of salmon canned) had declined from 8 million cases in 1935 to 2.4 million cases in 1955, the lowest level in 46 years, and complained:

> Nowhere, as in the Alaska fisheries fiasco, is the lesson clearer or the superiority, in purely material terms, of self-government to colonialism. In neighboring British Columbia and Washington State, where the fisheries are under home rule, and where fish traps have been abolished, the identical resource has not only been conserved but augmented.[29]

Several delegates proposed that the constitution specifically outlaw fish traps, and there was spirited debate on the topic. One concern was whether the fish traps were ecologically sound, but the major concern was whether the new state's constitution should legislate or only state general principles. Most delegates

[29] Ernest Gruening, "Let Us End American Colonialism," Address, Alaska Constitutional Convention, November 9, 1955 (Fairbanks: University of Alaska, Rasmuson Library).

believed that a matter of detail, such as the abolition of fish traps, should not be in the constitution. Instead, delegates agreed to present voters in the 1956 election with a special ordinance prohibiting the traps.

RATIFICATION OF THE CONSTITUTION IN 1956

Delegates to the Constitutional Convention debated whether the Tennessee Plan (which they called the Alaska-Tennessee Plan) should be linked to the ratification of the new state constitution. This plan would place on the ballot the election of two U.S. senators and one U.S. representative, who would lobby Congress for statehood upon election. The delegates reached agreement that Alaska voters should have a vote on ratification of the proposed constitution and should separately elect representatives who would defend the new state charter in the statehood debate in Washington, D.C.

The newly drafted constitution went on the ballot in April 1956, along with three ordinances: on ratification, the Alaska-Tennessee Plan, and the abolition of fish traps. Alaska voters approved the new constitution 17,447 to 8,180, and they banned the hated fish traps by 21,283 to 4,004.[30] They also approved of the Alaska-Tennessee Plan by a vote of 15,011 to 9,556.

In the fall election, voters selected Ernest Gruening and William A. Egan as designees to the U.S. Senate and Ralph Rivers as designee to the House of Representatives. The three Democrats immediately went to Washington, D.C., to lobby Congress for statehood.

AMENDMENTS TO THE CONSTITUTION

An unusual feature of the Alaska Constitution is a provision asking voters whether a constitutional convention should be called; it appears on the ballot every ten years. This has not been an attractive option to Alaskans, perhaps because a convention would expose the entire constitution to change. In 1992, despite popular support for term limits among other issues that a convention might address, voters turned down the ten-year call by a 2-to-1 margin.

The legislature may also call a constitutional convention, but as of 1996 it had not done so. It may also be possible for voters to call a convention through the initiative process, but there is legal uncertainty about this method.[31]

The only method used in Alaska to change the constitution is through the legislature initiating amendments by a two-thirds vote. Since statehood, only 33 attempts have been made, and only 24 have succeeded, considerably below the

[30] Claus-M. Naske, *An Interpretative History of Alaskan Statehood* (Anchorage: Alaska Northwest Publishing Company, 1973), 178.

[31] McBeath and Morehouse, *Alaska Politics and Government*, 132.

average rate for states in the postwar period. About half the changes were relatively insignificant, but ten have altered the meaning of the Constitution. (See the Appendix for a compilation of amendments to the Alaska Constitution.)

Minor changes have been made in the judiciary through constitutional amendment by establishing a Commission on Judicial Qualification (1968) and designating an administrative director, appointed by the chief justice, as the supervisor of court administration. Voters changed the position's name from secretary of state to lieutenant governor in 1970. The only significant change to government institutions was the 1984 amendment limiting legislative sessions to 120 days. This was a popular reaction to the long sessions of the oil-rich years in the early 1980s.

Five amendments expanded citizens' rights and popular controls over government. In 1972, Alaskans approved an amendment adding "sex" along with race, color, creed, and national origin as categories of protected civil and political rights. In the same election, and by a far wider margin, Alaskans added a "right to privacy" to the constitution. The supreme court interpreted this constitutional provision in 1975 to mean that individuals could keep small amounts of marijuana for personal use in their homes (*Ravin v. State*, 1975). However, with the developing war-on-drugs climate of the 1980s, voters passed an initiative recriminalizing the possession of any amount of marijuana in 1990.[32] As of 1996, the Alaska Supreme Court had not determined whether the new law was constitutional (as it reversed the *Ravin* decision without having amended the constitution).

The third amendment to Article I was an outgrowth of frustration over the failure of state and federal courts to support Alaska "local hire" laws, which favored residents over nonresidents seeking employment in Alaska. The amendment allowed the state to grant preferences to residents, but as of 1996 it had not been used successfully to increase the proportion of Alaska residents hired.

In 1994 voters adopted two amendments bearing on the rights of crime victims and gun owners. Section 24 was added to Article I, spelling out ways in which crime victims could be involved in judicial proceedings against perpetrators. Like constitutional amendments in other states, this amendment was an attempt to toughen criminal law. Section 19 was amended to prohibit the state or a political subdivision from abridging the right to keep and bear arms, in a western state's response to national gun control legislation.

A significant change was made in the natural resources article in 1972, when voters agreed to establish limited entry rights to state fisheries. Section 15 of Article VIII had prohibited any "exclusive right or special privilege of fishery," largely as a reaction to the hated fish traps used by absentee owners to deprive

[32] Ibid., 129.

Alaskans of fisheries income. The 1972 amendment allowed the state to limit the number of fishermen in salmon and other fisheries and to decide who would be granted valuable "limited-entry" permits. The ostensible purpose of this amendment was to improve "resource conservation, to prevent economic distress among fishermen . . . and to promote . . . aquaculture," because it did limit the number of fishermen who could exploit the resource. However, initially it served to strengthen the resident control of Alaska fisheries, as nonresidents were at a disadvantage in purchasing permits. The result over time has been to privatize public resources on a large scale, as those with limited entry permits now have a private property right to what was once a resource in common use.[33] Moreover, allowing the sale of permits has brought about the transfer of ownership of many valuable permits to outside interests.

Perhaps the most important amendment to the Alaska Constitution was the 1976 establishment of the Permanent Fund. The taxation article was progressive for its time in prohibiting the dedication of public funds to specific purposes. Anticipating large increases in state revenues from Prudhoe Bay oil revenues, voters approved a dedicated fund and required that 25 percent of oil lease bonuses, royalties, and rentals be deposited in it. By 1996, the principal of the Permanent Fund exceeded $18 billion.

Discussion at the time of this amendment's passage centered on using the Permanent Fund to support state government when oil revenues declined. In the two decades since passage, however, fund earnings have not been applied to pay for government operations, even when oil prices crashed in the mid-1980s. Instead, half of fund earnings has been distributed to state residents in the form of annual dividend checks; the other half has been redeposited in the fund to offset inflation.

The establishment of the Permanent Fund gave Alaska a unique role among American states as it made the state an investment banker with a direct financial trust relationship with its shareholder-citizens.[34] Former governor Walter J. Hickel said Alaska was an "owner state," and its citizens all held shares in its resource wealth.

A second change to the finance article was made in 1982 when voters approved an appropriations limit. The legislators and Governor Jay Hammond hoped to cap state spending when oil revenues were high, leaving money in the general fund for the lean years that were predicted to follow. However, the ceiling was too high, and it has had no impact on fiscal policy since enactment.

The third change occurred in 1990 when voters approved an amendment creating a Constitutional Budget Reserve Fund. This fund was designed to serve

---

[33] Ibid., 125–126.

[34] Ibid., 127–128.

as a receptacle for money that the state expected to win in litigation over oil taxes and royalties. It was designed to allow the legislature to tap it (only with an extraordinary [three-fourths] majority), when there were significant decreases in state revenues. The legislature used the fund in 1994, 1995, and 1996; repeated annual deficits because of oil revenue shortfalls will probably exhaust it by the late 1990s.

The history of amendments to the constitution reveals the flexible nature of the state's basic law in accommodating change in Alaska government and politics. When the constitution was written in the 1950s, Alaska had a small population with a relatively simple society, The statehood battle produced a consensus in state politics, and conflict was directed toward the federal government and outsiders who controlled Alaska's resources. In the 1990s, Alaska is a diverse and complex polity with conflict among residents, but this does not seem to have detracted from the constitution's workability, as seen particularly in the limited entry and Permanent Fund amendments. The limited entry amendment and the Permanent Fund dividends signaled important shifts in the values and purposes to be served by state government as they privatize public resources, thus facilitating their appropriation by nonresidents and newcomers, who can acquire them nearly as easily as residents.

CONCLUSIONS

Alaskans held a constitutional convention before statehood to prove that they were capable—and deserving—of self-government. Critics from outside Alaska questioned the ability of this sparsely populated territory to provide for its own governmental services and asked pointed questions about the preparedness of Alaskans for self-rule. Not all the questions came from outside of the state; the delegates were very much aware that the eyes of all Alaskans were on them, too. During a discussion on legislative salaries, Anchorage delegate Herb Hilscher, a public relations consultant, made note of the responsibility to make decisions that would stand up to close scrutiny:

> We have an end product to sell and that is the one thing that I hate to stress too much, but it must be kept constantly in front of us, and if we give the legislature a blank check to write their own salaries, that is the finest argument in the world to get people stirred up emotionally to vote against the ratification of the constitution. (*PACC*, 381)

The record of the proceedings of the Alaska Constitutional Convention reflects an overriding concern with demonstrating Alaska's political maturity. When put to the test, Alaska's representatives excelled in this task, ignoring their individual political agendas for the common cause of statehood.

As consultant to the convention John Bebout said on its 35th anniversary: "Alaska's is, on the whole, the best written constitution in the country. . . . Delegates hoped a well-written constitution would provide a vehicle for statehood. You adapted the concepts of good government to the special needs of Alaskans."[35]

What the framers created was indeed a model constitution, which drew an effective framework for government based on principles of the U.S. Constitution and the National Municipal League's *Model State Constitution,* and which has accommodated significant political and social changes in the state.

---

[35] Quoted at the 35th Reunion of the Alaska Constitutional Convention, April 27, 1991, Juneau, Alaska.

PART TWO

The Alaska Constitution and Commentary

Part II gives a section-by-section analysis of the Alaska Constitution. It describes each section and delineates its origin, including discussions from the constitutional convention. Most of the commentary is based on interpretations of the provision by the courts, and in a few cases, by attorneys general. Citations to cases discussed are found in the Table of Cases.

Attempts have been made to provide a comprehensive discussion of the constitutional issues arising from each section, but the treatment is not necessarily exhaustive, and the law is evolving. The discussion and analysis are not a substitute for specific legal research on a particular subject of interest to a reader.

PREAMBLE

> We the people of Alaska, grateful to God and to those who founded our nation and pioneered this great land, in order to secure and transmit to succeeding generations our heritage of political, civil, and religious liberty within the Union of the States, do ordain and establish this constitution for the State of Alaska.

A preamble introduces and states the purposes of a constitution. All but two state constitutions (West Virginia and Vermont) have preambles. Most are modeled on the preamble to the U.S. Constitution.

The preamble to the Alaska constitution clearly states its origin in popular sovereignty and its concern with popular rights, two abiding themes over Alaska's settlement. It follows the *Model State Constitution's* recommendation by stating Alaska's equality with other states in the federal system. It does not make specific reference to the aboriginal residents of Alaska—Aleuts, Indians, and Eskimos—who lived in Alaska long before the non-Native pioneers arrived.

The only significant discussion at the constitutional convention was whether the preamble should refer to "God Almighty" instead of "God," because of the many faiths and sects in Alaska (*PACC*, 1289). Delegates had no objection to toning down the reference to the deity, but they declined, on a voice vote, to remove the reference altogether.

Like other state constitutions, the preamble is not actually a part of the constitution itself and has no legal significance.

Article I

Declaration of Rights

Each state constitution begins with a declaration of rights, which is intended to acknowledge the importance of personal rights and liberties and the role that civil rights and political freedoms play in limiting government power. The Alaska declaration of rights, like that of most state constitutions, resembles closely the Bill of Rights of the U.S. Constitution. However, it includes several rights not found in the federal constitution, such as an explicit right to privacy (section 22) and the right to sexual equality (section 3), which were added by amendment in 1972.[1]

Over the course of the twentieth century, the Fourteenth Amendment of the U.S. Constitution has been interpreted to apply some (but not all) of the provisions of the federal Bill of Rights to citizens in their relations to state and local governments. This establishes a floor of protection for individual rights: if states provide less protection than the federal constitution, it takes precedence. State constitutions supported by court decisions, however, may strengthen protection for state citizens. The Alaska Supreme Court has declared that it is "not limited by decisions of the United States Supreme Court or the United States Constitution when we expound our Constitution; the Alaska Constitution may

[1] Citations to the *Minutes of the Daily Proceedings of the Alaska Constitutional Convention* (Juneau: Alaska Legislative Council, 1965), abbreviated as *PACC*, appear throughout the text.

have broader safeguards than the minimum federal standards" (*Roberts v. State*, 1969, pp. 342–343).[2]

In general, this has meant expanded protection for individuals in several areas. The Alaska Declaration of Rights provides stricter standards in support of equal protection of the laws (section 1). It assures greater due process safeguards, such as the provision of counsel at preindictment hearings (section 7). The Declaration of Rights also gives strong defense for rights of the accused (section 11) and broader guarantees against unreasonable searches and seizures (section 14) than the Fourth Amendment of the U.S. Constitution.

However, recent amendments have shifted the pendulum away from individual rights somewhat. In 1994, voters amended section 12 to toughen provisions of criminal administration (by calling for community condemnation of criminals, for example), and they added section 24, which provides for the rights of crime victims.

SECTION 1

Inherent rights. This constitution is dedicated to the principles that all persons have a natural right to life, liberty, the pursuit of happiness, and the enjoyment of the rewards of their own industry; that all persons are equal and entitled to equal rights, opportunities, and protection under the law; and that all persons have corresponding obligations to the people and to the State.

The first clause embeds in the Alaska Constitution the natural rights emphasis of the Anglo-American liberal tradition. It combines both John Locke's protections of "life, liberty, and property" from *The Second Treatise on Civil Government* and Jefferson's "life, liberty, and the pursuit of happiness" from *The Declaration of Independence*, making them inherent features of constitutional government in Alaska.

The second clause is a straightforward statement of the principle of equal protection, as found in the Fourteenth Amendment to the U.S. Constitution. It limits the government from discriminating, positively or negatively, against different groups without good reason. The Alaska equal protection statement is regarded as employing a stricter standard than the federal provision in determining whether challenged statutes bear a fair and substantial relationship to state purposes. In *State v. Anthony* (1991), Justice Allen Compton declared: "Alaska's equal protection clause is more protective of individual rights than the federal equal protection clause" (p. 157).

---

[2] See Charles Mann, "A Study in State Supreme Court Constitutional Interpretation: *Roberts v. State*, 458 P.2d 340 (Alaska 1969)," *Alaska Law Journal* 2 (January 1971): 83–95.

The third clause reflects the desire for good government of the delegates to the constitutional convention, who sought to balance individual rights and opportunities with citizens' responsibilities to others and to the state. In one instance, this clause influenced a high court decision. Rejecting a complaint that state taxes violated natural rights, the Alaska Supreme Court declared that one "corresponding obligation" was paying taxes (*Cogan v. State Department of Revenue*, 1983).

A series of court decisions has defined the extent of rights to life, liberty, and property in Alaska. One interesting pair of decisions clarifies citizens' rights regarding dress and hair length. In 1972, the supreme court declared that students could not be excluded from school because they wore their hair longer than school regulations allowed (*Breeze v. Smith*). Students had a fundamental "right to be let alone," which could be overridden only by a more compelling state interest. Eight years later, a district court required a male attorney to wear a coat and tie to court because of the importance of decorum in that venue (*Friedman v. District Court*, 1980). The court consistently has supported restrictions on citizens when driving. In 1984, the supreme court held that it was no violation of rights to penalize those refusing to take breathalyzer tests when suspected of driving while intoxicated (DWI) (*McCracken v. State*).

The courts also have defined the meaning of property rights under the constitution. In *Cogan v. State* (1983), the supreme court found that the state's taking of income through taxation did not impermissibly infringe on citizen rights. Several court decisions have supported administrative agencies that regulate the exploitation of fish and game resources, to which some citizens have claimed property rights. Perhaps the most persuasive was *Deubelbeiss v. Commercial Fisheries Entry Commission* (1984), in which the supreme court declared that there was no "fundamental right" to a limited entry permit (see Article VIII, section 15). (Limited entry permits restrict fishing in order to conserve the resource. In this case, only those with at least 16 of a possible 20 points based on one's economic dependence on a fishery were allowed to engage in the Cook Inlet salmon drift-gillnet fishery. Deubelbeiss had only 15 points and challenged the regulation as arbitrary. Although the court supported his challenge, it upheld a classification system for granting permits if it bore a "fair and substantial" relation to the purpose of regulation).

An important court interpretation concerned the property status of the Alaska Permanent Fund dividend, which is distributed to all Alaska residents annually and which, in 1995, amounted to $990. In 1988, the legislature made felons, if incarcerated during any period of a fiscal year, ineligible for a permanent fund dividend for that year. The supreme court held that the dividend was an economic interest entitled only to minimum protection, and that it could be seized to compensate crime victims (*State v. Anthony*, 1991).

The equal protection clause of section 1 has drawn the greatest attention from the courts. Federal courts tend to use a three-tier approach for equal protection analysis: (1) rational basis, (2) suspect class or strict scrutiny, and (3) intermediate or heightened scrutiny, which is used mainly for sex discrimination cases that fall between (1) and (2). Unequal treatment must be substantially related to important government objectives and to their achievement.[3] The Alaska courts tend to follow "a more flexible, less result-oriented analysis" (according to *State v. Erickson*, 1978, p. 12):

> First, it must be determined . . . what weight should be afforded the constitutional interest impaired by the challenged enactment. The nature of this interest is the most important variable in fixing the most appropriate level of review. . . . Second, an examination must be undertaken of the purposes served by a challenged statute. . . . The state may be required to show only that its objectives were legitimate, at the low end of the continuum, or, at the high end of the scale, that the legislation was motivated by a compelling state interest. Third, an evaluation of the state's interest in the particular means employed to further its goals must be undertaken. . . . At the low end of the sliding scale, we have held that a substantial relationship between means and ends is constitutionally adequate.
>
> At the higher end of the scale, the fit between the means and ends must be much closer. If the purpose can be accomplished by a less restrictive alternative, the classification will be invalidated. (*Alaska Pacific Assurance Co. v. Brown*, 1984, pp. 269–270)

Michael Wise calls the Alaska Supreme Court's sliding-scale approach a unique analytical doctrine as compared to the federal bench's haphazard method.[4]

To illustrate the Alaska courts' reasoning, I review cases at the high and, then, the low ends of the scale, following which I consider two of the most controversial issues of the Alaska constitution—residency requirements (including local hire) and durational residency.

Alaska courts consistently have invalidated laws and regulations making invidious and arbitrary distinctions among classes of people under the constitution's equality guarantees. In 1972, the high court voided the incarceration of an indigent who could not pay a $300 fine for reckless driving (*Hood v. Smedley*). The imprisonment was invidious under the federal equal protection clause, because it was imposed for indigency, and not for a valid penological purpose, as required in *Williams v. Illinois* (1970). However, in 1995 the high court defended the state's recoupment system (which recovers the costs of appointed counsel from indigents) against an equal protection challenge. The court held that the rule of criminal procedure did not restrict indigents' right of access to the courts,

---

[3] I am indebted to Fae Korsmo for this formulation. See also Harold W. Chase and Craig R. Ducat, *Edwin S. Corwin's THE CONSTITUTION and What It Means Today* (Princeton, NJ: Princeton University Press, 1978), 492–510.

[4] Michael Wise, "Northern Lights—Equal Protection Analysis in Alaska," *Alaska Law Review* 3, no. 1 (1986): 47.

or otherwise impinge on an interest protected by high or intermediate levels of scrutiny (*State v. Albert*).

A suit on behalf of 28 Alaska Native youth argued that they were treated differently from other Alaska school children in that they were deprived of the right to attend secondary schools in the (sparsely populated) communities in which they resided (*Hootch v. Alaska State-Operated School System*, 1975). The supreme court majority admitted that both federal and state equal protection guarantees might apply, but it delegated the resolution of this issue to the superior court. The court's majority indicated that the executive and legislature should address the issue of high school programs for small communities.[5] This led to the *Tobeluk v. Lind* (1979) consent decree calling for the provision of rural high school programs in all villages where there was at least one child of secondary school age.

The supreme court struck the clause "by female" from prostitution statutes, finding that the means of the statute did not further the goals of enactment (*Plas v. State*, 1979). Ten years later, the court invalidated the policy of an Anchorage landlord who declined to rent to unmarried couples, holding that this was unlawful discrimination based on marital status (*Foreman v. Anchorage Equal Rights Commission*, 1989).

The courts have also struck down attempts of local governments to tax absentee landlords (usually corporations owning oil and gas property) at higher rates than residents (*Kenai Peninsula Borough v. State Department of Community & Regional Affairs*, 1988).

Using a rational basis test, under which state actions are upheld if they serve a legitimate governmental end and are rationally related to its achievement, Alaska courts have defended discriminatory treatment when it served valid state interests. In 1978, the high court concluded that there was ample evidence of potential harm from cocaine use to sustain the legislature's inclusion of the drug in its narcotics classification, notwithstanding the fact that cocaine is not a narcotic (*State v. Erickson*, 1978). During the period when adults could possess marijuana for personal use (1975–1990), the courts supported penalties that the legislature had specifically applied to minors (*M.O.W. v. State*, 1982). After voters recriminalized marijuana use by adults, in 1990, the supreme court upheld the legislature's differentiation of penalties by age for marijuana possession (*Allam v. State*, 1992), declaring that the statute was rationally related to the legitimate state interest of protecting minors.

When Anchorage educators held the state's first teachers' strike in 1978, on being enjoined by the superior court, they complained to the supreme court of "unequal treatment." Other employees, teachers complained, were covered by the state's Public Employees Relations Act (PERA), which permitted strikes or

---

[5] In a strongly worded dissent, Justice Rabinowitz read the constitution as requiring the establishment of secondary schools in the communities in order to guarantee equality of access to education.

binding arbitration for essential employees. The court held that this discrimination was also permissible, as it served an important purpose of the state—namely, the promotion of cooperative employment relations and the assurance of smooth operation of a critical government service. (*Anchorage Education Association v. Anchorage School District*, 1982) More recently, an unlicensed guide objected to penalties more severe than those assessed others who practiced licensed professions without licenses, but the court was unsympathetic. The appeals court argued that the state had a legitimate interest in enacting firm measures to discourage unlicensed guiding because of the importance of Alaska's wildlife resources and the inherent difficulties in enforcing guiding statutes in remote areas (*Maeckle v. State*, 1990).

A pair of 1995 supreme court cases applied sliding scale analysis to provisions of the Alaska Worker's Compensation Act. Chiropractors alleged that regulations establishing standards for frequency of treatment discriminated against them because they would lose benefits they otherwise would have received. (They would no longer automatically receive payments for continuing multiple treatments in excess of the frequency standards.) However, the high court found that the state had a legitimate interest in curbing abuse by health providers and claimants, discouraging needless or fruitless treatments, and in general, ensuring the delivery of reasonable and necessary medical benefits to injured workers (*Chiropractors for Justice v. State*).

The court also rejected a challenge by a worker who claimed that amendments to the law treating workers with mental injuries differently from those with physical injuries deprived her of equal protection. The supreme court ruled that compensating workers for stress-induced injuries only if they met an "extraordinary and unusual test" did not violate equal protection guarantees. The amendments to the law, said the court, minimized fraud and abuse in claims for stress-related mental injuries, which was substantially related to the state's goal of efficiently and fairly distributing benefits while cutting costs for employers (*Williams v. State, Department of Revenue*, 1995). In both cases, the court said that workers' compensation benefits were "merely an economic interest, and entitled only to minimum protection under equal protection analysis." (See also *Pan-Alaska Construction, Inc. v. State, Department of Administration*, 1995).

Local option laws have also provided tests of the constitution's provisions on inherent rights. Alcohol has been a serious problem (with devastating social effects) in Alaskan villages since contact. In response to growing evidence of a strong relationship between alcohol abuse and crime, and also in response to the developing Native sobriety movement, the legislature enacted a local option law in 1980. Under the law, any municipal government seeking to regulate alcoholic beverages could conduct a referendum election, opting for anything from a complete prohibition of importation to regulated sales. Elections are conducted under state supervision, and violations have been subject to state criminal prosecution. The supreme court supported the village of St. Mary's, whose police arrested a state trooper bringing beer and vodka into the "dry" village, notwithstanding his contentions that local option laws violated equal protection, due process, and privacy rights (*Harrison v. State*, 1984). The supreme court also has held that differences in penalties across villages of the state do not violate equal protection of the laws (*Burnor v. State*, 1992).

Like the other states, Alaska has residency requirements for both statewide and local offices. The courts have upheld these distinctions after strict scrutiny because they serve the compelling state interest of affording greater voter knowledge of the candidates and greater candidate knowledge of the needs of the constituency (see, for instance, *Gilbert v. State*, 1974; and *Castner v. City of Homer*, 1979).

The supreme court also has upheld fish and game regulations that give preferences to residents. Two hunting guides challenged the constitutionality of regulations giving preference to residents in the taking of moose, deer, elk, and caribou for personal use. The high court pointed out that the state owned the fish and game resources and had to manage them as a trustee for the benefits of its citizens. The Equal Rights and Opportunities Clause of the constitution, said the court, required equal treatment only for those who were similarly situated. Alaska residents and nonresidents were not similarly situated with respect to their rights of access as recreational users of the state's fish and game (*Shepherd v. State, Department of Fish & Game*, 1995).

Residence requirements for employment have been exceedingly popular with citizens and legislators, for whom local hire is a huge issue, but they have been unpalatable to the state's high court. In 1973, the supreme court invalidated state personnel regulations that required one year's residency in Alaska before becoming eligible for state employment (*State v. Wylie*, 1973). Although the legislature and state agencies sought to lower the unemployment rate of Alaskans, the effect, said the high court, was to violate fundamental rights of Americans to travel (and the U.S. Constitution was intended to facilitate individual commerce and movement); it was impermissibly discriminatory under both the federal (Fourteenth Amendment) and Alaskan (Article I, section 1) constitutions.

As oil and gas development proceeded on Alaska's North Slope, legislators sought ways to focus employment opportunities to the benefit of Alaska residents. In 1975, the state department of labor first enforced an "Alaska Hire" law (enacted in 1972 and amended in 1976), which gave preference in oil pipeline construction work to Alaska residents, and several affected nonresidents then filed suit. Although the Alaska Supreme Court found that the law had not violated the privileges and immunities clause of the U.S. Constitution, it was found to violate equal protection guarantees and was ruled invalid (*Hicklin v. Orbeck*, 1977). An amended version of the Alaska Hire law was found to violate the privileges and immunities clause of Article IV, section 2, of the U.S. Constitution (*Robinson v. Francis*, 1986).

The legislature attempted to meet constitutional objections by crafting a new statute in 1986, which created four hiring preferences for public works projects. The preferences benefited individuals living in economically distressed areas, yet a divided court ruled that this also violated equal protection rules because it economically assisted one class over another (*State v. Enserch*, 1989). Frustration over these court outcomes on local hire issues is a large factor in explaining the successful mobilization of voters in 1988 in support of a constitutional amendment allowing resident preferences (Article I, section 23).

Upon statehood, Alaska provided residents with a series of benefits based on the *duration* of their residency. Some were like those of other states—for example, reduced tuition at the state university, while others were unique, such as care in state-financed old age homes (called "pioneer homes") and land disposal programs. When oil began flowing through the trans-Alaska pipeline in 1977 and the state's coffers began to overflow, legislators sought means to return benefits to residents based on their length of residency.

During its 1980 session, the Alaska legislature enacted two statutes giving preferential treatment to citizens based on duration of residency. The first completely exempted from taxation the income of individuals who had paid taxes in Alaska for three or more years, and proportionately reduced taxes for those paying taxes for one or two years only. Anchorage attorneys Ron and Patricia Zobel, new residents to Alaska, sued the state, claiming a violation of their rights to equal opportunities and protection. The supreme court agreed, stating that the law might actually force those with lower incomes to pay higher taxes, and invalidated the statute (*Williams v. Zobel*, called *Zobel*, 1980). Thereupon, the state legislature abolished the income tax entirely.

The second law, which is referred to as the Permanent Fund Dividend Statute, provided for a cash distribution of the income derived from the Alaska Permanent Fund and based on the number of years an individual had been a resident of the state since 1959 (the year when Alaska became a state). Following this scheme, the first distribution in 1980 would have given a 21-year resident $1,050, and a one-year resident only $50. In this case, however, the supreme court was divided. Three justices, led by Justice Jay Rabinowitz, supported the state's position: it was not necessary to subject the statute to the strict scrutiny test or to prove that the durational residency requirement was absolutely necessary to promote a compelling state interest. Indeed, they believed that the permanent fund distribution met sound state policy objectives, without compromising the rights of interstate migration (*Williams v. Zobel*, called *Zobel II*, 1980). Two judges dissented, however, finding the statute in violation of both state and federal equal protection guarantees.

The Zobels appealed to the U.S. Supreme Court, which found that Alaska had indeed violated federal equal protection principles (*Zobel v. Alaska*, called *Zobel III*, 1982). The state legislature then altered the permanent fund distribution program and the state began giving checks to all residents, with the amount determined by dividing the number of residents into one-half of the five-year average earnings of the fund.

From 1980 to the present, the state supreme court has become less protective of benefit programs aligned to duration of residency. It ruled that the Kenai Peninsula Borough violated constitutional equal protection provisions when it required participants in a land sale lottery to have been residents for one year preceding their applications and when it granted a 5 percent reduction in a parcel's sale price for each year of residency in the borough (*Gilman v. Martin*, 1983). A year later, Rodney Vest, a new senior citizen aged 65, claimed a longevity bonus from the state for which he was ineligible because he had lived in Alaska an insufficient length of time. Lawmakers had established the bonus system at the outset of the oil boom to reward long-time citizens. It gave each resident over 65 years of age who had lived in Alaska since 1959 a monthly payment of $250.[6] Vest's case reached the state high court, which supported his plea and ruled the longevity bonus program unconstitutional because it violated the equal protection clause (*Schafer v. Vest*, 1988). Vest received a bonus, as did every other senior citizen who applied, regardless of residence; however, the legislature curbed entry into the program in the early 1990s.

Provisions of section 1 of Alaska's declaration of rights have not fulfilled Justice Compton's prognosis regarding *individual benefits*. The protection of individual rights is probably greater through other parts of this article, such as sections 7 and 11.

SECTION 2

Source of government. All political power is inherent in the people. All government originates with the people, is founded upon their will only, and is instituted solely for the good of the people as a whole.

This section expresses the principle of popular sovereignty as the basic guiding idea of Alaska statehood and ultimate authority for government. The section has been invoked to clarify the rights of the people to determine public affairs when, for example, the attorney general stated that it prevented governmental restrictions on write-in voting.[7]

The Alaska Supreme Court has interpreted section 2 in one election case. When the state elections office prepared the ballot question for a referendum to determine if there should be a constitutional convention, the preparatory

[6] Gerald A. McBeath and Thomas A. Morehouse, *Alaska Politics and Government* (Lincoln: University of Nebraska Press, 1994), 206.

[7] Alaska Department of Law, Opinion of the Attorney General, 1963, No. 30 (Legality of Write-in Votes), Juneau.

language was challenged as biased. (It read "REFERENDUM As required by the Constitution. . . . Shall there be a constitutional convention?") The biased wording, challengers alleged—and the court agreed—led to an affirmative vote, whereas surveys had suggested that the result should have been negative. The court found that by departing from the constitutionally prescribed form of ballot question, the electorate's right to vote on the question was impeded (*Boucher v. Bomhoff*, 1972).

SECTION 3

Civil rights. No person is to be denied the enjoyment of any civil or political right because of race, color, creed, sex, or national origin. The legislature shall implement this section.

This section incorporates civil rights protections from the Fourteenth Amendment to the U.S. Constitution. Harrison found its specific origin in congressional statehood bills for Alaska that "required that the constitution . . . 'make no distinction in civil and political rights on account of race or color.'"[8] The committee version added *creed* and *national origin* but contained no reference to sex, a subject that was discussed heatedly at the constitutional convention. Delegate John Rosswog proposed specifying protection from discrimination on the basis of sex, and he was supported by Helen Fischer, who remarked, "Sex definitely should be in this proposal because there are still states in the Union where women are not allowed to serve on juries" (*PACC*, 1292). Delegate Ada Wien noted that the topic had come up for discussion in committee, but added that members had decided that the term *person* referred to women and men and that therefore, additional protection was not needed. She was supported by Mildred Hermann, who said that Alaska was one of the first political subdivisions under the American flag to give women the right of suffrage, which was accomplished in 1913, six years before national lawmakers passed the Nineteenth Amendment (*PACC*, 1292).

The convention defeated Rosswog's proposal by a vote of 37 to 15. Later, in the general provisions of the constitution (Article XII, section 10), the delegates said that personal pronouns were to be construed as referring to either sex. The issue remained, however, and voters amended the constitution in 1972 by adding the word *sex* to this section.

The courts have emphasized the need for sex neutrality in examining statutes. In striking the clause "by a female" from an Anchorage prostitution ordinance, Supreme Court Justice Roger Connor remarked: "In creating criminal offenses

[8] Gordon S. Harrison, *Alaska's Constitution: A Citizen's Guide*, 3d ed. (Juneau: Alaska Legislative Research Agency, 1992), 18.

it is particularly important that any distinctions as to gender rest upon some logical justification having a basis in the actual conditions of human life" (*Plas v. State*, 1979, p. 968).

Delegate Victor Fischer sought to expand protections under section 3 by adding the word *economic* in order to guarantee economic rights. He argued that a significant portion of Alaska's population was nonwhite and needed protection for equal rights to employment (*PACC*, 1298). Other delegates were concerned that such an addition might be misconstrued as a right-to-work or collective-bargaining issue. The Hawaii Constitution (Article XIII, sections 1–2) included the "right of labor to organize and bargain collectively," which scared business leadership in Alaska. As a result, Fischer's proposal was defeated.

The legislature has implemented section 3 through statutes proscribing discrimination in hiring, housing, government operations, and other areas (title 18, chapter 20). In addition, the legislature established a State Commission on Human Rights to make investigations into discrimination complaints and rectify them.

SECTION 4

Freedom of religion. No law shall be made respecting an establishment of religion, or prohibiting the free exercise thereof.

This section is taken nearly verbatim from the first sentence of the First Amendment to the U.S. Constitution. It guarantees religious freedom and restricts the state from interfering in the operations of religious institutions without a compelling reason.

A small number of court cases have interpreted this section. One concerned the city of Ketchikan's lease of a hospital (built with federal, state, and local funds) for operation by the Sisters of St. Joseph of Newark. The state supreme court found that the religious order was a nonprofit corporation organized for charitable purposes; its articles of incorporation did not indicate that its objective was to further religious beliefs or dogmas (*Lien v. City of Ketchikan*, 1963). For these reasons, the lease did not violate the constitutional prohibition on establishment of religion.

The most publicized case of religious freedom in Alaska is *Frank v. State* (1979). Carlos Frank, an Athabascan Native from the Minto area, was convicted of illegally shooting a cow moose out of season. He contended, and the high court agreed, that moose meat was an essential Native food for the village's funeral potlatch; consequently, to convict him for taking game would violate his religious liberty. The court held that the state had not met its burden of proving a compelling state interest that would justify curtailing the religiously based practice.

However, when a Seward church protested against a city zoning ordinance that excluded nonpublic schools from the residential area in which the church (and its parochial school) were located, the supreme court upheld the city ordinance. The court noted that parochial schools had not been banned; rather, their location had been subject to zoning in order to lessen the impact on surrounding parcels (*Seward Chapel, Inc. v. City of Seward*, 1982).

SECTION 5

Freedom of speech. Every person may freely speak, write, and publish on all subjects, being responsible for the abuse of that right.

This section is taken from the Idaho Constitution and also resembles closely the first sentence of Article 1, section 5, of the 1947 New Jersey Constitution. The guarantee is stated as a direct and explicit right of the people, and not merely a limit on government action, as is contained in the First Amendment to the federal constitution. Alaska, like several other states, explicitly recognizes that the right to free speech and press must be balanced against other public interests, such as protection from defamation and fraud.[9] Writing for the supreme court in a 1981 case, Justice John Dimond commented:

> [T]hese rights, in a free society such as ours, have never been recognized as absolute and without limitations. . . . [I]t is the function of this court to create a workable equilibrium and synthesis between the two polar ideas of freedom and authority. . . . [T]here must be here a balancing of conflicting rights and interests. (*Messerli v. State*, 1980).

In election cases, the supreme court has supported modest disclosure and petition-filing requirements, but insisted that they meet strict tests of scrutiny. The high court found against an Anchorage opponent of local bond propositions, who had placed political advertisements without filing a written report with the Alaska Public Offices Commission (APOC). However, the court recognized that further regulations were necessary to protect individuals' rights to anonymity, to the extent they might be subject to reprisals (*Messerli v. State*, 1981). The high court upheld a judgment against VECO, a large oil-field services company that had formed groups with employees to make campaign contributions to candidates but had failed to follow reporting requirements. Although VECO argued that the Alaska Campaign Disclosure Act was unconstitutionally overbroad, vague, and violative of the right to privacy, the court found compelling grounds for disclosure in the deterrence of corruption and detection of

---

[9] Although the federal constitution lacks such an explicit recognition, the courts have regularly interpreted the First Amendment as requiring that speech rights be balanced against other legitimate public interests. As Chase and Ducat state, "The court's majority takes each case on its own merits and balances the competing private and public interests" (*Edwin S. Corwin's THE CONSTITUTION*, 307).

violations of contribution limitations (*VECO International, Inc. v. Alaska Public Offices Commission*, 1988).

When Joe Vogler, an Alaska Independence Party candidate for governor in the 1982 elections, challenged the petition requirements for individual candidates and parties to appear on the ballot (3 percent and 10 percent, respectively, of votes cast in the previous election), the supreme court agreed that such requirements were impermissible bars to the ballot and unconstitutionally infringed on the right of Alaskans to vote and to associate freely (*Vogler v. Miller*, 1982, 1983). The legislature thereafter changed the requirements to 1 and 3 percent, respectively (in AS 15.25.160).

The Alaska Supreme Court also has struck down local ordinances that restrict access to the public forum (any place where public business is transacted) and limit free expression. In 1978, the court declared that once a government-controlled forum for the dissemination of information and expression of ideas exists, the government may not deny equal access to the forum based solely on the content of materials (in this case, information on a homosexual organization). The city of Anchorage thus was ordered to include the Alaska Gay Coalition in the municipality's *Blue Book* (*Alaska Gay Coalition v. Sullivan*, 1978). The court struck down a Kodiak city ordinance banning nude dancing because there were no clear reasons under Alaska statutes to discriminate on the basis of the content of a protected form of expression (*Mickens v. City of Kodiak*, 1982). Interestingly, the Alaska Supreme Court provided stronger protection, under section 5, than is available under the federal constitution, as the Twenty-First Amendment permits the state regulation of nude dancing where liquor is sold (*California v. LaRue*, 1972).

Similarly, the court invalidated a city of Anchorage ordinance banning disorderly conduct. It found that those parts of the ordinance that could be applied to protected speech—for example "threatening," "tumultuous behavior," "unreasonable noise," "offensively coarse utterance, gesture, or display," and "addressing abusive language to any person present"—were unconstitutionally overbroad, while other parts of the ordinance were impermissibly vague (*Marks v. City of Anchorage*, 1972).

The court has stated its obligation to review actions by agencies of the state in order to ensure compliance with all provisions of the Alaska Constitution; on free speech matters, this review extends to lower courts and the grand jury. The publication of a grand jury report became controversial in 1990 following its investigation into the conduct of the Anchorage School District, police department, and district attorney's office relating to a high school teacher's sexual relationship with students. Part of the report mentioned deficiencies in teachers' actions, and the court precluded publication of names where allegations were unsubstantiated, against the protest of Anchorage newspapers and the police chief. In 1991, the supreme court found that the rule providing for the court review of grand jury reports before they were published was constitutional, and that it did not violate freedom of speech or press (*O'Leary v. Superior Court*, 1991).

(For a discussion of the constitutionality of Alaska's primary statute, see Article V, section 3.)

SECTION 6

Assembly; petition. The right of the people peaceably to assemble, and to petition the government shall never be abridged.

This section resembles the last clause of the First Amendment to the federal Constitution, but it appears stronger because the right to petition is not limited to grievances. Like the right to free speech, the right to assemble and petition the government is an affirmative right. It not only limits what the government may do, it also grants rights that may be enforceable against those who are not part of the government, such as mall owners whose property and parking lots are used for other than private purposes.

Governments may regulate the time, place, and manner of assembly, but they do so subject to a standard of reasonableness. The Anchorage disorderly conduct ordinance failed this test because it included both constitutionally protected conduct as well as conduct that the state can legitimately regulate within the ambit of its prohibitions (*Marks v. City of Anchorage*, 1972).

SECTION 7

Due process. No person shall be deprived of life, liberty, or property, without due process of law. The right of all persons to fair and just treatment in the course of legislative and executive investigations shall not be infringed.

The first sentence of section 7 incorporates in the Alaska Constitution the due process language of the Fifth and Fourteenth Amendments to the U.S. Constitution. The customary interpretation of the language is that certain procedures must be followed before one can be deprived of property or other interests, and that the substance of one's property and other interests is protected from government intrusions.[10] The second sentence is an obvious reference to the abuse of the investigative process during the McCarthy era. The framers of the constitution sought to avoid such a development in Alaska by instituting a doctrine of fairness for government inquiries.

---

[10] Ibid., 476.

Chief Justice Dimond commented on the meaning of due process in *Green v. State* (1969):

> The term "due process of law" is not susceptible of precise definition or reduction to a mathematical formula. But in the course of judicial decisions it has come to express a basic concept of justice under law, such as "our traditional conception of fair play and substantial justice," the "protection of the individual from arbitrary action," "fundamental principles of liberty and justice," whether there has been a "[denial of] fundamental fairness, shocking to the universal sense of justice," "that whole community sense of decency and fairness that has been woven by common experience into the fabric of acceptable conduct," and a "respect for those personal immunities which . . . are so rooted in the traditions and conscience of our people as to be ranked as fundamental . . . or are implicit in the concept of ordered liberty." (pp. 996–997)

Over the period of Alaska statehood, courts have further interpreted the meaning of due process with respect to these six aspects: (1) the character of laws and regulations (whether overly broad, vague, or arbitrary), (2) criminal arrest procedures, (3) trial procedures, (4) sentencing and penalty considerations, (5) inmate rights, and (6) notice, hearing, and open meeting requirements. These will now be considered in some detail below.

In the first category of due process, reviewing state statutes and administrative regulations, the courts have tended to rule against overly broad and vague laws, as well as those that create arbitrary classifications. Moreover, they have scrutinized the administrative rule-making process and deliberated over the fairness of prospective legislation.

Two challenges to game regulations occasioned court commentary on the doctrine of overbreadth. When a big game guide violated game regulations by killing a moose the "same day airborne," his plane, although owned by an innocent third-party, was seized. The supreme court invalidated the seizure, finding the regulation to be overly broad. It required a limiting construction indicating that it applied only to those who "knew or should have known" that game were being illegally transported (*State v. Rice*, 1981). This was more protective of property than the U.S. Supreme Court has been in the area of forfeiture. The second case concerned two hunters who were convicted of killing a Dall sheep in a closed area. The high court found that their due process rights had been abridged because the regulation prohibiting the transportation of illegally killed game conflicted with a statute prohibiting the wanton waste of big game animals (*Gudmundson v. State*, 1991).

The courts also have determined whether statutes and regulations are impermissibly vague. For example, a regulation prohibiting the taking of cub bears was not found to be vague in defining cubs as young bears in their first or second year of life (*Nelson v. State*, 1964). In one of the first trials of a state environmental protection law, the high court held that the definition of the term *pollution* in the state Environmental Conservation Act was not unconstitutionally vague (*Stock v. State*, 1974). However, an Anchorage city ordinance that banned loitering for the purpose of soliciting prostitution was declared void for vagueness and thus violative of the due process clause. The supreme court held that the ordinance gave too much discretion to government officials, raising the possibility of uneven and discriminatory enforcement (*Brown v. Municipality of Anchorage*, 1978).

In *Holton v. State* (1979), the Alaska Supreme Court specified the three factors it would consider when reviewing criminal statutes for vagueness:

> First, a statute may not be so imprecisely drawn and overbroad that it "chills" the exercise of first amendment rights. The second consideration is that in order to be consistent with notions of fundamental fairness a statute must give adequate notice of the conduct that is prohibited. The final element in an analysis of statutory vagueness is whether the statute's imprecise language encourages arbitrary enforcement by allowing prosecuting authority undue discretion to determine the scope of its prohibitions, (pp. 1235–1236)

A pair of city ordinances in the early 1990s tested the state's local option law for vagueness. In the first case, *Burnor v. State* (1992), defendants appealed their conviction for selling alcohol without a license or permit in the city of Kotzebue, which had exercised its authority under the state's local option law to prohibit the sale of alcohol. The defendants contended that penalty provisions were vague and gave inadequate notice, and that the penalties were disproportionately severe. The court of appeals disagreed with each contention and affirmed the conviction. In the second case, *Shetters v. State* (1992), a defendant appealed his conviction for importing more than twelve liters of distilled spirits into Kiana, a village that, by local option election, had voted to prohibit the sale and importation, but not the possession, of alcoholic beverages. Shetters argued that the ordinance was unconstitutionally vague: it banned "importation," implying for the purpose of sale, but seemingly not personal consumption. Moreover, he alleged that it was unclear whether the village had banned importation. In this case, too, the court of appeals affirmed the conviction, finding the ordinance clear and adequately publicized.

Finally, the court of appeals held that a fish and game emergency order specifying boundaries of an extended fishing area was not so vague as to violate due process. In the opinion of the court, optimal clarity was unnecessary for regulations directed at a limited group of persons (*State v. Martushev*, 1993).

The courts have also determined whether classifications in the law are arbitrary. In *Belgarde v. State* (1975), the court found that classifying marijuana as a dangerous drug was not so arbitrary as to deny due process to persons possessing it. Similarly, the court declared that the classification of cocaine as a narcotic was neither irrational nor arbitrary, when viewed from the legislative purpose of preventing the use of a drug that is harmful to health and social welfare (*State v. Erickson*, 1978). The supreme court disagreed with a defendant who challenged as arbitrary and irrational a sentence of three years for guiding without a license, in that it far exceeded penalties for unlicensed operation in other professions. The supreme court said the criminal penalty did not violate due process because it was proportionate to the state's interest in regulating this conduct (*Maeckle v. State*, 1990).

When several pipeline companies contended that their due process rights had been violated by the Alaska Public Utilities Commission (APUC), which arbitrarily charged them for the costs incurred in a pipeline tariff investigation, the supreme court qualified its judgment on administrative discretion. The court ruled that it was unnecessary for APUC to adopt regulations before allocating costs because the process it followed provided ample notice and opportunities for pipeline owners to object to cost allocations (*Amerada Hess v. Alaska Public Utilities Commission*, 1986). Finally, the high court supported prospective legislation by approving a statute that changed the rules for admission to the bar. Persons once eligible for admission to the state bar without examination would be considered ineligible if they took and failed to pass the bar examination after June 30, 1965 (*Application of Brewer*, 1967).

The second category of due process cases concerns criminal arrest procedures. A large number of judicial decisions have delineated the due process protections available to citizens facing arraignment and arrest. Generally, Alaska is much more protective of defendants' rights than the U.S. Supreme Court, but the Alaska courts have permitted practices by undercover police officers that seem to border on intrusiveness and entrapment. For example, in *Municipality of Anchorage v. Flanagan* (1982), the appeals court ruled that a prostitute's sexual contact with an undercover policeman was independent and unconnected to the commission of the offense of assignation. She accepted money from the undercover officer and agreed to sexual relations prior to his acquiescence. Thus, the police conformed to the standard established by the Alaska Supreme Court in *Pascu v. State* (1978): "[I]t is quite proper for the police to provide the opportunity for one engaged in criminal activities to ply his trade" (p. 960). Similarly, the court of appeals held that a defendant's right to due process was not violated by the failure of police to seek prior judicial approval for an undercover drug investigation relied on in prosecution (*Folsom v. State*, 1987). Furthermore, the court of appeals also declared that when the police forced a suspected drunk driver who had injured a pedestrian to have a blood sample drawn for alcohol testing in a medically acceptable manner and in an hospital environment, it was not so great an intrusion as to violate his right to due process (*Municipality of Anchorage v. Ray*, 1993).

Alaska's speedy trial law has been tested several times by defendants who believed that delays in filing charges had abridged their due process rights. In 1979, the supreme court held that an eight-month delay in filing formal charges was not a violation because the defendant lacked diligence in locating witnesses to support his case (*Prenesti v. State*, 1979). The court of appeals specified that the due process clause protected the accused only against *unreasonable* preaccusation delays. In the case of a defendant charged with the sexual abuse of a minor, a delay of twenty months was found not to have adversely affected the outcome. The defendant's complaint of anxiety resulting from this delay was not, in the opinion of the court, justification for the dismissal of charges (*State v. Mouser*, 1991). The court of appeals later ruled that an even longer delay, of 38 months between apprehension and the filing of formal charges, did not prejudice due process rights. The defendant, who was charged with unloading crabs outside a regulatory area and underreporting the number of crabs taken, was unable to satisfy the court that the witness he had reputedly lost because of the delay would have been able to attest to significant errors in his arrest (*Millman v. State*, 1992).

Usually, the court's analysis is as follows: (1) Was there a violation of a right? (2) If so, was it prejudicial (harmful) to the defendant? For example, the courts would not reverse if the right to a speedy trial were violated but the violation did not harm the defendant. For some rights, prejudice makes no difference, as with the right to counsel.

In its *Miranda* decision, the U.S. Supreme Court significantly liberalized criminal arrest procedures. The court specified these procedural safeguards: "Prior to any questioning, the person must be warned that he has a right to remain silent, that any statement he does make may be used as evidence against him, and that he has a right to the presence of an attorney, either retained or appointed" (*Miranda v. Arizona*, 1966, p. 445). The following year, the U.S. Supreme Court specifically extended the right to counsel to postindictment police lineups.

Alaska courts adopted the *Miranda* standards and applied them broadly. For example, in interpreting the state constitution, the Alaska Supreme Court held that "a suspect who is in custody is entitled to have counsel present at a preindictment lineup unless exigent circumstances exist so that providing counsel would unduly interfere with a prompt and purposeful investigation" (*Blue v. State*, 1977, p. 642).

The courts also have described how suspects may be questioned in the absence of "Miranda" warnings without violating their due process rights. The court of appeals ruled that police questioning of a defendant about ongoing drug activity after he had invoked his right to counsel in another drug case did not violate the due process provision (*Abdullah v. State*, 1991). This court also found legal the deceptive tactics used by the state in persuading the wife of a defendant to call him in prison and elicit incriminating statements about sexually abusing his stepdaughter (*Carr v. State*, 1992). In this case, nothing the wife said to the defendant was regarded as having taken advantage of his position as a sentenced prisoner. "Given the lack of coercion and the absence of any tendency to produce an untruthful confession," said the court, "the deceptive tactic . . . did not run afoul of the Alaska Constitution" (p. 1004).

The third category includes several cases treating the efficacy of trial procedures as they bear on due process rights. The courts have successively spelled out what assistance of counsel means in criminal prosecutions. In *Merrill v. State* (1967), the high court ruled that it was unnecessary for the accused to have a court-appointed counsel present to confront and cross-examine all witnesses at preliminary hearings. Most Alaska decisions, however, have expanded protections to indigents in misdemeanor cases. In *Alexander v. City of Anchorage* (1971), the court declared that defendants had a right to representation by a public defender if misdemeanor convictions would result in their incarceration, loss of valuable licenses, or heavy fines. To incarcerate an indigent, who was unprotected by counsel, because he could not afford a $300 fine imposed for reckless driving was also found to violate the defendant's due process rights (*Hood v. Smedley*, 1972). The court held that under due process guarantees, an indigent wife had the right to a court-appointed counsel in a private child custody proceeding where the husband was represented by Alaska Legal Services (*Flores v. Flores*, 1979). Moreover, the high court affirmed this right but disagreed with a defendant's contention that she should be able to select her counsel in a case concerning the termination of her parental rights (*V.F. v. State*, 1983; see also section II).

Several other cases pertain to the impact of due process rights on trial procedures. The supreme court has ruled that due process was not violated by introducing evidence of a defendant's prior grand larceny conviction in order to impeach his testimony in an embezzlement prosecution (*Lowell v. State*, 1978). Nor was the defendant's due process right considered abridged when the state reinstated a previously dismissed charge after the accused had successfully appealed it. The high court ruled that the state was not behaving vindictively, for like the accused, the state was simply restoring the case to its original position (*Morgan v. State*, 1983). Further, the supreme court held that the due process rights of a driver were violated at a license revocation hearing by the state's failure to preserve the videotape of his taking of a second set of field sobriety tests one hour after his arrest (*Thomas v. Department of Public Safety*, 1989).

The courts have supported citizens' right to be present at preliminary trial stages, in both criminal and civil cases. *Dixon v. State* (1980) spelled out the defendant's constitutional right to be present during jury deliberations whenever there are communications between judge and jury. *Odum v. University of Alaska Anchorage* (1993) confirmed the right of a terminated associate professor to be present at a predetermination hearing because participation at a postdetermination hearing did not satisfy due process standards.

Finally, even the means of communication with jurors has been reviewed with respect to the impact of due process rights on trial procedures. When the plaintiff in a personal injury suit claimed that telephoning jurors to notify them to appear in court violated his due process rights (because it eliminated from the pool those who could not afford telephones), the court affirmed the practice (*Bachner v. Pearson*, 1970).

The fourth category of due process cases concerns sentencing and penalty considerations. Several cases have focused on the fairness of sentencing procedures. In *Shagloak v. State* (1979), the supreme court declared that the imposition of more severe sentences after retrial (than were obtained in the original trial) violated due process, because it might cause apprehension in the accused, deterring him or her from exercising the right to appeal. The *Allain v. State* (1991) ruling permitted the merger of two counts of sexual abuse into one when they concerned closely related conduct with the same victim, provided that the terms of resentencing did not exceed the total duration of the sentences. In addition, the Alaska Supreme Court has resolved differences between courts as to sentence length. In a burglary case, the court of appeals reversed a superior court sentence of 23 years—the longest burglary sentence in state history. The supreme court, however, saw no greater fairness in the appeals court's sentence of fifteen years, and required that it consider the permissible range of reasonable sentences and fully justify its analysis (*State v. Bumpus*, 1991).

This focus on fairness applies to civil cases, including workers' compensation. In 1979, the supreme court declared there to be a fair and substantial relationship between the legislative objective of providing guaranteed, expeditious compensation to an injured employee and limitation on the employer's total liability, regardless of the employer's percentage of fault. It did so even though that limiting liability had the effect of denying the right of a third party who was liable for damages to compel others—particularly the negligent employer—to share in discharging the common liability (*Arctic Structures v. Wedmore*, 1979).

Finally, in an important 1988 election case, the high court ruled that fines nearly twice the amount of unreported campaign contributions were not unreasonable and did not violate due process (*VECO International, Inc. v. Alaska Public Offices Commission*). The primary purpose of the disclosure requirement, which was to fully inform the electorate, had been frustrated, said the court, which justified a large penalty.

The fifth category of due process concerns the rights of inmates. Parolees and inmates of state correctional facilities have sought the protection of section 7, and Alaska courts have been supportive. In 1973, the supreme court held that suspending a parolee's civil rights, which was then the state practice, denied his or her right to initiate a civil suit and thus violated due process (*Bush v. Reid*). A group of disgruntled state prison inmates charged the state with due process infringements. They alleged that correctional authorities had arbitrarily canceled statutory good time (reduction of sentence length for good behavior), arbitrarily administered internal prison discipline, and made arbitrary decisions relating to their institutional placements and participation in work release and educational programs. The supreme court ruled that prisoners coming before administrative tribunals had rights comparable to those of nonprisoners: to be represented by counsel, to call witnesses and produce documentary evidence in their favor, and to have the entire hearing recorded for the purpose of administrative appeal (*McGinnis v. Stevens*, 1975).

The sixth and final category of due process concerns notice and hearings requirements. Alaska courts have heard many complaints about due process problems in the notice and hearings requirements for public agencies. A Ketchikan bar owner objected to the loss of his liquor license without a hearing; the supreme court agreed, stating that due process required adequate notice and a meaningful opportunity to be heard before the state beverage control commission (*Frontier Saloon v. Alcoholic Beverage Control Board*, 1974). The same court required the state to provide notice and a hearing before it terminated a state grazing lease for noncompliance with the purpose of the lease (grazing livestock), which had been issued by the Division of Lands of the state Department of Natural Resources (*McCarrey v. Commissioner of Natural Resources*, 1974). In another resource case, the supreme court ruled that an unsuccessful applicant for a permit to enter the gill-net fishery was entitled to a hearing to determine his economic dependence on income from that fishery (*Matson v. State Commercial Fisheries Entry Commission*, 1990).

The supreme court has interpreted section 7 to require hearings in several wrongful discharge cases. It declared that nontenured teachers who were dismissed midyear for incompetence had a right to a hearing before termination. Although a hearing was not required by statute, due process considerations applied because the teachers were being deprived of an interest in property—their teaching posts (*Nichols v. Eckert*, 1973).

The supreme court halted the city of Nome from dismissing its city manager peremptorily and required that he be given notice and an opportunity to be heard by the city council (*Breeden v. City of Nome*, 1981). The court extended this analysis to the wrongful discharge of a union employee in the city of Fairbanks (*Casey v. City of Fairbanks*, 1983).

Alaska courts have balanced concerns for the fairness and impartiality of commission and board proceedings with concerns for efficiency in deliberations. When air taxi operators claimed that the hearing on their application before the Alaska Transportation Commission violated due process because not all commissioners were present, the court found otherwise. In its judgment, due process was observed because all the evidence was presented and the parties had opportunities to rebut (*Alaska Transportation Commission v. Gandia*, 1979).

Finally, in several cases the supreme court has interpreted the relationship between due process rights and the state's Open Meetings Act, which requires that the business of government be done primarily in public. In *Brookwood Area Homeowners Ass'n v. Municipality of Anchorage* (1985), the high court established a three-step analysis for determining the appropriate remedy for a decision made in violation of the act:

> First, the transgressing governmental body must show that a subsequent ratification of the original decision involved a substantial reconsideration of that decision. If full and fair reconsideration did not occur, then it must be determined whether reconsideration is possible without invalidating the earlier flawed decision. If reconsideration is not possible without invalidating the decision, then the court must conduct a balancing test to determine whether invalidation is in the public interest. In deciding the public interest issue, the court should weigh the "remedial benefits" to be gained in light of the goals of the [Open Meetings Act] against the prejudice likely to occur to the public. (*Brookwood Area Homeowners Assn. v. Municipality of Anchorage*, 1985; see also *Alaska Community Colleges' Fed'n of Teachers, Local No. 2404 v. University of Alaska*, 1984, p. 1325)

The former head librarian of Anchorage claimed that his due process rights had been violated when the library advisory board met in violation of the Open Meetings Act and recommended that he be fired. The supreme court disagreed that he had a right to be present at the meeting. The court said he was an "at-will" employee who could be fired for any reason, and thus he had no constitutionally protected property interest in his job that would give him a right to attend meetings where his reputation was at issue. Nor, said the court, did the former librarian have a liberty interest, as the library advisory board simply gave him a negative job evaluation and did not impugn his integrity, honesty, or morality (*Revelle v. Marston*, 1995).

SECTION 8

> **Grand jury.** No person shall be held to answer for a capital, or otherwise infamous crime, unless on a presentment or indictment of a grand jury, except in cases arising in the armed forces in time of war or public danger. Indictment may be waived by the accused. In that case the prosecution shall be by information. The grand jury shall consist of at least twelve citizens, a majority of whom concurring may return an indictment. The power of grand juries to investigate and make recommendations concerning the public welfare or safety shall never be suspended.

Grand juries are composed of laypersons who investigate and consider evidence of criminal violations. Their most common decision is for an indictment—a formal, written charge against a person. This informs the defendant and court of the facts said to constitute a criminal offense, allowing the defendant to prepare a defense and the court to examine the sufficiency of the charges. Section 9 allows the grand jury to issue a presentment (a formal accusation) in cases of public concern where the evidence is insufficient to issue an indictment. Although the accused have a right to grand jury deliberations, they may waive this right, allowing the prosecutor to charge them (this is an indictment "by information").

The grand jury section attracted considerable discussion at the constitutional convention. At that time, only half the state constitutions provided for grand juries, with the rest using less formal charging procedures. (This contrasts with the federal constitution, which requires indictment by grand juries in all felony cases.) Delegate Warren Taylor proposed the deletion of section 9: "I think the grand jury is in the same class as the dodo; it's done for, it is gone and we might as well relegate it to oblivion where it belongs because it serves no useful purpose except for just investigative purposes" (*PACC*, 1324).

Most delegates supported the grand jury system, however, and the discussion focused on two amendments. Delegate Edward Davis moved to amend the committee version, which had made the information and indictment "concurrent remedies." He thought this would encourage district attorneys to overuse the information, because it was a more convenient means to bring a case to trial. His amendment, which was incorporated in the final version, allowed district attorneys to prosecute by information only if defendants waived their rights to grand juries. The amendment was supported by three-fourths of the delegates. The second amendment, which was also incorporated in the final version, was the last sentence added by delegate Frank Barr, which gave grand juries general investigative powers. Although some delegates believed this might give grand juries the power to defame, the amendment and the entire section were adopted without further debate.

In 1972, the supreme court required that all proceedings before the grand jury be recorded, but it did not invalidate unrecorded grand jury proceedings before that date (*Griggs v. State*, 1972). In *Morgan v. State* (1983), the court of appeals held that the dismissed charges of defendants who had waived their right to trial by pleading guilty could be reinstated without the defendants' reindictment.

Grand jury proceedings have received critical scrutiny from the courts and the public. In 1985, a grand jury called to investigate charges of bid-rigging against Governor William Sheffield issued a report suggesting that the state senate should initiate impeachment proceedings against the governor (see Article II, section 20). This grand jury report led to the first impeachment inquiry conducted into any state's governorship in 75 years.

In a controversial morals case concerning a popular Anchorage teacher (which was allegedly covered up by the school district and the Anchorage Police Department), the court reviewed the investigative grand jury report before releasing it to the public, in an action challenged by Anchorage newspapers (*O'Leary v. Superior Court*, 1991). The supreme court held that grand juries were arms of the court system and subject to restraint under rules of the court. For the court to review grand jury reports before they were published did not violate the constitutional provision that the power of grand juries to investigate and make recommendations shall never be suspended.

SECTION 9

Jeopardy and self-incrimination. No person shall be put in jeopardy twice for the same offense. No person shall be compelled in any criminal proceeding to be a witness against himself.

The Alaska Constitution's prohibition of double jeopardy resembles that of the Fifth Amendment to the federal constitution: "Nor shall any person be subject for the same offense to be twice put in jeopardy of life and limb." It protects against a second prosecution for the same offense after acquittal or conviction, and it protects against multiple punishments for the same offense. The second sentence incorporates the right against self-incrimination, which is also found in the Fifth Amendment to the federal constitution and in most state constitutions.

Courts in Alaska have inquired into whether successive prosecutions are for the same or a different offense than that prosecuted earlier. The question often asked by the Alaska Supreme Court is whether differences in intent or conduct between the statutory offenses are substantial in relation to the basic social interests protected or vindicated by statutes: "[T]he test to be applied to determine whether there are two offenses or only one, is whether each provision requires proof of a fact, which the other does not" (p. 1028). In one instance, an Anchorage defendant drove recklessly while trying to evade the police; in the same incident, he was charged with assault with a dangerous weapon because he drove his automobile into the police officer pursuing him. When convicted by a jury of the lesser offense of reckless driving, the defendant claimed a violation of his constitutional right against double jeopardy. The high court found that the factual basis for the two reckless driving convictions consisted of separate conduct; consequently, sentencing for both did not violate section 9 (*Calder v. State*, 1980).

A more recent double jeopardy case concerned a defendant who was convicted of two counts of sexual abuse of a minor. The appeals court ruled that the two counts should have been merged into a single count for both judgment and sentencing, because they involved conduct that was closely related—a single criminal episode of sexual contact with the same victim. To resentence the defendant on the second count did not violate his double jeopardy rights, the court held, so long as the term did not exceed the composite sentence originally imposed (*Allain v. State*, 1991).

A third case, which also came before the court of appeals, concerned a defendant who fraudulently filed for, and received, unemployment insurance benefits. When this was discovered, she agreed to repay the benefits plus the 50 percent penalty specified in statute. Upon being served with a criminal complaint charging her with unsworn falsification, she sued for dismissal, asserting that the criminal charges violated her rights against double jeopardy. The court found no violation of double jeopardy protections, largely because the relevant federal case used by the defendant (*United States v. Halper,* 1989) was not analogous. The imposition of "civil" penalties for fraud that were completely disproportionate to the injury suffered by the government could potentially constitute jeopardy said the court, but that did not apply in this case.

The double jeopardy defense became popular in the mid-1990s, prompted by a U.S. Supreme Court case in 1994 that prohibited the state of Montana from imposing a heavy "marijuana tax" against a family of convicted pot growers who had first been punished in criminal court (*Montana Department of Revenue v. Kurth Ranch*). It also has been used in other drug cases, where criminal defendants have claimed the government has already punished them by using forfeitures to seize their homes and other property.

Scores of Alaskans charged with drunken driving invoked the defense, arguing that criminal prosecution after a routine civil procedure to revoke their licenses subjected them to double jeopardy. The issue divided the Alaska judiciary, and one Anchorage superior court judge invalidated thirteen DWI cases in 1995. However, a unanimous decision of the court of appeals reinstated the cases. Judge David Mannheimer concluded that double jeopardy did not apply to the drunken driving cases, or to similar cases where the charge is refusal to take a breathalyzer test. The 90-day license revocation imposed by the Division of Motor Vehicles, the appeals court ruled, is less a punishment of the driver than a "remedial" action intended to protect the public from dangerous motorists (*State v. Zerkel,* 1995). The pattern of most state courts has been to apply the double jeopardy clause only to criminal proceedings.

Alaska courts have followed the federal judiciary in the interpretation of the right against self-incrimination. The relevant federal decision is *Miranda v. Arizona* (1966), which disallows evidence obtained through the compulsion inherent in the coercive setting that exists when police conduct custodial interrogations. A recent Alaska test of this decision occurred when a defendant appealed his conviction of first-degree sexual abuse of his minor stepdaughter, based largely on incriminating statements he made to his wife in a telephone conversation prompted by state troopers. The court of appeals ruled that the circumstances were not coercive in that the defendant, although incarcerated at the time, was imprisoned on unrelated charges and had no knowledge of police involvement in the telephone call (*Carr v. State,* 1992).

SECTION 10

Treason. Treason against the State consists only in levying war against it, or in adhering to its enemies, giving them aid and comfort. No person shall be convicted of treason, unless on the testimony of two witnesses to the same overt act, or on confession in open court.

The section repeats nearly verbatim Article I, section 17, of the New Jersey Constitution, and it mirrors provisions of the federal constitution. It is the only constitutional provision that defines a criminal offense. No one has been indicted for treason in Alaska's history as a state.

SECTION 11

Rights of accused. In all criminal prosecutions, the accused shall have the right to a speedy and public trial, by an impartial jury of twelve, except that the legislature may provide for a jury of not more than twelve nor less than six in courts not of record. The accused is entitled to be informed of the nature and cause of the accusation; to be released on bail, except for capital offenses when the proof is evident or the presumption great; to be confronted with the witnesses against him; to have compulsory process for obtaining witnesses in his favor, and to have the assistance of counsel for his defense.

Most of the clauses in this section are taken directly from Article XVI of the New Jersey Constitution of 1776 and from Article VI of the federal Bill of Rights. They give constitutional protection to individuals accused under the law. The "speedy trial" provision guards against delays that may unfairly disadvantage defendants, while the trial's public nature protects the defendant against persecution by the state. The impartiality requirement assures the defendant that the jury has not already formed opinions about the case. The notice of charges allows the accused to prepare a defense. The right to bail allows the accused to be released from custody if he or she posts money as a guarantee of appearance for trial. The right to confront witnesses enables the defendant to cross-examine them and the judge to assess their credibility. The right to compulsory process means that the court will issue subpoenas or orders to ensure the attendance of witnesses at trial. Finally, the right to counsel ensures that the defendant will have help navigating through the complexity of the legal process.

Discussion of this section at the constitutional convention focused on jury size. Delegate Robert McNealy complained of the expense of paying twelve jurors, a cost he thought excessive for trials of assault and battery, drunken driving, and parking violations. Delegate Jack Cross pointed out that there were places in the Territory where it was difficult to seat a jury of twelve (*PACC*, 1317). The delegates agreed to leave latitude for the legislature to have smaller juries for district courts (those "not of record"). The legislature set the size of district court juries at six members, which is the practice in a number of other states.

The supreme court interpreted the right to a jury trial when a defendant requested a trial on an assault charge under a Fairbanks city ordinance. The court held that defendants had a right to a jury trial for criminal prosecutions whose penalty was incarceration, loss of a valuable license (such as a driver's license or occupational license), or penalties short of incarceration that connoted criminal conduct (*Baker v. City of Fairbanks*, 1970). The court said: "We should be alert against attempts by government to whittle away fundamental rights on grounds of expediency" (p. 401). It went on to declare:

> [W]e are under a duty to develop additional constitutional rights and privileges under our Alaska Constitution if we find such fundamental rights and privileges to be within the intention and spirit of our local constitutional language and to be necessary for the kind of civilized life and ordered liberty which is at the core of our constitutional heritage. (p. 402)

The *Baker* ruling frees the Alaska Supreme Court from the more conservative interpretations of the U.S. Supreme Court.

In a related case, the high court investigated the authority of courts to punish summarily for contempt (justified traditionally as necessary to preserve the "dignity, decorum, respect, authority, order and effectiveness of the judicial process" (*State v. Browder*, 1971, p. 934). It held that an accused who had brought a shotgun (unloaded) into court was entitled to a jury trial to determine if he was guilty of contumacious conduct (*State v. Browder*, 1971).

In a third case, the court held that children, too, were constitutionally entitled to jury trials in the adjudicative stage of delinquency proceedings (*RLR v. State*, 1971). Justice Rabinowitz argued that the "benevolent social theory supposedly underlying juvenile court acts" (p. 30) was an inadequate premise for dispensing with constitutional safeguards (in this case, the right of a juvenile, who allegedly sold LSD, to attend a hearing).

Alaska has no statutory provisions by which to measure the definite time within which trials must be held, but the supreme court has adopted a rule that normally requires trial within 120 days of being charged.[11] In *Nickerson v. State* (1971), the high court noted the purposes served by the speedy trial guarantee: (1) it prevents harming a defendant through a weakening of his or her case as evidence and witnesses' memories fade with the passage of time; (2) it prevents prolonged pretrial incarceration; and (3) it limits the infliction of anxiety on the accused because of long-standing charges.

The meaning of "speedy trial" has been clarified by several court cases. The supreme court found that a delay of some fourteen months in bringing a defendant to trial, during most of which time he was incarcerated, was a deprivation of his rights (*Glasgow v. State*, 1970). In *Rutherford v. State* (1971) the high court reported that "the longer the period of delay, the more willing the court should be to find a denial of the right to speedy trial without a showing of actual prejudice to the accused" (p. 947).

The court ruled that an eight-month delay after the arrest of a suspect on a narcotics charge before bringing him to trial did not deny the defendant's right to a speedy trial (*Nickerson v. State*, 1971). The defendant in the case of this

---

[11] Harrison, *Alaska's Constitution*, 28.

shorter delay had offered no proof of any impaired ability to defend himself, such as loss of witnesses or anxiety. However, the high court dismissed the indictment of a defendant arrested for burglary who was not brought to trial until 29 months after his arrest (*Whitton v. State*, 1973). Although the defendant was responsible for nine months of the delay, the remainder (about twenty months) far exceeded even the fourteen-month period held impermissible in earlier cases. (See clarification in section 7.)

Although neither the federal nor the state speedy trial guarantees apply until the commencement of formal proceedings, Alaska courts have considered whether delays prior to accusation deprive individuals of due process of the law. In *Marks v. State* (1972), the supreme court established two factors as relevant to determining whether a substantial delay between the commission or discovery of an alleged offense and the initiation of formal charges constituted a denial of due process—the reasonableness of the delay and the probable prejudice attributable to the delay. Following this logic, the supreme court rejected a defendant's charge that a five-month delay between an alleged rape and return of the indictment prejudiced his case (*Dixon v. State*, 1980). The delay in this case was appropriately justified because of the need to conduct investigations in two parts of the state; and in the high court's view, whatever prejudice occurred to the defendant was insufficient to overturn his conviction. The supreme court also has ruled that defendants must be given notice sufficiently in advance of court proceedings to allow reasonable time to prepare (*Doe v. State*, 1971).

The Alaska judiciary has spelled out the requirements of impartiality in a series of cases that focus on jury selection. In *Green v. State* (1969), the high court ruled that the constitutional standard would be met if prospective jurors were drawn from a fair cross-section of the community and if the method used by the state prior to a change of law in 1969—drawing from the list of residents who had voted in the preceding general election—was fair. However, when jurors were drawn from an area in a radius of 15 miles from Anchorage to try a defendant who had allegedly raped his sister-in-law in the village of Chignik (some 450 air miles southwest of Anchorage), the supreme court declared that his rights had been denied (*Alvarado v. State*, 1971). The court's objection was to an urban jury trying a rural Native, not to the distance from the location of the crime. Unlike most of the other states, Alaska's constitution does not require that the jury trial be held in the area where the crime was committed (but statute and court rules do limit the distance a trial may be moved).

In *Tugatuk v. State* (1981), the supreme court defined the nature of groups requiring representation in the jury pool in order to ensure impartiality:

> A group to be "cognizable" . . . must have a definite composition. That is, there must be some factor which defines and limits the group. A cognizable group is not one whose membership shifts from day to day or whose members can be arbitrarily selected.

> Secondly, the group must have cohesion. There must be a common thread which runs through the group, a basic similarity in attitudes or ideas or experience which is present in members of the group and which cannot be adequately represented if the group is excluded from the jury selection process. Finally, there must be a possibility that exclusion of the group will result in partiality or bias on the part of juries hearing cases in which group members are involved. That is, the group must have a community of interest which cannot be adequately protected by the rest of the populace, (p. 100)

In this case, the defendant contended he had been unfairly convicted of murder because the jury was drawn from a 30-mile instead of a 50-mile radius of the court's urban center (to lower transportation costs). The high court ruled, however, that residents of Native Alaskan villages (the "cognizable" group) were not systematically excluded from the jury selection process (as some lived within a 30-mile radius). Moreover, the defendant had not presented statistics proving the underrepresentation of Natives, and Tugatuk had asked that the trial be moved away form the Dillingham area, where the murders were committed, to Anchorage.

The court of appeals reversed the conviction of a Native defendant whose jury did not include representation from the area where the crime was committed and where he resided (*Erich v. State,* 1982). However, when a defendant complained that his jury did not have representation from a group to which he belonged (Caucasian members of the Russian Orthodox church within the community), the court of appeals declined to reverse the conviction (*Kelly v. State,* 1982). The court held that the defendant had failed to offer evidence regarding the attitudes, ideas, experiences, or beliefs of members that would qualify them as a "cognizable" group.

The courts have applied the right to bail to all criminal offenses, because Alaska has not had a death penalty (previously imposed for "capital" crimes only) since 1957. The supreme court has interpreted the bail clause in three cases. In *Reeves v. State* (1966), the court held that an indigent defendant did not have an absolute right to be released on his own recognizance prior to trial. In this case, the defendant was not a resident of the locality and had no family ties to hold him there, which made him a flight risk.

The supreme court ruled that the right to bail does not extend to hearings on the revocation of probation (*Martin v. State,* 1974 A). Moreover, it has ruled that the bail clause does not apply to the period following the conviction for a crime and prior to sentencing (*State v. Wassillie,* 1980).

The court also has clarified the meaning of confrontation of witnesses (as well as documentary evidence). In *Lemon v. State* (1973), Justice Robert Boochever stated:

> This right of confrontation protects two vital interests of the defendant. First, it guarantees him the opportunity to cross-examine the witnesses against him so as to

> test their sincerity, memory, ability to perceive and relate, and the factual basis of their statements. Second, it enables the defendant to demonstrate to the jury the witness' demeanor when confronted by the defendant so that the inherent veracity of the witness is displayed in the crucible of the courtroom. (p. 1153)

The high court reversed the conviction of the defendant in this case. His right of confrontation had been spoiled by the admission of hearsay testimony in statements of an alleged accomplice who was not available for effective cross-examination (because he had invoked his right not to incriminate himself).

A second case, *Blue v. State* (1977), further established the inadmissability of hearsay statements as evidence in court even if they were made in the defendant's presence and he appeared to agree with them. The court found that this violated the defendant's right to confront his accusers.

Although the constitutional right to confront and cross-examine witnesses is expressly limited to criminal trials, the supreme court has considered it incorporated within due process rights in administrative hearings. Thus, when the state failed to preserve a videotape of a driver's second set of field sobriety tests taken one hour after his arrest, the court ruled that his due process rights had been violated (*Thomas v. Department of Public Safety*, 1989).

Finally, in several cases the courts have interpreted the meaning of the right to counsel. The supreme court held in 1967 that neither the federal nor the state constitution required the appointment of counsel at a preliminary hearing that did not constitute a "critical stage" in criminal proceedings (*Merrill v. State*). Nor did counsel need to be provided during investigative police efforts. Before a person could claim the right, the state had to take adversary action, changing a person's status from that of a suspect to the accused in a criminal prosecution (*Carr v. State*, 1992).

However, the high court found that a defendant arrested on a forgery charge had a right to counsel while in jail awaiting trial. This right was violated when police acquired handwriting samples from him by threatening him with contempt (*Roberts v. State*, 1969). Moreover, in misdemeanor cases, the court ruled that counsel had to be provided if a conviction would result in incarceration, loss of a valuable license, or a heavy fine (*Alexander v. City of Anchorage*, 1971).

In Alaska, indigent defendants are provided lawyers by a state office, the Public Defender Agency. The counsel provided to the accused, said the supreme court in 1974, must be effective: he or she must perform at least as well as a lawyer with ordinary training and skills in criminal law, conscientiously protect the client's interest, and be undeflected by conflicting considerations (*Risher v. State*). If a defendant waived the right to counsel and sought to represent him or herself, the high court called on trial court judges to scrutinize the waiver carefully. The record had to show that the person was informed of the role of a defense attorney and the advantages of being represented by one in a criminal proceeding; that the defendant had the capacity, in a legal sense, to make a knowledgeable waiver of his or her right to counsel; and that a court had made a penetrating and comprehensive examination of all circumstances under which such a plea had been made (*Gregory v. State*, 1976).

Like a number of states, Alaska has a recoupment system requiring indigent defendants to repay the costs of appointed counsel. The Alaska Supreme Court considered challenges to the system's constitutionality in the 1995 decision of *State v. Albert*. The court ruled that the recoupment system did not violate indigents' counsel rights, although the repayment obligation might deter some indigents from accepting the services of counsel. It noted that the recoupment system resulted in civil, not criminal, judgments; normal conditions for civil judgments (such as payment by installment) applied; the judgment was not enforceable by contempt; and failure to pay would not affect services available to defendants on appeal.

SECTION 12

Criminal administration. Excessive bail shall not be required, nor excessive fines imposed, nor cruel and unusual punishments inflicted. Criminal administration shall be based upon the following: the need for protecting the public, community condemnation of the offender, the rights of victims of crimes, restitution from the offender, and the principle of reformation.

Originally, this section was titled, "Excessive Punishment," but the title was changed in a 1994 amendment. The first sentence, which is found in many state constitutions and was taken verbatim from Article VIII of the federal Bill of Rights, includes protections against three impositions of government. The excessive bail prohibition is connected to the right to bail in section 11. The clause proscribing excessive fines refers to actions of the legislative branch and to administrative agencies. The "cruel and unusual" clause harkens back to barbarous punishments of the Middle Ages; in Alaska, it has been judicially defined and broadened.

The original clause enumerating two principles of penal administration—reforming the criminal and protecting the public—was added in the constitutional convention at the request of delegate Ralph Rivers. There was, however, no intention to abolish capital punishment (which remained in use until 1957). In 1994, voters amended this section by adding three factors to the list of principles—community condemnation of the criminal, the rights of victims of crimes, and restitution from the criminal. A new section on the rights of crime victims was placed at the end of the Declaration of Rights (section 24).

Supporters of the amendment argued that the constitution provided rights primarily to persons charged with criminal offenses. Protection *from* an accused person and for the victim and the victim's family, it was argued, was statutory, but not constitutional. The amendment would redress the balance by providing constitutional protection for victims, and voters agreed.[12] Opponents countered that the amendment was unnecessary, its construction was flawed, and the new provisions, particularly the phrase "condemnation of the offender," were vague and confusing.[13]

Responding to this constitutional amendment, Anchorage State Senator Dave Donley sponsored a "no-frills" prison bill in the legislature. Saying that "prisons should be prisons, not country clubs,"[14] Donley's measure would ban inmates from having computers, television sets, compact disc players, and videocassette recorders. Personal weightlifting and bodybuilding equipment would be banned, too. Inmates would be prevented from making unmonitored phone calls and told they could smoke only in designated areas.

Corrections Commissioner Margaret Pugh opposed the bill, remarking that prisoners with diminished hope were not good candidates for compliance with prison authorities and preparation for return to civil society. In a March 4, 1996, editorial, the state's largest newspaper, *Anchorage Daily News*, echoed the commissioner's criticisms. Senator Donley argued for his bill, saying that he was "bringing the prison system into line with the 'community condemnation' of criminals provision of the constitution adopted two years before."[15]

The excessive bail and fines clauses have drawn little attention from Alaska's courts. *Reeves v. State* (1966) established that to deny an indigent defendant release on his or her own recognizance was not in violation of this clause.

Judicial interpretation of the first sentence of section 12 has centered on the "cruel and unusual" clause. Courts have applied a single test to determine whether a statutory penalty constitutes cruel or unusual punishment or violates substantive due process; amounting to a punishment so disproportionate to the offense committed as to be completely arbitrary and shocking to the sense of justice (*Dancer v. State*, 1985).

In 1973, the supreme court held that denying parolees access to the civil courts violated their due process and equal protection rights but was not so severe a punishment as to be considered "cruel and unusual" (*Bush v. Reid*). The high court ruled that denying a prisoner conjugal visits was not a cruel and unusual punishment (*McGinnis v. Stevens*, 1975). When a Native prisoner who had been convicted of murder complained that incarceration in any facility other than Bethel's was cruel and unusual punishment because he spoke little English and required a traditional Native diet, the court disagreed (*Abraham v. State*, 1978).

---

[12] State of Alaska, "Official Election Pamphlet" (Juneau, November 8, 1994), B-22.

[13] The phrase, which is drawn from Justice Rabinowitz's decision in *State v. Chaney* (1970), is a refined substitute for retribution.

[14] *Anchorage Daily News*, March 2, 1996.

[15] *Anchorage Daily News*, March 4, 1996.

The high court found that the imposition of criminal punishment for possession of marijuana also did not meet cruel and unusual punishment standards (*Belgarde v. State,* 1975). The court of appeals found "totally without merit" the contention that the marijuana statute subjected minors to cruel and unusual punishment because they were incarcerated for conduct that would not be a crime for adults or would be penalized by a fine only (*M.O.W. v. State,* 1982). Finally, the court of appeals determined that punishment for the unlicensed sale of alcohol in a local option community that prohibited sale of alcohol as a class C felony was not constitutionally disproportionate (*Burnor v. State,* 1992).

In several cases, the supreme court has demonstrated that action can be taken based on the principles of criminal justice administration. The clause on reformation has been interpreted to include rehabilitation. For instance, in *Rust v. State* (1978), the supreme court agreed with a petitioner who sought treatment for his dyslexic condition. Similarly, in 1991, the high court supported an inmate who challenged his removal from a prison industry program after he registered positive for drug use on an unconfirmed urine test. The court ruled that the prisoner had an enforceable interest in continued participation in the program because it was a rehabilitation program and section 12 of the constitution gives prisoners rights to rehabilitation (*Ferguson v. Department of Corrections,* 1991).

In 1970, the Alaska Supreme Court took exception to the leniency of the sentence imposed on a defendant adjudged guilty on two counts of forcible rape and one count of robbery (the sentence comprised concurrent one-year terms with a provision for parole). Following 1969 legislation that authorized the appellate review of criminal sentences, Justice Rabinowitz of the high court read these sentencing criteria into the broad constitutional standards:

> [R]ehabilitation of the offender into a noncriminal member of society, isolation of the offender from society to prevent criminal conduct during the period of confinement, deterrence of the offender himself after his release from confinement or other penalogical treatment, as well as deterrence of other members of the community who might possess tendencies toward criminal conduct similar to that of the offender, and community condemnation of the individual offender, or in other words, reaffirmation of societal norms for the purpose of maintaining respect for the norms themselves. (*State v. Chaney,* 1970, p. 444)

The court required a substantially longer sentence to manifest the seriousness of the appellee's dangerous and unlawful conduct and to reaffirm society's condemnation of forcible rape and robbery.

In a 1978 decision (*Smothers v. State*), the high court declared that retribution was inconsistent with the goals of criminal administration. However, the court supported the legislature's presumptive sentencing statute, which significantly reduced judicial discretion in sentencing (*Nell v. State,* 1982).

Alaska courts have been extensively involved in litigation concerning conditions and services in correctional facilities. In 1981, prisoners brought a class action suit against the state, contending that substandard prison conditions, such as overcrowding, violated state statutes and both state and federal constitutional guarantees. The *Cleary* case was a landmark consent decree on prison conditions (*Michael Cleary et al. v. Robert Smith et al, Superior Court, Third Judicial District*). It has led to negotiated agreements and court orders that have increased rehabilitation programs in prisons, in addition to other improvements.

SECTION 13

Habeas corpus. The privilege of the writ of habeas corpus shall not be suspended, unless when in cases of rebellion or actual or imminent invasion, the public safety requires it.

A writ of habeas corpus (Latin for "you have the body") is used in court to challenge the legality of a person's incarceration. It is traditionally called the Great Writ for the judicial protection of individual rights.

During the constitutional convention, delegates questioned why the committee had added "or imminent peril" to the section. Delegate Dorothy Awes remarked that the committee was inspired by a speech she heard at Ladd Air Base about modern conditions of warfare, with Alaska being only one and a half hours from Russia (*PACC*, 1358). Most delegates, however, thought the phrase "imminent peril" was too ambiguous and replaced it with "imminent invasion" in the final version. This section has not been subject to judicial interpretation.

SECTION 14

Searches and seizures. The right of the people to be secure in their persons, homes and other property, papers and effects, against unreasonable searches and seizures, shall not be violated. No warrants shall issue, but upon probable cause, supported by oath of affirmation, and particularly describing the place to be searched, and the persons or things to be seized.

This section mirrors the New Jersey Constitution and the language of the Fourth Amendment to the U.S. Constitution. It is designed to prohibit warrantless searches and to require that warrants issued by the courts are specific as to the object of search.

Discussion at the constitutional convention on this section focused on preventing electronic surveillance, with many delegates expressing opposition to the wiretapping practices of the McCarthy era. Delegate Jack Hinckel of Kodiak sought to amend the section by adding, "The right of privacy of the individual shall not be invaded by use of any electronic or other scientific transmitting, listening or sound recording device" (*PACC*, 1488). Delegate Seaborn Buckalew noted that the committee's version prohibited wiretapping generally, if not specifically. Other delegates believed that the matter of preventing electronic surveillance should be handled by the legislature, and the amendment failed to pass.

The supreme court noted in *Ellison v. State* (1963) that section 14 contains "an even broader guarantee against unreasonable searches and seizures than does the Fourth Amendment to the Constitution of the United States." It concluded this from the fact that the Fourth Amendment does not have the phrase, "and other property." Moreover, the Alaska Constitution since 1972 has had an explicit right to privacy, which reinforces the protections of section 14.

Section 14 has been applied by the courts to two kinds of situations: investigations of those suspected of crime, and "area-wide exploratory investigations, carried out by specialized law enforcement officers, in order to prevent crime (including violation of health and safety regulations)" (*D.R.C. v. State*, 1982).

A number of Alaska court cases have defined the conditions under which investigating officers may conduct searches without violating constitutional protections. The supreme court allowed evidence from the warrantless search of clothing a defendant was wearing when arrested, nearly two days after an alleged burglary, because the search was incident to the arrest (*Lemon v. State*, 1973). The high court also admitted amphetamines, heroin, and other evidence accumulated from a search for which the warrant was based on a questioned affidavit, because the affidavit was based on statements from a credible informant with personal knowledge of supporting facts (*Keller v. State*, 1975).

Finally, the supreme court held that the exclusionary rule (that evidence obtained in an unconstitutional search or seizure may not be introduced at trial) did not apply to evidence of heroin found in a napkin after a defendant was ordered by police to expectorate. Chief Justice Boochever commented: "The exclusionary rule is not the type of doctrine designed to protect against conviction of the innocent. Rather, it is a prophylactic device to curb improper police conduct and to protect the integrity of the judicial process" (*Moreau v. State*, 1978, p. 280).

However, the supreme court held that the recording of a drug transaction between a defendant and an informant without a search warrant or other court order was constitutionally impermissible, even though the recording was done by police officers stationed outside the defendant's home (*State v. Glass*, 1978). In this case, the court observed that the "transcendent values" preserved by the constitutional guarantees against unreasonable searches and seizures were of greater social importance than use of the evidence to obtain a criminal conviction. The decision is far more protective of privacy than those of the U.S. Supreme Court. However, the court of appeals admitted the testimony of a state shellfish biologist who, in the course of his normal observation, noted that crabbers were in possession of undersized tanner crabs, thus violating state regulations (*Dye v. State*, 1982). The court found that it was unnecessary for the official to follow state procedures for conducting a warrantless search because the information he gathered was routine and in a highly regulated industry.

Generally, Alaska courts have relied on the history of regulation in a field in upholding warrantless searches, pursuant to statutory authorization as well as on a theory of implied consent or an urgent state or federal interest in the warrantless inspection (*Woods & Rohde, Inc., v. State, Department of Labor*, 1977). The supreme court noted approvingly a variety of legitimate administrative searches, such as state liquor law inspections; inspections of food establishments, junkyards, pharmacies, and nursing homes; and safety inspections conducted after a fire and as a condition of airplane boarding. However, the high court ruled that a warrantless Occupational Safety and Health Administration (OSHA) inspection authorized by Alaska's Occupational Safety and Health Act unconstitutionally violated this section. The court read section 14 as protective of the privacy of owners of business premises; the burden of obtaining warrants would not frustrate the purpose of OSHA inspectors (*Woods & Rohde, Inc. v. State, Department of Labor*, 1977).

In two cases establishing the constitutionality of Alaska's driving while intoxicated (DWI) statutes, the court of appeals found first that the breathalyzer examination, made without a warrant, is a valid search (*McCracken v. State*, 1984); criminalizing refusal to consent to a breathalyzer examination did not violate the federal Fourth Amendment. Moreover, it ruled that for purposes of search and seizure analysis, a blood test was not materially more intrusive than testing the breath for alcohol content (*Municipality of Anchorage v. Ray*, 1993).

SECTION 15

Prohibited state action. No bill of attainder or ex post facto law shall be passed. No law impairing the obligation of contracts, and no law making any irrevocable grant of special privileges or immunities shall be passed. No conviction shall work corruption of blood or forfeiture of estate.

Most of section 15 repeats protections of the federal Constitution in Article I, section 10. A bill of attainder is a legislative declaration in a statute that specific individuals are guilty, without judicial trial. An ex post facto law makes acts that have already been committed innocently illegal, or increases the penalties for criminal behavior after the crime was committed. Prohibiting the impairment of contract is another protection against retroactive laws. Prohibitions of irrevocable privileges or immunities are designed to restrict private legislation benefiting persons or interests permanently. The final sentence of this section prohibits laws penalizing the family of convicted criminals.

Most judicial interpretations of section 15 have concerned alleged ex post facto laws. For example, the supreme court upheld the state's mandatory three-year license revocation for third-time DWI offenders (*Danks v. State*, 1980). The court found that even if prior convictions had occurred before the enactment of the revocation statute, the revocation was based on the latest crime, which was more serious because it was a repetitive one; it was not barred by the prohibition on ex post facto laws. The court of appeals extended the logic of this decision to prior convictions in other states of third-time DWI offenders (*Carter v. State*, 1981).

When a defendant contended that his conviction for importing alcohol into a "dry" village was a violation of the prohibition against ex post facto laws (because federal approval of the local option election laws was pending at the time of his offense), the court of appeals disagreed (*Harrison v. State*, 1984). The court pointed out that the federal preclearance of state election law was not germane to the local option case (federal approval ultimately was attained).

The supreme court also upheld the legality under both state and federal constitutions of an extension of the period for bringing charges of sexual abuse of a minor. The defendant had argued that sexual assault charges should be dismissed because the statute of limitations had expired and thus, to convict him based on the enlarged period for bringing charges violated ex post facto prohibitions (*State v. Creekpaum*, 1988). In reaching its decision, the court relied on the tests in *Weaver v. Graham* (1981), which stated that for a law to fall within the ex post facto prohibition, it "must be retrospective, that is, it must apply to events occurring before its enactment," and "it must disadvantage the offender affected by it" (p. 29). In this case, the court found that the defendant did not suffer because of a change in the crime defined, the punishment prescribed, or the quantity or degree of proof necessary to establish guilt.

The clause prohibiting irrevocable grants of privileges and immunities has been subject to little judicial interpretation. The supreme court, however, declared that the provision did not bar the legislature from granting to municipalities all rights and immunities that were not also held by private entities, for without this provision, municipalities would lose the power to govern. In the specific case, it upheld a statute conferring immunity to municipalities for liability arising from safety inspections of private property (*Wilson v. Municipality of Anchorage*, 1983).

The clause on maintaining the obligation of contracts has been interpreted to allow revisions of such items as tariff rates on the property of developers (*Stepanov v. Homer Electric Association*, 1991). Contract rights remain subject to police power regulation (to protect public health, for example) as well as to changes in methods of enforcing contracts.

SECTION 16

Civil suits; trial by jury. In civil cases where the amount in controversy exceeds two hundred fifty dollars, the right of trial by a jury of twelve is preserved to the same extent as it existed at common law. The legislature may make provision for a verdict by not less than three-fourths of the jury and, in courts not of record, may provide for a jury of not less than six or more than twelve.

Section 16 can be read in connection with section 11, as extending the protections of jury trial to civil cases. The reference to common law might potentially limit the number of matters that could be submitted to jury trial, for example, modern statutory cases concerning discrimination. The specification of a dollar amount, however, expands the opportunity for jury trial. The legislature has provided for juries of six in courts not of record (district courts), and for verdicts by five-sixths of jury members.

At the constitutional convention, the discussion on this section concerned whether a dollar figure should be mentioned at all. Initially, a majority substituted for the dollar figure, "a sum set by law." On reconsideration, however, delegates agreed to keep a dollar amount, which would remove this right from alteration by the legislature. Delegate Walter Smith reminded his fellow delegates: "If we had trust in the Legislature, then why would we need a bill of rights? The bill of rights is to guarantee rights, not to leave them to future legislatures" (*PACC*, 1423).

The supreme court has been careful in expanding trial by jury rights to civil cases. When the state sought injunctive and restitutory relief under the Uniform Land Sales Practices Act, the court held that the developer was not entitled to trial by jury (*State v. First National Bank of Anchorage*, 1982). The eligibility for trial depended, in the court's interpretation of common law, on whether the claim being asserted was legal or equitable in nature. If it were equitable only, as was the state's claim, there was no right to a jury trial. The court also denied a jury trial to a discharged city employee whose employment contract contained grievance procedures (*Diedrich v. City of Ketchikan*, 1991).

SECTION 17

Imprisonment for debt. There shall be no imprisonment for debt. This section does not prohibit civil arrest of absconding debtors.

This section is a standard provision of state constitutions, which protects those who have incurred debts in private contracts from incarceration. Unlike most other state constitutions, the section is silent on the criminal offense of fraud. It does permit civil actions against debtors who depart without paying their bills.

The courts have interpreted the provision as allowing the imprisonment of those who do not pay fines and criminal penalties or who defy court orders to pay divorce or child support bills.[16]

---

[16] Harrison, *Alaska's Constitution*, 42.

SECTION 18

Eminent domain. Private property shall not be taken or damaged for public use without just compensation.

Section 18 recognizes the sovereignty of state government and its ability to take private property, as long as it is appropriated for public purposes. When property is taken, however, the taking must be compensated. The addition of the word *damaged* affords the property owner broader protection than that explicitly conferred by the Fifth Amendment of the federal constitution. The section is thus closely related to the due process guarantees of section 7. "Just" compensation is specified by the legislature and interpreted by the judiciary.

The Alaska high court has applied the eminent domain provision in several different areas. In *B & G Meats, Inc. v. State* (1979), the court declined to compensate the operator of a wholesale/retail meat store when the state changed the frontage road providing access to the store. Although the operator had a right to access to the highway, the diversion of traffic flow in order to improve public safety did not restrict access and thus, ruled the court, was not compensable.

The court struck out in a different direction when a private attorney refused a court appointment to represent an indigent criminal defendant without compensation and then appealed the resulting contempt citation. The court held that an appointment compelling the attorney to work pro bono (representing indigent criminal defendants for little or no compensation) was the taking of property, for which just compensation was required under the eminent domain provision of the constitution (*DeLisio v. Alaska Superior Court*, 1987).

However, the court ruled that the state could increase the hours worked by union employees without salary increases, after the parties to negotiation had reached an impasse. Once the collective bargaining agreement expired, the continuation of existing terms and conditions, said the court, was "a mere expectancy" (p. 1034). Therefore, the employees were not deprived of property by the extension of their work week from 37.5 to 40 hours (*Alaska Public Employees Association v. State, Department of Administration*, 1989).

Most of the eminent domain cases concern land taken for highways, and the courts have pondered over what "just" compensation entails. When road construction in Petersburg displaced a bar business, the supreme court upheld an award to the owner, Richard Kito, for loss of profits incurred by the relocation, because his property had been "damaged for public use" (*State v. Hammer*, 1976, p. 821). The court noted that traditionally, such incidental damages were not recognized in eminent domain proceedings; however, they were justified in this case:

> To deny compensation for such damages would contravene the policy behind the constitutional provision that the condemnee should not pay a higher price for a public improvement than do other members of the public. The Constitution does not require Kito to make a special sacrifice for the Petersburg Highway, (p. 826)

The supreme court repeatedly has set fair market value as the standard for just compensation. In *Gackstetter v. State* (1980), the high court referred to the treatise, *Nichols on Eminent Domain,* for a definition of fair market value as the amount of money "a purchaser willing but not obliged to buy the property would pay to an owner willing but not obliged to sell it, taking into consideration all uses for which the land was suited and might in reason be applied."[17] In this decision, the court rejected the argument of property owners who wanted a higher value placed on the land lost to the state because of the value to the state of fill and gravel on the property. The high court held that "just compensation is determined by what the owner has lost and not by what the condemnor has gained" (*Gackstetter v. State,* 1980, p. 566).

Normally, Alaska courts have not included the value enhancement attributable to the project for which property is being taken when making fair market determinations. However, the supreme court has ruled that owners may receive compensation for value added to property by an unrelated public project that took no part of the tract of land involved (*State v. Alaska Continental Development Corp.,* 1980).

SECTION 19

Right to keep and bear arms. A well-regulated militia being necessary to the security of a free state, the right of the people to keep and bear arms shall not be infringed. The individual right to keep and bear arms shall not be denied or infringed by the State or a political subdivision of the State.

The first sentence of section 19 is taken verbatim from the Second Amendment to the federal constitution. It is the primary justification for the ownership of constitutionally protected weapons, which include rifles, shotguns, revolvers, pistols, and knives. Nevertheless, the state does regulate firearms through registration requirements (extending to concealed weapons) and the prohibition of such weapons as sawed-off shotguns.

The second sentence was added by voters in the 1994 general elections and the title was changed to add "keep and." Supporters of this amendment were motivated by the growing strength of gun control forces outside Alaska. They alleged that there were "continuing attacks on the . . . constitutional right to keep and bear arms," making it necessary to "clarify the right . . . to own and use arms for traditional purposes." Opponents said the amendment was unnecessary because they believed Alaska's laws were among the least restrictive weapon laws of any state. Further, they alleged that the amendment was flawed and would undo laws currently in place restricting weapons from school grounds

[17] Julius Sackman, *Nichols' The Law of Eminent Domain,* 3d ed. (New York: Matthew Bender, 1964), 12.

and from use by felons.[18] The amendment passed resoundingly in the 1994 general elections.

Section 19 has not been interpreted by the judiciary. However, an attorney general's opinion cautioned that expanded right-to-bear-arms provisions in other states had prohibited law enforcement authorities from enforcing concealed weapons statutes.[19]

SECTION 20

Quartering soldiers. No member of the armed forces shall in time of peace be quartered in any house without the consent of the owner or occupant, or in time of war except as prescribed by law. The military shall be in strict subordination to the civil power.

The first sentence reflects the Third Amendment to the U.S. Constitution. It refers to the colonial heritage of the American states and the strong opposition to housing British soldiers in American homes. The second sentence is an expression of American constitutionalism—civilian control over the military. Neither part of this provision has been the subject of judicial interpretation.

SECTION 21

Construction. The enumeration of rights in this constitution shall not impair or deny others retained by the people.

This "saving" clause indicates that there may be other rights not yet expressed and that these should not be excluded from protection. It resembles the Ninth Amendment to the U.S. Constitution. The source of other rights could be the common law tradition or natural law.

The one "saved" right interpreted by the supreme court is the right of a person to act as his or her own attorney. In *McCracken v. State* (1974), the court acknowledged that the right to self-representation was not absolute, for it depended on knowledge of the allegations and of what one was giving up. However, the court found ample precedent for this right: "At the time that the Alaska Constitution was enacted and became effective, the right of self-representation was so well established that it must be regarded as a right 'retained by the people'" (p. 91).

---

[18] State of Alaska, "Official Election Pamphlet" (Juneau, November 8, 1994), B-20.

[19] Ibid., B-21.

SECTION 22

Right of privacy. The right of the people to privacy is recognized and shall not be infringed. The legislature shall implement this section.

During the constitutional convention, privacy rights were discussed in the context of electronic eavesdropping, but the general sentiment supported delegate Seaborn Buckalew's observation: "I don't think we have ever had any problem in Alaska with wire-tapping or invasion of the right of privacy of the average Alaskan" (*PACC*, 1439).

Concerns about the possible abuse of computerized information systems as well as police surveillance, which developed in the early 1970s, prompted legislators to draft this constitutional amendment.[20] Voters approved it in 1972. The amendment gives broader protection to individual privacy than is available through the U.S. Constitution, where the right to privacy is found in the penumbra cast by the First Amendment's right of association, the Third Amendment's prohibition against quartering soldiers, the Fourth Amendment's search and seizure clause, the Fifth Amendment's guarantees against self-incrimination, and the Ninth Amendment.[21]

The judiciary has interpreted section 22 extensively, starting with the *Ravin v. State* decision in 1975. Irvin Ravin, an attorney, was arrested for possessing a small amount of marijuana. The superior court found against Ravin, supporting the state prosecutors. The supreme court reversed the lower court's decision, declaring that the constitutional right to privacy permitted a citizen to possess a small amount of marijuana for personal use. The court defined the right as associated with a "penumbra of home-related rights" (p. 494), which provided immunity from prosecution only when the private activity did not endanger or harm the general public.

The high court clarified the status of marijuana possession in a second 1975 decision, *Belgarde v. State*. In this case, the defendant had been convicted for possession of marijuana in public, in connection with sale of a large amount of the drug. The supreme court upheld the conviction, saying that privacy rights in public places warranted less constitutional protection.

Then, in a 1978 decision, the high court ruled that the criminalization of personal use and possession of cocaine in the home was not an invalid infringement on the right of privacy (*State v. Erickson*). Unlike the Ravin case, which concerned a relatively harmless drug, the court found cocaine to be substantially more of a threat to health and welfare. The court concluded: "No one has an

---

[20] Harrison, *Alaska's Constitution*, 44–45.

[21] See *Griswold v. Connecticut* (1965) and Chase and Ducat, *Edwin S. Corwin's THE CONSTITUTION*, 441–442, 466–473.

absolute right to do things in the privacy of his own home which will affect himself or others adversely" (p. 21).

In 1990, by a ratio of five to four, Alaska voters passed an initiative in favor of making possession of marijuana a criminal offense. Alaskans for Privacy filed suit in the spring of 1991, and on the day the new law was to go into effect, it landed back in court.[22]

The contention of Alaskans for Privacy was that the initiative clearly contravened the privacy section of the Alaska Constitution, and moreover, that a popular initiative could not overturn a supreme court decision based on it (*Ravin v. State*, 1975),—a constitutional amendment was required. Anchorage Superior Court Judge Karen Hunt disagreed and ruled that marijuana possession was illegal. Alaskans for Privacy then petitioned for review by the supreme court, but this was denied and the case appeared to fade away.

In 1993, Ketchikan Superior Court Judge Michael Thompson dismissed a marijuana conviction, stating that an initiative could not overturn a supreme court decision (*State v. McNeil*). The state did not appeal this decision. Thus, with superior court decisions on both sides of the issue and without a further supreme court clarification, the status of marijuana possession in Alaska as of 1996 is undecided.[23] The judgment of those applying the law, however, is that no one much cares about marijuana possession in private, and the 1975 *Ravin* decision is still recognized in reality.

The supreme court also has employed the private/public distinction in applying the privacy right to electronic surveillance. In *State v. Glass* (1978), it held that the right to privacy was abridged by warrantless participant monitoring of private conversations, regardless of the locus of police surveillance. (In this case, the police were stationed outside the defendant's house while monitoring the frequency of a transmitter worn by an informant who was talking with the defendant.) Using the two-pronged test developed by Justice John Harlan in *Katz v. United States* (1967), the court held: "One communicating private matters to another exhibits an actual [subjective] expectation of privacy whether or not the listener is equipped with electronic devices. The key question is whether that expectation of privacy is one that society is prepared to recognize as reasonable" (p. 880).

In another case, however, it was clearly unreasonable for a DWI defendant to expect that his conversation with a fully uniformed police officer would not be recorded, and the court found no violation of privacy rights (*City and Borough of Juneau v. Quinto*, 1984).

---

[22] McBeath and Morehouse, *Alaska Politics and Government*, 204.

[23] I am indebted to Anchorage attorney Robert Wagstaff, who represented Alaskans for Privacy, for these observations, February 16, 1996.

When a defendant used the privacy of his home to engage in lewd and lascivious conduct with a child, the supreme court held that he lacked the standing to challenge the statute with the theory that it infringed on sexual privacy rights of juveniles (*Anderson v. State*, 1977). In such a situation, the court continued, the child's apparent consent was overridden by the state's interest in the well-being of children.

The appeals court noted that the right to privacy "clearly shielded the ingestion of food, beverages and other substances, subject to overriding public health considerations" (p. 337). However, consumption of alcohol was not a protected privacy right that could be used to invalidate a local option law prohibiting the importation of alcohol into a village (*Harrison v. State*, 1984).

Consistently, Alaska courts (like the federal bench) have stated that privacy is a protection of "people, not places" (p. 421), but places outside the home tend to be given less protection. Fishing vessels, for example, are subject to frequent necessary inspections, and observations of their holds during unloading are not covered by the privacy provision (*Dye v. State*, 1982).

The court of appeals ruled that searches of students by school officials who followed properly enacted school regulations were consistent with section 22 (*D.R.C. v. State*, 1982). Even one's choice of apparel might fall outside privacy protections, said the supreme court; for example, requiring an attorney to wear a coat and tie was a reasonable court requirement to induce an air of seriousness, solemnity, and respect for the court (*Friedman v. District Court*, 1980).

Personnel records and internal investigations of citizens' complaints about the police, declared the supreme court in 1990, are not protected by privacy rights from discovery (*Jones v. Jennings*). Even so personal a substance as one's blood may be drawn by the state without violating privacy rights, if one were driving while intoxicated and involved in an accident bringing death or injury to another (*Municipality of Anchorage v. Ray*, 1993).

Challenges to Alaska's campaign disclosure laws, which have been administered by the Alaska Public Offices Commission (APOC), have concerned the constitutional privacy provision. APOC charged a physician who served on a school board with violating public disclosure regulations when he declined to list patients of his medical center on the conflict of interest form. In *Falcon v. Alaska Public Offices Commission* (1977), the supreme court upheld the ruling, noting that only certain types of information communicated in the context of the physician-patient relationship fell in the protected privacy zone.

Based on this ruling, a group of chiropractors sought to overturn amendments to the Alaska Worker's Compensation Act, alleging that its requirements for the administrative review of payment claims for multiple treatments (in excess of new frequency standards) constitutionally infringed on the physician-patient relationship. Writing for the court, Justice Robert Eastaugh dismissed the challenge, saying that "the right to privacy is not absolute" (p. 972). The physician-patient relationship was allowed to be invaded only to the extent necessary to administer the worker's compensation program (*Chiropractors for Justice v. State*, 1995).

When an opponent for an Anchorage bond proposition advertised his opposition in the newspapers but declined to report personal data and expenditures, he was held in violation of the Campaign Disclosure Act; however, the court found the act itself incomplete with respect to the protection of free speech rights. The supreme court acknowledged an interest in anonymity for those fearing reprisals and held that APOC would need to adopt regulations providing such protections (*Messerli v. State*, 1980).

The high court ruled against the complaint of an oil-field services company that the act violated its privacy because the company failed to establish that its rights had been abridged (*VECO International Inc. v. Alaska Public Offices Commission*, 1988).

Alaska's constitutional protection of privacy figured prominently in one of the larger issues of the 1980s and 1990s—AIDS testing. The supreme court considered this issue in relationship to section 22 in *Chizmar v. Mackie* (1995). In this case, a doctor tested a married woman for the human immunodeficiency virus (HIV), the presence of which indicates AIDS, when she entered the hospital in 1989 with an unexplained and unresolved case of pneumonia, because he believed she was from an island near Haiti (which then had a high incidence of the disease). The initial test was positive, and the doctor told the husband before informing his patient of the result. Subsequently, the husband divorced his wife, who sued the doctor for malpractice and sought damages based on the violation of her privacy rights, among other reasons. The supreme court, referring to its decision in *Luedtke v. Nabors Alaska Drilling, Inc.* (1989), held that the right to privacy was a right against *government action*, not against the actions of private parties. Moreover, the court found that the physician's actions were not so outrageous as to support a claim for damages.

The legislature has not yet implemented this section of the constitution. The courts have been extensively involved in interpreting the meaning of the right to privacy.

SECTION 23

Resident preference. This constitution does not prohibit the State from granting preferences, on the basis of Alaska residence, to residents of the State over nonresidents to the extent permitted by the Constitution of the United States.

Voters added this amendment to the constitution in 1988, after both federal and state courts had struck down resident-preference schemes (see section 1). It means that resident preference is legal and constitutional unless it violates the federal constitution. The courts may not rule that such a preference violates the Alaska Constitution. This section has not yet been subject to judicial interpretation.

SECTION 24

Rights of crime victims. Crime victims, as defined by law, shall have the following rights as provided by law: the right to be reasonably protected from the accused through the imposition of appropriate bail or conditions of release by the court; the right to confer with the prosecution; the right to be treated with dignity, respect, and fairness during all phases of the criminal and juvenile justice process; the right to timely disposition of the case following the arrest of the accused; the right to obtain information about and be allowed to be present at all criminal or juvenile proceedings where the accused has the right to be present; the right to be allowed to be heard, upon request, at sentencing, before or after conviction or juvenile adjudication, and at any proceeding where the accused's release from custody is considered; the right to restitution from the accused; and the right to be informed, upon request, of the accused's escape or release from custody before or after conviction or juvenile adjudication.

The Declaration of Rights (section 24) is an amendment to the constitution, which was added by voters in 1994. The rights listed in this section, such as the right to reasonable protection from an accused person, the right to confer with the prosecution, and to be treated with dignity, respect, and fairness, are victims' rights and the rights of the family of a victim of a crime.

Supporters of the amendment pointed out in the general election campaign that previously, victims' rights had had only a statutory basis and thereby were inferior to a criminal defendant's constitutional rights.[24] Incorporating victims' rights in the Declaration of Rights, supporters said, redressed the imbalance.

Opponents thought that the new section was unnecessary, as all aspects were already covered in state law. Further, they feared that the amendment might lead to attempts to justify cruel and unusual punishment. The judiciary has not yet interpreted this section.

[24] State of Alaska, "Official Election Pamphlet" (Juneau, November 8, 1994), B-22–23.

Article II

The Legislature

The constitution's legislative article establishes the legislative branch of government. It assigns to it the power to make laws (which is plenary), specifies the ways in which representatives are selected and legislative processes are structured, and provides limits on legislative power.

Like the federal constitution and a number of state constitutions, the Alaska Constitution does not provide an express, textual statement of the separation of powers doctrine. However, the Alaska Supreme Court recognized the existence of the separation of powers doctrine in *Public Defender Agency v. Superior Court, Third Judicial District* (1975):

> Although the Alaska Constitution does not expressly address itself to the doctrine of separation of powers, we have noted that often what is implied is as much a part of the constitution as what is expressed. The doctrine must be implied by the vesting of legislative, executive, and judicial powers in three separate branches, as done in section 1 of articles II, III, and IV. (p. 950)

Several sections of Article II demonstrate the separation of legislative from executive and judicial power and the checks and balances of the branches as they affect the legislative process. For example, section 5 prohibits dual office holding, and section 6 shields legislators from administrative harassment while in session, both of which protect the independence and integrity of the legislative branch. Section 15 expresses the powers of the governor to veto legislation, giving him or her a strong role to play in the making of laws.

The Alaska legislature has many unicameral features, such as uniform rules of procedure (section 12) and joint sessions for the reconsideration of gubernatorial vetoes (section 16). The framers placed fewer limits on the legislature's power than are found in most other state constitutions. However, voters have monitored legislative salaries carefully (section 7), and in 1984, they limited the session length to 120 days (section 8).

SECTION 1

Legislative power; membership. The legislative power of the State is vested in a legislature consisting of a senate with a membership of twenty and a house of representatives with a membership of forty.

Like all other states except Nebraska, the constitution establishes a bicameral, or two-house, legislature. With only 60 members, the Alaska legislature is the nation's second smallest (Nebraska's unicameral legislature has 49 members).

The issue of unicameral versus bicameral legislatures was the first difficult question of government that the constitutional convention delegates faced; it was the subject of prolonged debate in committee and on the convention floor.

Delegate John McNees was the primary proponent of a unicameral body. He argued that a bicameral legislature was a holdover from the days when the English wanted to limit the powers of the king. The British houses were composed of two entirely different kinds of people, unlike the houses of Congress or American state legislatures. He pointed to the success of unicameral legislatures in Canada and Finland. His observation was that one-house systems were more efficient, less time-consuming and less costly than those of two houses. McNees thought that influence of lobbyists would decline in a unicameral system and, because conferences between houses would be unnecessary, there would be more floor debate and openness (*PACC*, 432–433).

Victor Fischer supported a unicameral system because he believed it would operate more efficiently: "You could have twice as much study for each bill and . . . you would not have duplication" (*PACC*, 429). Delegate Frank Barr thought that the unicameral system was "ideal," but explained that was also what was wrong with it: "The unicameral system would work very well if human beings ceased to be human" (*PACC*, 446).

Most of the delegates, however, favored bicameralism because of its familiarity. George Cooper spoke for many when he said the bicameral system suits "our age-old American custom of checks and balances" (*PACC*, 425). Other reasons were mentioned as well. Delegate Robert McNealy had grown up in Nebraska, living under its unicameral system only a few years before moving to Alaska. Although he thought the system worked well for Nebraska, he was "unalterably opposed" to its use in Alaska, largely because the population was much less homogeneous and stable than Nebraska's (*PACC*, 423). Delegate Dora Sweeney clinched the argument against unicameralism when she opined that Alaska voters and the Congress would be unlikely to endorse such a radical proposal.

The Alaska Supreme Court has discussed the assignment of legislative power in three contexts. When the legislature established the Alaska State Development Corporation in 1961, its constitutionality was challenged as an unlawful delegation to the corporation of legislative authority, which transferred public funds and the use of public credit for other than a public purpose. The court found the delegation proper and declined to second-guess the legislature:

> Where the legislature has found that a public purpose will be served by the expenditure or transfer of public funds or the use of the public credit, this court will not set aside the finding of the legislature unless it clearly appears that such finding is arbitrary and without any reasonable basis in fact. (*DeArmond v. Alaska State Development Corporation*, 1962, p. 721).

However, in 1986, the high court held an action of then Governor William Sheffield to be an unconstitutional delegation of legislative power. When oil prices fell below ten dollars per barrel, the governor impounded 10 percent of agency budgets and the school foundation grant, basing this action on a section of the executive budget act authorizing the governor to reduce or withhold expenditures. The Fairbanks School Board, Fairbanks North Star Borough Assembly, and mayor sued, calling the governor's action unconstitutional. In *State v. Fairbanks North Star Borough* (1987), the high court agreed that the legislation had provided insufficient standards for the governor to reduce spending in this way.

The high court's first separation of powers case concerned a dispute between a Democratic legislature and a Republican governor. The legislature had passed, over the governor's veto, a statute that provided that the appointment of deputy heads of each principal executive department and nineteen directors of divisions was subject to confirmation by the legislature. The governor saw this action as violating his appointment powers and the separation of powers implied in the constitution.

In *Bradner v. Hammond* (1976), the supreme court held that the separation of powers doctrine was "a brooding omnipresence by virtue of its conceptually central role in the structure of American constitutional government" (p. 5). Interpreting the issue, the court held that the appointment of executive officers of state government was an executive, and not a legislative, function; moreover, the confirmation of executive appointments was an attribute of the appointive power of the governor, not a distinct legislative power. Consequently, the court ruled the legislative statute unconstitutional.

SECTION 2

Members' qualifications. A member of the legislature shall be a qualified voter who has been a resident of Alaska for at least three years and of the district from which elected for at least one year, immediately preceding his filing for office. A senator shall be at least twenty-five years of age and a representative at least twenty-one years of age.

This provision establishes the eligibility requirements for membership in the legislature. One must be a qualified voter, which in turn requires U.S. citizenship (Article V, section 1). The residence requirement is designed to ensure familiarity with issues the legislators will address and with their constituents. The greater age requirement for the Senate than the House reflects a traditional bias found in about one-fourth of upper Houses nationally and in the U.S. Senate.

The supreme court defended the residency requirements for legislative office in an equal protection challenge (*Gilbert v. State*, 1974). It found two compelling justifications for the requirement. First, those who governed needed to be acquainted with the conditions, problems, and needs of their constituents. Indeed, Alaska's unique geography, economy, and ethnic diversity made this interest of greater importance than in any other state. Second, electors needed a period in which to become familiar with the character, habits, and reputation of candidates for office. In an era of media campaigns and packaged candidacies, it was essential, the court held, that voters have the opportunity to develop some direct knowledge of candidates in order to judge their sincerity and the truth of their claims.

SECTION 3

Election and terms. Legislators shall be elected at general elections. Their terms begin on the fourth Monday of the January following election unless otherwise provided by law. The term of representatives shall be two years, and the term of senators, four years. One-half of the senators shall be elected every two years.

This paragraph provides for biennial legislative elections and a continuing two-year session of the legislature. The term lengths—two years for representatives and four for senators—are the same as those of the Territorial Legislature and most U.S. states.

The only discussion on this section at the constitutional convention was introduced by delegate Victor Rivers, who proposed that terms for House members be for four years instead of two (*PACC*, 1784). At that time, only four states had four-year House terms, and there was little support for the amendment.

The legislature has set the beginning dates of terms in statute. Following presidential elections, the legislature begins on the second Monday in January; following gubernatorial elections, the legislature starts on the third Monday in January (AS 24.05.080).

SECTION 4

Vacancies. A vacancy in the legislature shall be filled for the unexpired term as provided by law. If no provision is made, the governor shall fill the vacancy by appointment.

This section provides for the filling of vacancies due to death or resignation by appointment. The legislature has not sought to fill vacancies by election, except when a senate vacancy leaves a seat open for more than 29 months. The legislature's statute on vacancies allows the governor to appoint a person to serve the remainder of the term, but that person must be of the same party as the predecessor and confirmed by a majority in that party and of the same house as the predecessor (AS 15.40.320–470). This paragraph has not been subject to significant judicial interpretation.

SECTION 5

Disqualifications. No legislator may hold any other office or position of profit under the United States or the State. During the term for which elected and for one year thereafter, no legislator may be nominated, elected, or appointed to any other office or position of profit which has been created, or the salary or emoluments of which have been increased, while he was a member. This section shall not prevent any person from seeking or holding the office of governor, secretary of state, or member of Congress. This section shall not apply to employment by or election to a constitutional convention.

The first sentence establishes the independence of the legislature from the executive and judiciary by making it impossible for legislators to have a second position that might compromise their legislative integrity (dual office holding). It also guards against conflicts of interest and self-aggrandizement. The second sentence was patterned after Article I, section 6, clause 2, of the U.S. Constitution; it is commonly found in state constitutions. It expresses apprehension over possible collusion between the executive and legislators, whose decisions might be influenced by the promise of jobs in the state administration.[25] It thus serves to eliminate suspicions that legislators are acting for selfish motives when voting for or against bills.

The first sentence of section 5 was added by delegate Steve McCutcheon, chairman of the Committee on the Legislative Branch. The intent was "that there should be no dual office holding from the standpoint of a legislator," and to clarify what the original section had left unclear (*PACC*, 3095).

---

[25] See Chase and Ducat, *Edwin S. Corwin's THE CONSTITUTION*, 32–34, for differences between presidential and cabinet systems.

In *Begich v. Jefferson* (1968), the Alaska Supreme Court held that the term "position of profit" was intended to prohibit all other salaried, nontemporary employment under the United States or the state of Alaska. It declared unconstitutional a state statute that had excluded teachers from this consideration, and ruled that teachers and a school superintendent of the Alaska State-Operated School System, who were then serving in the legislature, could not hold both offices simultaneously.

The attorney general has ruled that legislators may not serve on legislative-executive commissions or boards that carry out significant executive functions.[26] Service on advisory joint committees or boards, however, is permissible.[27]

The supreme court interpreted the second sentence in its 1976 decision *Warwick v. State*. Warwick was a member of the Eighth Legislature who was appointed commissioner of administration within the time period proscribed by section 5. The Eighth Legislature had raised salaries, including that of the commissioner of administration, but Warwick argued that they had been raised again by the succeeding legislature and that he had demonstrated no improper intent. The court held that the appointment was in violation of the constitutional provision (but ruled that its decision should not be applied prospectively); the purpose of the provision was to prevent all legislators from being influenced by either conscious or unconscious selfish motives. (A proposed 1980 amendment to the constitution would have eliminated this sentence, but it failed to pass.)

SECTION 6

Immunities. Legislators may not be held to answer before any other tribunal for any statement made in the exercise of their legislative duties while the legislature is in session. Members attending, going to, or returning from legislative sessions are not subject to civil process and are privileged from arrest except for felony or breach of the peace.

This section is similar to the federal Constitution's "Speech and Debate Clause" (Article I, section 6, clause 1). Historically, its purpose is to protect disfavored legislators from hostile executives (thereby enhancing their independence) and to protect them from the burdens of forced participation in private litigation. The common objective is to increase legislative effectiveness. The phrase "are not subject to civil process" was adopted from the Washington Constitution (*PACC*, 1684). It does not represent a broad exclusion from arrest, however, because of the specific mention of "felony or breach of the peace."

---

[26] Alaska Department of Law, Formal Opinion, Office of the Attorney General, 1977, No. 42 (Constitutionality of Legislators Serving on the State Bond Committee), Juneau.

[27] Harrison, *Alaska's Constitution*, 58.

In *State v. Dankworth* (1983), the court of appeals provided a definitive interpretation of the first sentence of section 6. Dankworth, who was then president of the state Senate, was indicted on two counts of conflict of interest. During the 1982 legislative session, he had inserted a line in the state capital budget in order to purchase a pipeline camp of which he was a part owner at a price which would bring him substantial profits. The state alleged that he was using his influence to secure an appropriation that would benefit him. However, the appeals court accepted Dankworth's arguments (as used in federal courts) that once it had been established that legislative business was being done, "the propriety and the motivation for the action taken, as well as the detail of the acts performed, are immune from judicial inquiry" (p. 151). The court clarified by noting: "[O]ur constitutional provision protects any statements made or actions taken by a legislator that directly affect the enactment of legislation or the contents of bills to be submitted to the legislature, whether or not the statements or actions occur in public" (p. 151).

The immunities clause of the constitution was used in an interesting episode during the Sheffield administration (1982–1986). The ruling coalition in the House of Representatives declined to attend a joint session called by the governor to confirm his appointments to cabinet posts, whereupon the attendance of some House members was compelled by state troopers. (A separate suit by a legislator [who alleged civil rights violations, false arrest, and imprisonment] was dismissed by the federal court because attendance was compelled for legitimate legislative activities; see *Schultz v. Sundberg*, 1985). The Senate president, who was not a coalition supporter, presided over the joint session that confirmed the appointments. House majority coalition members then challenged the legality of the joint session and the validity of the confirmation votes. They subpoenaed the Senate president to testify concerning conversations he had had with the governor pertaining to the joint session. In *Kerttula v. Abood* (1984), the high court found that the Senate president's conversations with the governor fell within the definition of legislative duties, and thus he was protected by the immunity clause from revealing information at the meeting.

SECTION 7

Salary and expenses. Legislators shall receive annual salaries. They may receive a per diem allowance for expenses while in session and are entitled to travel expenses going to and from sessions. Presiding officers may receive additional compensation.

Section 7 avoids the practice some states follow and leaves the amounts of legislative salaries out of the constitutional text. It also does not limit legislators from raising (or lowering) salaries during their terms of office. Making legislative compensation a matter for the legislature itself is a mark of the strong legislature enshrined in the National Municipal League's *Model State Constitution;*[28] however, it has been quite controversial in Alaska politically.

The salary to be paid legislators was a divisive issue during the constitutional convention. Some delegates wanted to limit the discretion of the legislature by placing a salary figure or percentage in the constitutional provision. One proposal was to pay legislators a daily amount, but other delegates thought this would give legislators little incentive to hurry. A second proposal was to set legislative salaries at 10, 15, 20, and 33 percent of the governor's salary. At several points, the 10 percent figure seemed to have a bare majority in support. Delegate Herb Hilscher expressed the views of many critics of legislative salaries when he said that to "give the legislature a blank check to write their own salaries" would be the easiest way to encourage votes *against* ratification of the constitution (*PACC*, 1652).

However, other delegates pointed to the importance of having adequate legislative salaries. John McNees read the delegates a *Reader's Digest* article that warned that low pay made legislators more susceptible to bribery. Throughout this discussion, several amendments were offered to the committee's proposal, which left salaries to be disposed of by the legislature. Delegate Seaborn Buckalew expressed the views of an evolving majority when he said: "Now we trust the legislators to enact all our laws and I think we can trust them to set their salaries" (*PACC*, 1641). That is what delegates did in the final version of the salaries provision.

The experience of Alaskans with legislative pay has raised question about this constitutional provision. In 1975, the legislature passed a bill increasing salaries of legislators, judges, and department heads. Opposition developed quickly, however, and a referendum petition to nullify the bill passed overwhelmingly at the next election.[29] In 1983, legislators changed the per diem/stipend system of paying themselves to an annual salary; at $46,800, it neared the top nationally. Legislators liked the salary increase because, among other benefits, it equalized their pay. While some leaders were earning more than $60,000 a year, lawmakers who claimed no interim per diem pay made about $26,000. Failing to understand or appreciate the inequities in the existing system, citizens recognized only that lawmakers wanted the equivalent of year-round pay for part-time work.[30] To head off a public outcry and forestall another referendum, the legislature rescinded its action and cut salaries in half, but it also restored its per diem.

---

[28] National Municipal League, *Model State Constitution*, 5th ed. (New York, 1954), 4, 27.

[29] Harrison, *Alaska's Constitution*, 62.

[30] McBeath and Morehouse, *Alaska Politics and Government*, 162–163.

SECTION 8

Regular sessions. The legislature shall convene in regular session each year on the fourth Monday in January, but the month and day may be changed by law. The legislature shall adjourn from regular session no later than one hundred twenty consecutive calendar days from the date it convenes except that a regular session may be extended once for up to ten consecutive calendar days. An extension of the regular session requires the affirmative vote of at least two-thirds of the membership of each house of the legislature. The legislature shall adopt as part of the uniform rules of procedure deadlines for scheduling session work not inconsistent with provisions controlling the length of the session.

The first sentence of section 8 has been changed by statute to specify the second Monday, except following a gubernatorial election, when the legislature convenes on the third Monday of January, giving the governor an extra week to get started. Most of this constitutional provision has undergone significant change through amendment. During the constitutional convention, several changes were suggested to the committee's recommendation, which proposed unlimited annual sessions of the legislature (the hallmark of the *Model State Constitution*). One suggestion was to have biennial sessions, but this notion was defeated when delegate John McNees noted that a strong legislature was needed to counterbalance the strong executive, which could not be accomplished in biennial sessions (*PACC*, 1665).

Delegate George Sundborg introduced an amendment to limit legislative sessions to 60 days. That was the limit for the Territorial Legislature, which met biennially. After some discussion, this proposal was defeated. The chair of the legislative committee objected that the theory of this constitutional article required an annual salary, unlimited sessions, and special sessions that could be called by the governor (*PACC*, 1674). The original constitutional provision followed this advice, and the legislature's sessions were of unlimited length until 1984.

In the oil-rich years of the late 1970s and early 1980s, the legislature vastly increased the session length. For example, the 1981, 1982, and 1983 sessions exceeded the norm (by then around 100 days). In fact, the 1981 session dragged on for a record 165 days, which left little time for state and local government departments and agencies to start the new fiscal year on time. The focus of discontent, however, settled on a legislature that lingered too long in Juneau.[31] Repentant lawmakers placed a constitutional amendment on the ballot in 1984 to limit the session to 120 days; voters approved it by a 3-to-2 margin.[32] (A supreme court opinion established that the length of the session was actually 121 days

---

[31] Ibid., 162.

[32] Former state legislator Niilo Koponen observed on March 5, 1996, that the session limit amendment was crafted to exclude any requirement for legislation amended in one house to be passed back to the house of origin for public hearings and committee examination. Thus, now a bill from the House

because the day the legislature convened should not be included within the 120-day limit (see *Alaska Christian Bible Institute v. State*, 1989). The last sentence of section 8 attempts to institute deadlines so that the legislature will conclude its work expeditiously. It has not been subject to judicial interpretation.

SECTION 9

Special sessions. Special sessions may be called by the governor or by vote of two-thirds of the legislature. The vote may be conducted by the legislative council or as prescribed by law. At special sessions called by the governor, legislation shall be limited to subjects designated in his proclamation calling the session, to subjects presented by him, and the reconsideration of bills vetoed by him after adjournment of the last regular session. Special sessions are limited to thirty days.

The special sessions provision places Alaska toward the high side of state practice with respect to the powers of the governor versus the legislature. The governor may independently call a special session; the governor's agenda, and thus his or her influence over the outcomes, is not limited.

Some states allow only the governor to call special sessions, others permit a majority of the legislature to call a special session, and still others require an extraordinary majority of two-thirds or three-fourths. The Alaska provision for legislative calls is two-thirds; it has been little used.

The legislature has spelled out procedures for calling special sessions in statute (AS 24.05.100). The governor is required to give legislators fifteen days' notice before calling them into special session (which is in apparent conflict with Article III, section 17, authorizing the governor to convene the legislature whenever the public interest required). House and Senate leaders need to poll members to see if they should make a call (with 40 of 60 legislators needing to favor a call). Most of Alaska's fourteen special sessions (as of 1996) have been called by the governor; only two have been called by the legislature.

The last clause of the third sentence was added by amendment of the voters in 1976. It expands the opportunity of the legislature to override gubernatorial vetoes. This section has not been subject to judicial interpretation.

SECTION 10

Adjournment. Neither house may adjourn or recess for longer than three days unless the other concurs. If the two houses cannot agree on the time of adjournment and either house certifies the disagreement to the governor, he may adjourn the legislature.

(the budget, for example) can be amended in the Senate and held until immediately before adjournment, when the originating house must vote it up or down without further legislative or public scrutiny.

Section 10 exposes a problem of bicameralism—tension between the two houses leading to breakdown, whereby one house completes its agenda and adjourns, using that tactic to force compliance to its agenda by the other. This provision is fairly standard in state constitutions and has caused much interhouse conflict. In the 1980s, on several occasions the two houses engaged in adjournment disputes, based partly on differences in partisan or coalition control and partly on different visions of the optimal state operating and capital budgets. With reduced revenues in the 1990s and fewer interhouse differences in coalition control, adjournment disputes have lessened. On no occasion since statehood, however, has it been necessary for the governor to adjourn the legislature. The provision had been added in an amendment to the committee version at the constitutional convention because a number of states with unlimited sessions gave the governor limited power to adjourn the legislature (*PACC*, 1666).

SECTION 11

Interim committees. There shall be a legislative council, and the legislature may establish other interim committees. The council and other interim committees may meet between legislative sessions. They may perform duties and employ personnel as provided by the legislature. Their members may receive an allowance for expenses while performing their duties.

The provision gives flexibility to the legislature to provide for activity during sessions. The legislative council supervises work of the Legislative Affairs Agency (a housekeeping agency). Other interim agencies include the legislative budget and audit committee, the ethics committee, and the administrative regulation review committee.

In 1978 and 1980, attempts were made to amend this section to allow the legislative budget and audit committee to review and determine budget revisions jointly with the governor between legislative sessions.[33] Such an amendment would have satisfied objections to the improper delegation of legislative power and violation of the separation of powers doctrine, which appeared in Alaska (*Kelly v. Hammond*, 1977) and in other states' courts. However, voters rejected both attempts, making it necessary for the whole legislature to approve modifications to all appropriations.

SECTION 12

Rules. The houses of each legislature shall adopt uniform rules of procedure. Each house may choose its officers and employees. Each is the judge of the election and

[33] Harrison, *Alaska's Constitution*, 68.

qualifications of its members and may expel a member with the concurrence of two-thirds of its members. Each shall keep a journal of its proceedings. A majority of the membership of each house constitutes a quorum to do business, but a smaller number may adjourn from day to day and may compel attendance of absent members. The legislature shall regulate lobbying.

Section 12 begins with an aspect of unicameralism: both houses operate under uniform rules. Each, however, selects officers and staff, develops its own procedures, and records daily proceedings for the public. Importantly, this provision puts each house in charge of judging the qualifications of, and disciplining (including expulsion of), its members, which is an essential prerequisite of an independent legislative branch. The section also establishes the quorum as a majority of the members of each house (or a simple majority of all members for joint sessions), allows less than a majority for calls of the membership, and mandates legislation on lobbying.

Three supreme court cases have interpreted the rules section of the legislative article. In June 1981, Democrat Russ Meekins, a dissident member of the state House of Representatives, took the Speaker's chair to reorganize the body. Meekins called for a vote on a new Speaker, House officers, committee chairs, and members of the powerful Finance Committee. Displaced majority members protested on grounds of illegality and unconstitutionality, but the rump caucus prevailed. The new leadership installed itself and proceeded to rewrite the state budget (which was then in the Conference Committee) from scratch.

Republicans and some Democrats, including more south-central and rural interests than sat in the previous leadership, joined Meekins. The dissidents felt bitter about the way in which the state was allocating its oil wealth. They were also extremely dissatisfied with the method of distributing capital construction dollars, which left the Republican minority outside the loop.[34]

Ousted majority members cried foul to the press and filed a suit in the supreme court, asking the justices to nullify the reorganization. They made four charges: (1) removal of the Speaker required that two-thirds of each house vote to suspend or amend the legislature's Uniform Rules of Procedure; (2) new majority leader Rick Halford had usurped the authority of the Speaker by convening the first meeting of the reorganized House; (3) reasonable notice of this meeting was not given to the old majority and the public; and (4) the old majority was denied its right to speak freely on the floor of the House.

The high court interpreted the rules provision as giving each house exclusive power to remove, as well as choose, its own officers, without any participation by the other house; it found that a majority vote of the members was sufficient to either elect or remove an officer. The court declined to declare the House

[34] McBeath and Morehouse, *Alaska Politics and Government*, 135.

Speaker's election invalid, even if the representative convening the meeting was without authority to do so. Such a declaration, said the court, would be an unwarranted intrusion into the business of the House. The judicial branch, it remarked, owed respect to the independent and coequal legislative branch of government (*Malone v. Meekins*, 1982).

In the absence of a court objection, the new leaders of the House continued in power. This event signified the importance of solidity in the majority, to which coalition leaders paid attention when they developed organizations based on shares in leadership positions and budget slices thereafter.

The second supreme court case concerned the Sheffield confirmation controversy of 1983 (discussed in section 6). The Speaker of the House and 22 other members of the majority asked the court to invalidate the appointments, allegedly because they were improper. The high court interpreted the rules section's provisions, as they applied to joint legislative sessions, by saying that a quorum was a majority of members of the legislature, counting members from both houses without distinction between the two. Further, the Speaker's absence from confirmation voting did not invalidate it (*Abood v. Gorsuch*, 1985).

In both cases, for part of its argument, the high court invoked principles of justiciability, any one of which might limit its involvement:

> These elements included: 1) a textually demonstrable commitment of the issue to a coordinate political department; 2) the impossibility of a court's undertaking an independent resolution of the case without expressing lack of respect due coordinate branches of government; and 3) the need for adherence to a political decision already made. (Reference to *Baker v. Carr*, 1962, in *Malone v. Meekins*, 1982, p. 357)

In short, the extent to which majorities in either or both branches of the legislature would use constitutional rules to their advantage was a political question, which was beyond the authority of the courts.

Finally, the supreme court declined to review the charge by the League of Women Voters of Alaska that closed meetings of the legislature violated the joint rules (*Abood v. League of Women Voters of Alaska*, 1987).

SECTION 13

> **Form of bills.** Every bill shall be confined to one subject unless it is an appropriation bill or one codifying, revising, or rearranging existing laws. Bills for appropriations shall be confined to appropriations. The subject of each bill shall be expressed in the title. The enacting clause shall be: "Be it enacted by the Legislature of the State of Alaska."

This section makes several provisions for the full disclosure of legislation; these are found in many state constitutions. The single-subject requirement is an attempt to prevent logrolling, whereby a majority coalition of legislators is brought together in support of several unrelated bills, none of which has enough votes to pass on its own. As the high court said in *Suber v. Alaska State Bond Commission* (1966), the purpose "is to prevent the inclusion of incongruous and unrelated matters in the same bill in order to get support for it which the several subjects might not separately command, and to guard against inadvertence, stealth and fraud in legislation" (p. 557).

The second sentence on appropriations bills, the traditional "confinement rule," is an attempt to avoid making changes in legislation or the development of substantive law through the operating or capital budget bills that the legislature passes. It protects the governor's veto power, because without it, the governor might be forced to veto a needed budget appropriation in order to avoid an offensive statutory change.

The superior court applied the confinement rule in 1980 when the legislature made an appropriation to the Department of Health and Social Services to conduct a study on minority hire. The court found that although the department had no statutory authority to conduct such a study, the effect of the appropriation measure would be to give it the power. To satisfy the confinement rule required two separate acts, one establishing authority in the department to cover the proposed study, and the second funding the study (*Alaska Legislature v. Hammond*, 1983).

Attorneys general will, on occasion, advise governors that legislative intent language in appropriation bills violates the confinement rule. Harrison noted that in 1989, Governor Steve Cowper's attorney general pointed out that an intent statement to reduce employee health insurance premiums was illegal because it would have amended a collective bargaining act.[35]

The third sentence requires a title that gives general notice on the contents of the bill. This is an additional safeguard against deceitful legislation. Finally, the enactment clause requirement is intended to announce an action of the formal law-making power, rather than less important actions such as resolutions, statements of advice, or opinions.

Several court decisions have focused on the single-subject rule of section 13, and all have construed the rule broadly. In 1974, the high court reversed a lower court, which had found that projects authorized for a bond proposition—flood control and small-boat harbor projects—were totally unrelated, violating the one-subject rule. The majority of the supreme court, however, disagreed, finding that both flood control and small-boat harbors pertained to a single, ongoing plan for the development of water resources (*Gellert v. State*, 1974).

---

[35] Harrison, *Alaska's Constitution*, 73.

When a complaint was filed to enjoin issuing bonds for construction and improvements of correctional and public safety facilities, the supreme court ruled that the bond sale did not violate the single-subject provision of section 13 (*Short v. State*, 1979). Chief Justice Rabinowitz applied the *Gellert* test and found that it was sufficient, for the purposes of the one-subject rule, that "the various provisions of single legislative enactment fairly relate to the same subject or have a natural connection therewith" (p. 24).

A 1982 supreme court case challenged the 1977 amendments to the Uniform Land Sales Practices Act (ULSPA) as violating the single-subject section of the constitution. The amendments brought in-state sales of subdivided land within ULSPA's scope and added an antifraud section; they also added to the Alaska Lands Act sections on the leasing of state-owned lands and the land division's zoning power. Sympathizing with those who objected to the legislation, the court noted: "Were we writing on a clean slate, we would be inclined to find this subject impermissibly broad. Permitting such breadth under the one-subject rule could conceivably be misconstrued as a sanction for legislation embracing 'the whole body of the law'" (p. 415). However, the court decided to broadly construe Article II, section 13, because the legislation had met loose tests: it embraced one "general subject" and expressed "one general idea" because all parts concerned lands (*State v. First National Bank of Anchorage*, 1982).

The same year, the court approved an amendment to state liquor laws that changed a driving while intoxicated statute. The amendment was germane, said the appeals court, because it was limited to one general subject—intoxicating liquor (*Van Brunt v. State*, 1982, *Van Brunt I*).

In 1985, the court of appeals upheld an act amending various sections of the criminal code, finding that it did not violate the single-subject rule (*Galbraith v. State*, 1985). Finally, the supreme court in the same year upheld the validity of an initiative proposition that would repeal statutes regulating intrastate motor and air carriers and require the governor to seek repeal of a federal statute. To the court, these different subjects were inextricably related and on one general topic (*Yute Air Alaska, Inc. v. McAlpine*, 1985).

Justice Daniel Moore dissented from this court decision, challenging the history of enforcement of the constitutional one-subject rule: "This court has mistakenly continued to give the rule such an extremely liberal interpretation that the rule has become a farce. Prior decisions tell us that in Alaska any hodgepodge of laws will comply if broadly construed to "relate to" such general topics as water, or land, or taxation" (p. 1182). He was joined in this dissent later by Justice Burke. However, the pattern of the court has been to liberally construe section 13. In fact, as of 1996 it has not struck down any provision as violating the single-subject rule. As the court said in *Gellert v. State* (1974): "Otherwise statutes might be restricted unduly in scope and permissible subject matter, thereby multiplying and complicating the number of necessary enactments and their interrelationships" (p. 1122).

SECTION 14

> **Passage of bills.** The legislature shall establish the procedure for enactment of bills into law. No bill may become law unless it has passed three readings in each house on three separate days, except that any bill may be advanced from second to third reading on the same day by concurrence of three-fourths of the house considering it. No bill may become law without an affirmative vote of a majority of the membership of each house. The yeas and nays on final passage shall be entered in the journal.

Another standard provision of state constitutions, the intent of this passage is to induce informed and careful deliberation on legislation. Initially, the provision contained no allowance for advancing from second to third reading with a three-fourths majority vote. Delegate Katherine Nordale offered the amendment at the constitutional convention because it was less rigid than the original proposal. This section also requires that those supporting the legislation be identified.

The court of appeals has ruled that the requirement that bills be read three times does not extend to an amended bill, even though the amendments substantially alter the bill. Only if the amendments change the subject of the bill does the three readings requirement apply (*Van Brunt v. State; Van Brunt II*, 1982).

In 1985, a defendant argued that the five-year presumptive sentence given him was unconstitutionally enacted because the identical bill was not passed by both houses, as required by section 14. (Court rules adopted as part of the legislation by a two-thirds majority in the House passed with only a majority in the Senate, which was less than required for adoption.) The court of appeals did not invalidate the legislation because the substance was passed by majorities in both houses and only one version was transmitted to the governor. The requirement that "an affirmative vote of a majority of the membership of each house" had not been violated, said the court (*Galbraith v. State*, 1985, p. 884).

The final sentence of section 14, requiring a recorded vote of individual legislators, was interpreted by the supreme court in *Plumley v. Hale* (1979). In that case, petitioners challenged the constitutionality of a statute establishing advisory panels for medical malpractice suits because the last action on the legislation in one house was a simultaneous voice vote. During the 1970s, one or both houses of the legislature had used voice-voting procedures to approve free Conference Committee amendments with increased frequency. (Free conference committees added new statutory items to bills in conference; they operated without much restraint.) The court held that "final passage" did mean the last vote of the House and that recording votes was justified for these reasons:

> To ensure deliberation prior to passage, to ensure that the requisite majority of each house affirmatively votes to enact a bill into law, and to provide a public record of the vote cast by each legislator. It is thus designed to engender a responsible legislative process worthy of the public trust, (p. 500)

Resolutions of either house or joint resolutions are not subject to procedures of section 14 and other sections pertaining to the enactment of laws. Proposed constitutional amendments are treated as resolutions and are not subject to gubernatorial vetoes.

In one area—attempts to nullify administrative regulations—the Alaska legislature has used joint resolutions improperly. The supreme court ruled that for the legislature to annul regulations of executive agencies would require the enactment of bills, following the procedures of sections 13 and 14, and subject to gubernatorial veto (*State v. A.L.I.V.E. Voluntary*, 1980).

The constitution provides for a legislative veto in two instances only: (1) to disapprove of a governor's reorganization of the executive (Article III, section 23) and (2) to disapprove of local boundary changes (Article X, section 12). After the negative ruling in *State v. A.L.I.V.E. Voluntary*, the legislature sought voter approval three times (in 1982, 1984, and 1986) to permit the control of administrative agencies through annulling their regulations with joint resolutions. On each occasion, however, the voters were opposed.

The legislature has used two other methods to attempt to exercise control over administrative agencies. Most successful has been use of the appropriations process to reward and punish agencies. Less successful have been attempts of individual legislators to control outcomes on policy matters that historically have been the responsibility of the executive. For example, during the eighteenth legislature, Anchorage Republican Representative Mulder introduced two bills (HB 471 and HB 366) designed to alter the allocation of salmon in the Cook Inlet and Kenai River. (Neither bill passed.) These areas are under the control of the Board of Fisheries and, thus, of an executive function. This encroachment varies based on differences in partisan affiliation of the governor and legislators.

SECTION 15

Veto. The governor may veto bills passed by the legislature. He may, by veto, strike or reduce items in appropriation bills. He shall return any vetoed bill, with a statement of his objections, to the house of origin.

Section 15 is a simple expression of the governor's power to negate bills passed by the legislature. In the case of substantive legislation, the governor's veto covers the entire bill, not parts of it. However, the second sentence gives the governor a line-item veto authority on appropriation bills that is among the strongest in the nation. Most state constitutions give governors the power to veto individual items in appropriations bills, but the Alaska provision gives the governor the additional flexibility of reducing without vetoing. The governor is obliged to explain his objections to legislation that he has vetoed.

The original committee proposal at the constitutional convention did not contain line-item veto authority. Delegate Barrie White moved the amendment, which was a *Model State Constitution* recommendation, and it was endorsed in a 30-to-22 vote. Only one delegate, Warren Taylor, spoke against the amendment, believing that the executive should not have the power to amend appropriations (*PACC*, 1758).

The judiciary interpreted section 15 in a case where the governor's use of the item veto of a general obligation bond authorization was challenged (*Thomas v. Rosen*, 1977). The supreme court noted the desire of delegates to create a strong executive with "a strong control on the purse strings" of the state (*PACC*, 1740), but ruled that the power to strike or reduce was meant to apply to the appropriation process, and not debt financing.

SECTION 16

Action upon veto. Upon receipt of a veto message during a regular session of the legislature, the legislature shall meet immediately in joint session and reconsider passage of the vetoed bill or item. Bills to raise revenue and appropriation bills or items, although vetoed, become law by affirmative vote of three-fourths of the membership of the legislature. Other vetoed bills become law by affirmative vote of two-thirds of the membership of the legislature. Bills vetoed after adjournment of the first regular session of the legislature shall be reconsidered by the legislature sitting as one body no later than the fifth day of the next regular or special session of that legislature. Bills vetoed after adjournment of the second regular session shall be reconsidered by the legislature sitting as one body no later than the fifth day of a special session of that legislature, if one is called. The vote on reconsideration of a vetoed bill shall be entered on the journals of both houses.

Section 16 contains relatively detailed procedures to be followed upon gubernatorial vetoes. There are important distinctions with respect to the age of the legislative session and the type of legislation vetoed. Items vetoed after the conclusion of the first regular session, or after a special session held before the second regular session, may be reconsidered during the first week of the second regular session. However, items vetoed after the second regular session can only be reconsidered at a special session, which increases the governor's influence because there is no automatic provision to call such a session. (Both these provisions were added by constitutional amendment in 1976 to clarify procedures for reconsidering bills following adjournment.) Bills vetoed during either the first or second regular sessions are treated identically. In addition, vetoes of taxing and spending bills are made more difficult to override, with a three-fourths requirement, which is rare in state constitutions. The section incorporates aspects of unicameralism by the provision requiring the legislature to consider vetoes in joint session, which is designed to make vetoes somewhat easier to override than they would be in separate sessions.

The two innovative parts of section 16 received some discussion at the constitutional convention. Delegates noted that the joint session requirement invaded the province of bicameralism. Delegate Maurice Johnson proposed an amendment to allow both houses to vote separately to override a veto and was supported by other delegates who thought joint sessions would consume more time because of the negotiations they would require. This amendment failed (*PACC*, 1731). Delegate George Sundborg was concerned that confusion would result from requiring different extraordinary majorities to overturn financial and other vetoes. He proposed that the constitution follow provisions of the Alaska Organic Act, which specified that all vetoes must be overridden by a two-thirds vote (*PACC*, 1738). This amendment was defeated, too.

SECTION 17

Bills not signed. A bill becomes law if, while the legislature is in session, the governor neither signs nor vetoes it within fifteen days, Sundays excepted, after its delivery to him. If the legislature is not in session and the governor neither signs nor vetoes a bill within twenty days, Sundays excepted, after its delivery to him, the bill becomes law.

This section completes the options available to the governor upon receipt of bills passed by the legislature. The clock begins when the governor receives the bill, and not when it is passed by both houses. (Sometimes, bills are not delivered for several weeks, especially following the end of legislative sessions, when most bills are adopted.) The section spells out the time line during which the governor must either act or see legislation enacted without his signature. The period—fifteen days during sessions and twenty days after sessions—is generous compared to the practice in most states. Section 17 does not permit a "conditional veto," which is found in some other state constitutions and allows the governor to negotiate with the legislature. Nor does it permit the "pocket veto," whereby a governor's delay in acting on a bill at the end of the second year of a legislative session effectively kills it.

SECTION 18

Effective date. Laws passed by the legislature become effective ninety days after enactment. The legislature may, by concurrence of two-thirds of the membership of each house, provide for another effective date.

Section 18 establishes the date on which legislation becomes law, giving those affected by the legislation opportunity to prepare for it. The two-thirds requirement guarantees that there will be broad legislative support for any deviation from the 90-day postenactment effective date.

This constitutional provision was used in a major challenge by oil companies to a change in oil tax statutes, which had retroactive provisions (*ARCO Alaska, Inc. v. Alaska*, 1992). In 1989, the legislature eliminated the Economic Limit Factor, which had been regarded as a significant tax break for oil companies, and made the tax change retroactive to January 1. The companies argued that section 18 permitted retroactive provisions of legislation only when two-thirds of the members of each house agreed. The supreme court called this a misinterpretation and held that retroactive dates of laws served only to identify the conduct to which the law would apply. The court said: "While a retroactive law applies to pre-enactment conduct, the legal effect produced by the law occurs only after the law's effective date" (p. 711). Moreover, the court held that courts in other states had also held that extraordinary majority voting requirements for deviations from effective dates did not apply to tax laws having retroactive dates.

SECTION 19

Local or special acts. The legislature shall pass no local or special act if a general act can be made applicable. Whether a general act can be made applicable shall be subject to judicial determination. Local acts necessitating appropriations by a political subdivision may not become effective unless approved by a majority of the qualified voters voting thereon in the subdivision affected.

Section 19 attempts to restrict what has become practice in most American states at one time or another: the passage of legislation that explicitly favors one interest or region or gives preferences to some individuals (such as granting divorces or dismissing fines) to the exclusion of others. This provision clearly assigns to the judiciary the power to determine if legislation justifiably is special, or local. The section also ensures, in those cases where local legislation is permissible, that residents of the political subdivision have an opportunity to vote on it.

Delegates to the constitutional convention accepted the draft version prepared by committee, but not without some discussion. Delegate Warren Taylor sought to remove the last sentence, asking why it was necessary to have a local vote (*PACC*, 1762). Several delegates spoke in favor of it and gave examples, such as sanitation districts, which local voters should have the opportunity of approving or rejecting.

Several cases have clarified the meaning of section 19. In *Boucher v. Engstrom* (1974), the supreme court held that an initiative to relocate the state capital did not amount to special or local legislation and could be placed on the ballot. The court argued that legislation did not become "local" merely because it operated on a limited number of geographical areas instead of on a statewide geographical basis, or because of a statewide concern or interest it addressed.

However, in *Abrams v. State* (1975), the court found that a statute pertaining to the organization of an Eagle River–Chugiak Borough was special and local in nature. The act created a new borough that was peculiar to that locality, and the act as a whole was limited to the Greater Anchorage Area Borough. For these reasons, the court struck down the statute, even though Article X, section 3, gave the legislature broad powers over the organization of boroughs. Section 19 of the legislative article, in the view of the court, governed the exercise of all legislative powers expressly granted by other portions of the constitution.

In an earlier decision (*Walters v. Cease*, 1964), the supreme court had upheld the Mandatory Borough Act of 1963, which incorporated eight specific areas of the state as organized boroughs. Opponents had sought to repeal the act by referendum, but the court ruled out that course of action by declaring the act local and special legislation, and thus not subject to referendum under Article XI, section 7.

In 1977, the high court was asked to strike down a three-way exchange of land between Alaska, the United States, and Cook Inlet Region, Inc. (*State v. Lewis*, 1977), as violative of the constitutional prohibition on local and special legislation. The court held that although the land exchange was a unique matter, it was an issue of statewide concern. The court examined legislative goals and the means used to achieve them, and found there to be a "fair and substantial relationship." To the court, "legislation need not operate evenly in all parts of the state to avoid being classified as local or special" (p. 643).

The constitutional prohibition against local or special acts has not been applied to appropriations, which frequently are designated for specific cities and boroughs.

SECTION 20

Impeachment. All civil officers of the State are subject to impeachment by the legislature. Impeachment shall originate in the senate and must be approved by a two-thirds vote of its members. The motion for impeachment shall list fully the basis for the proceeding. Trial on impeachment shall be conducted by the house of representatives. A supreme court justice designated by the court shall preside at the trial. Concurrence of two-thirds of the members of the house is required for a judgment of impeachment. The judgment may not extend beyond removal from office, but shall not prevent proceedings in the courts on the same or related charges.

In its impeachment provisions, the Alaska Constitution diverges from the federal constitution and that of most states in three respects. All civil officers, and not only the highest elected and appointed officials, are subject to impeachment.

The Senate impeaches, and the trial is held in the House (the opposite of common practice). Moreover, impeachable offenses are not defined, leaving this for statutory and judicial determination. The two-thirds majority requirement for impeachment and the involvement of the supreme court resemble requirements of other state constitutions. The final sentence of section 20 clearly distinguishes the remedy for impeachment (removal from office), while allowing criminal prosecution for crimes committed in office.

Debate at the constitutional convention concerned where the impeachment charges should be brought and where they should be tried. Several delegates objected to the committee's version (which became the constitutional text), but all attempts to amend failed (*PACC*, 1616–1622). The consensus of delegates was that a trial of impeachment charges should be held in the house with the closest ties to the people.

Alaska has used the impeachment provision once only. In 1985, a grand jury recommended that the Senate conduct impeachment inquiries about Governor William Sheffield's involvement in bid rigging and other improprieties in the state's lease of an office building in Fairbanks.[36] This was the first time in 75 years that any state legislature had considered impeaching a governor. The Senate Rules Committee (with a Republican majority) found insufficient evidence for impeachment, however.

SECTION 21

Suits against the state. The legislature shall establish procedures for suits against the state.

Most states waive their sovereign immunity from suits through statutes, but Alaska has a general constitutional provision charging the legislature with setting up procedures. The language is drawn from the Arizona Constitution. There were several attempts to clarify it at the constitutional convention, but there was no interest on the part of delegates in denying individuals the opportunity to sue the state for liability.

This constitutional provision was interpreted in a supreme court deliberation over whether a state statute could confer on municipalities an immunity from liability arising from safety inspections of private property (*Wilson v. Municipality of Anchorage*, 1983). The court found that the statute barred only certain liability claims, and not all; moreover, it referred to municipalities, while the constitutional provision applied only to "suits against the state" (p. 571).

[36] McBeath and Morehouse, *Alaska Politics and Government*, 174–175.

Article III

The Executive

The third Article of the constitution establishes the executive as a unified and strong focus of governmental authority in Alaska. It specifies the qualifications for governor, describes the election and terms of office, provides extensively for succession, and defines most of the office's formal powers (Article II, section 15, and Article IX, section 12, list the remaining powers).

The delegates to the constitutional convention often discussed the weakness of the territorial governorship. Appointed by the president, large federal bureaucracies and legislative boards and commissions hobbled the governor's administrative authority. Delegate Victor Rivers, who chaired the committee that developed the executive proposal, remarked that all delegates were agreed thoroughly on the need for a strong executive (*PACC*, 1984).

The committee reviewed various other state constitutions and found many restrictions on powers of the executive. They paid special attention to the revised New Jersey Constitution of 1947 and the new constitution of Hawaii (1950)—as well as the *Model State Constitution*[37]—all three of which incorporated principles of unity in the executive, the centralization of power, and a streamlined administrative organization. These principles influenced the design of the strong executive that the framers created.

[37] National Municipal League, *Model State Constitution*, 9–10, 23–24, 31–33.

Particularly noteworthy is the fact that only the governor and lieutenant governor are elected. All remaining executive officers are appointed by the governor and accountable to him or her. Additionally, the constitution limits the number of executive departments and emphasizes organizational integration and efficiency.

SECTION 1

Executive power. The executive power of the State is vested in the governor.

Section 1 directly endows the governor with the executive power of the state. Like similar statements in Articles II and IV, this provision grants the executive branch the authority found under the separation of powers doctrine. It is the basis for the implied powers of the governor, and also for the strength of the governorship as an institution.

Although the constitution does not mention explicitly the separation of powers doctrine, the courts consistently have found that it exists. In *Public Defender Agency v. Superior Court, Third Judicial District* (1975), the supreme court said that "it can be fairly implied that this state does recognize the separation of powers doctrine" (p. 950). Moreover, when the legislature sought (by statute) to subject appointments of deputy heads to legislative confirmation, the court held that it had violated the separation of powers requirements of the state constitution.

SECTION 2

Governor's qualifications. The governor shall be at least thirty years of age and a qualified voter of the State. He shall have been a resident of Alaska at least seven years immediately preceding his filing for office, and he shall have been a citizen of the United States for at least seven years.

This provision sets out the basic qualifications for the office of governor, which are comparable to those of the other states. It has not been subject to judicial interpretation.

The committee proposal contained a twenty-year U.S. citizenship requirement, but an early action of the delegates was to amend this to seven years. Delegate Barrie White said he thought the delegates should set up as few barriers as possible "to service to the people of Alaska" (*PACC*, 2052).

Similar discussions were held about the required length of residence. Some wanted a period as brief as five years, but Frank Barr wanted a long period of residency in Alaska, at least ten years: "The governorship is our highest office and a man should be entitled to it not only by his ability but by his sympathy with our aims and ideals and his acquaintanceship with our problems here in Alaska" (*PACC*, 2061). The seven-year state residency requirement was thus a compromise.

SECTION 3

Election. The governor shall be chosen by the qualified voters of the State at a general election. The candidate receiving the greatest number of votes shall be governor.

Section 3 is straightforward and exact. It provides that one need only gain a plurality of the votes, and not a majority, to win the gubernatorial election. This provision has allowed a succession of plurality winners to become governor, the most recent being Governor Hickel (who won with only 39 percent of the vote in 1990) and Governor Tony Knowles (who in 1994 won 40 percent, collecting just 562 votes more than the runner-up). A majority requirement might have changed the outcome in these and other races. The issue was discussed briefly at the constitutional convention, but the attempt to change it failed.

Elections for Alaska's governor are held in the off-year cycle, between presidential elections. Section 3 has not been subject to judicial interpretation.

SECTION 4

Term of office. The term of office of the governor is four years, beginning at noon on the first Monday in December following his election and ending at noon on the first Monday in December four years later.

Section 4 states the length and dates of the governor's term of office. The governor's term begins within a month of election, which is an earlier start than in any other state except Hawaii. The purpose of the early inauguration is to give the new governor time to develop a budget and legislative agenda before the session begins in January. (Article II, section 8, starts the legislative session one week later after gubernatorial elections for the same reason.) Section 3 has not been subject to judicial modification.

SECTION 5

Limit on tenure. No person who has been elected governor for two full successive terms shall be again eligible to hold that office until one full term has intervened.

This provision establishes a two-term limit for the governor, who may run again only after an intervening term. The Alaska provision limiting gubernatorial terms resembles that in most states and was constructed for the same reasons—to avoid concentrated power in the executive and to encourage political competition. The section was engaged only once in state constitutional history, when Governor Bill Egan sought to succeed himself the second time. Because he was elected in November 1958, Egan's first term began late (Alaska was admitted to the Union in January 1959, and the first governor's term was one month short of full). In addition, the secretary of state was acting governor for two months while Egan was in ill health. Egan contended that he had not served two "full" terms, yet it was a major election issue. The attorney general and courts agreed with Egan's position, but the voters did not consent and instead elected Walter J. Hickel governor in 1966.

SECTION 6

Dual office holding. The governor shall not hold any other office or position of profit under the United States, the State, or its political subdivisions.

This paragraph, which is similar to Article II, section 5, for legislators, prohibits the governor from holding any other state or federal office. It has not been subjected directly to any judicial interpretation, but it has been referred to by the court.

In *Begich v. Jefferson* (1968), the supreme court declared: "The framers intended to prohibit members of the legislature, judiciary, judicial council, and the state's chief executive officer from holding any other salaried non-temporary employment under the United States or the State of Alaska" (p. 31). The most imperative requirement, in the view of the courts, has been to protect the operations of one branch of government from the contamination of conflicts of interest with another.

SECTION 7

Lieutenant governor duties. There shall be a lieutenant governor. He shall have the same qualifications as the governor and serve for the same term. He shall perform such duties as may be prescribed by law and as may be delegated to him by the governor.

The original version of this section called the position "secretary of state." It was amended to the current language by the voters in 1970. Other sections of the constitution (Article XI, sections 2 through 6; Article XIII, sections 1 and 3) give the lieutenant governor responsibilities in the administration of elections. The legislature has found little for the lieutenant governor to do. The statutory responsibilities include the administration of election law, guarding the state seal, appointing notaries public, and supervising the process of regulations promulgation. Governors have differed in the tasks assigned to their lieutenants, but none has made the position an indispensable part of state government.

Section 7 was a controversial part of this article at the constitutional convention. The delegates were nearly evenly divided about the necessity for the position. Some thought it wiser to eliminate "a figurehead who receives a high salary and does nothing," in the words of delegate Frank Barr (*PACC*, 2070). Others thought it important to have a "governor-in-training" in the event the governor died or fell ill. This group opposed the idea of succession falling to the president of the Senate, as provided for in the revised New Jersey Constitution of 1947.

SECTION 8

Same—election. The lieutenant governor shall be nominated in the manner provided by law for nominating candidates for other elective officers. In the general election the votes cast for a candidate for governor shall be considered as cast also for the candidate for lieutenant governor running jointly with him. The candidate whose name appears on the ballot jointly with that of the successful candidate for governor shall be elected lieutenant governor.

Section 8 provides that candidates for lieutenant governor move through the nomination process individually. (Current law stipulates that candidates run in primary elections. The candidate with the highest number of votes in his or her party then becomes that party's nominee.) In the general election, candidates for lieutenant governor and governor of the same party run together, on the same ticket. This section has not been subject to judicial interpretation.

Section 8 was even more controversial than section 7 among delegates to the constitutional convention. Some delegates wanted the secretary of state (as the position was named before being amended to "lieutenant governor" in 1970) to be an appointed official, but the general consensus was that the office should be elective. Delegate Victor Rivers pointed out that the Hawaiian constitution had an elected lieutenant governor, and others remarked that if the governor died, the replacement should be an elected official (*PACC*, 2084).

Disagreement continued over pairing the governor and secretary of state on the same ticket. Some supported this as a "package deal" that ensured that the governor would not be "stuck with a sidekick" from another party. Others wanted the secretary of state to be elected independently of the governor. At this point in the debate, delegate Seaborn Buckalew objected, saying, "We are leaving it up to the people to rubber-stamp a 'flunky' selected by the man that's running for governor" (*PACC*, 2089).

In a rare move, convention president William Egan left the chair and spoke passionately against an appointive secretary of state and a "package deal" that would not allow the people the opportunity to vote on a nominee (he did support a measure giving the people a say through the primary election) (*PACC*, 2135). Calling the election of the second-in-command on the same ticket as the chief executive the "granddaddy" practice of the American system of government, a majority of the delegates agreed.

SECTION 9

Acting governor. In case of the temporary absence of the governor from office, the lieutenant governor shall serve as acting governor.

Section 9 provides for the interim empowerment of the lieutenant governor if the governor, for any reason, is temporarily unable to serve. It is distinct from sections 10 through 12, which define conditions for the permanent succession to the governorship.

Section 9 has been used once, when the state's first governor, Bill Egan, was unable to perform the duties of office because of ill health. Then, Secretary of State Hugh Wade served as acting governor.

SECTION 10

Succession; failure to qualify. If the governor-elect dies, resigns, or is disqualified, the lieutenant governor elected with him shall succeed to the office of governor for the full term. If the governor-elect fails to assume office for any other reason, the lieutenant governor elected with him shall serve as acting governor, and shall succeed to the office if the governor-elect does not assume his office within six months of the beginning of the term.

Section 10 spells out the two different sets of signals for succession. The first set includes death, resignation, and disqualification (with the latter meaning impeachment or the assumption by the governor of another office). This set brings on the immediate succession of the lieutenant governor. The second set of signals includes all other reasons, for example, medical conditions, including insanity, or indictment. The incumbent has six months to remedy this condition, during which time the lieutenant governor is in an "acting" capacity; if the condition is not remedied, the governor-elect forfeits office to the lieutenant governor.

SECTION 11

Vacancy. In case of a vacancy in the office of governor for any reason, the lieutenant governor shall succeed to the office for the remainder of the term.

Section 11 does not define a vacancy, but its meaning can be inferred from the foregoing and following sections—it refers to an absence from office that is likely to extend beyond six months. The most obvious causes of vacancy are death, resignation, serious mental or physical impairment, and disqualification, such as through impeachment.

On one occasion in Alaska's history as a state, succession occurred under terms of section 11. When President Richard Nixon appointed Governor Walter J. Hickel as U.S. secretary of the interior in 1969, Secretary of State Keith Miller became governor.

The Alaska Constitution does not provide for special gubernatorial elections in the event of vacancy (as is the case in some other states), except when an unelected lieutenant governor succeeds to the governorship (as specified in section 13).

SECTION 12

Absence. Whenever for a period of six months, a governor has been continuously absent from office or has been unable to discharge the duties of his office by reason of mental or physical disability, the office shall be deemed vacant. The procedure for determining absence and disability shall be prescribed by law.

Section 12 further defines vacancy as lack of the governor's continuous presence over a period of six months or his or her serious mental or physical impairment. The section is designed to allow the removal from office of a disabled chief executive who declines to resign, whereupon the lieutenant governor succeeds to the office until the end of the term. Absence of the governor for shorter periods, however, makes the lieutenant only an "acting governor."

The legislature is obliged to determine how the office of governor can be declared vacant, but it had not done so as of 1996.

SECTION 13

Further succession. Provision shall be made by law for succession to the office of governor and for an acting governor in the event that the lieutenant governor is unable to succeed to the office or act as governor. No election of a lieutenant governor shall be held except at the time of electing a governor.

This section requires the legislature to specify succession to the lieutenant governorship, and it has done so by having the governor upon taking office appoint a successor from among the heads of principal state departments, who is then confirmed by a majority of the legislature meeting in joint session (AS 44.19.040). The second sentence explicitly disallows a special election just for the purpose of electing a lieutenant governor. If the elected lieutenant governor succeeds to the office of governor and then vacates the office, the appointed lieutenant governor becomes acting governor, but only until a special election is held to elect a new governor and lieutenant governor (AS 44.19.044).

SECTION 14

Title and authority of successor. When the lieutenant governor succeeds to the office of governor, he shall have the title, duties and emoluments of that office.

Section 14 makes a further distinction between an "acting" and permanent governor. Only the latter has all the powers and privileges of the gubernatorial office, such as the full salary.

SECTION 15

Compensation. The compensation of the governor and the lieutenant governor shall be prescribed by law and shall not be diminished during their term of office, unless by general law applying to all salaried officers of the State.

There was some discussion at the constitutional convention about the appropriate salary for the governor. It was resolved in the first clause of section 15 by allowing the legislature to set the salary, which keeps the details out of the constitutional text. The second clause protects the governor from a reduction in salary by an antagonistic legislature; it is a basic protection of executives in separation of powers systems. The provision has not been the subject of judicial interpretation.

SECTION 16

Governor's authority. The governor shall be responsible for the faithful execution of the laws. He may, by appropriate court action or proceeding brought in the name of the State, enforce compliance with any constitutional or legislative mandate, or restrain violation of any constitutional or legislative power, duty, or right by any officer, department, or agency of the State or any of its political subdivisions. This authority shall not be construed to authorize any action or proceeding against the legislature.

The first sentence of section 17 follows the "take care that the laws be faithfully executed" clause (Article II, section 3) of the U.S. Constitution, and is found in most state constitutions. It heads the listing of specific gubernatorial powers and elaborates the assignment of executive power to the governor, as mentioned in section 1 of the executive article. The phrase, "faithful execution of the laws" covers a range of necessary implied gubernatorial powers, which are often called "inherent" by the courts.

The second sentence of section 17 follows closely Article V, section 11, of the revised New Jersey Constitution.[38] The governor is empowered, under its terms, to intervene in legal actions on behalf of individuals or the state, whether or not the state has standing to sue. The "enforce[ment] of compliance" may occur through the use of executive orders.

The third sentence disallows the governor from acting against the legislature to assure the faithful execution of the laws, but it does not restrict the governor from suing the legislature to protect executive powers in a separation of powers dispute.

The supreme court found that section 16, along with section 1, "clothed" the governor "with the power to appoint subordinate executive officers to aid him in carrying out the laws of Alaska," when that appointment power was challenged by the legislature (*Bradner v. Hammond*, 1976). No other ruling has amplified the meaning of this section.

SECTION 17

Convening legislature. Whenever the governor considers it in the public interest, he may convene the legislature, either house, or the two houses in joint session.

Section 17 allows the governor to call the houses of the legislature to meet jointly, or one or both of the houses to meet separately. It specifies no time limit for the meeting, and the legislature may already be in session when the governor convenes it.

One controversial use of the governor's power to convene the legislature occurred in 1983, when Governor William Sheffield sought to gain legislative confirmation of his executive appointments after they had been held up by house leaders. Leaders of the majority coalition in the House argued that the governor's action in calling a joint session to confirm his appointments was unconstitutional, because it prevented the house from conducting hearings on some of the appointees. The high court held, however, that the legislature's inquiries into gubernatorial appointees did not limit the governor from calling a joint session, and if the legislature disagreed, it could, through a majority vote, adjourn the session (*Abood v. Gorsuch*, 1985; *see also Kerttula v. Abood*, 1984; and *Schultz v. Sundberg*, 1985).

The relationship between Article III, section 17, and the special session powers of governor and legislature (Article II, section 9) is not entirely clear.

---

[38] See Robert F. Williams, *The New Jersey State Constitution: A Reference Guide* (Westport, CT: Greenwood Press, 1990), 84–85.

Harrison noted that in 1987, Governor Cowper used section 17 to convene the legislature so that it could finish its work on some budget bills. The legislature was then in its 120th day, and so the effect of the proclamation was to extend the session, a power the constitution assigns to the legislature alone.[39] In 1994, Governor Hickel also used section 17 to convene the legislature to finish its work, as did Governor Knowles in 1996. The judiciary has not clarified these applications of section 17.

SECTION 18

Messages to legislature. The governor shall, at the beginning of each session, and may at other times, give the legislature information concerning the affairs of the State and recommend the measures he considers necessary.

The governor's annual "state of the state" message to the legislature (which in recent years has been followed by a budget message) has been an important tool of executive leadership. The governor's ability to address the legislature at other times enables him or her to establish an agenda of issues and focus public and legislative attention on them. Section 18 is the constitutional basis for the governor's introduction of bills in the legislature.

SECTION 19

Military authority. The governor is commander-in-chief of the armed forces of the State. He may call out these forces to execute the laws, suppress or prevent insurrection or lawless violence, or repel invasion. The governor, as provided by law, shall appoint all general and flag officers of the armed forces of the State, subject to the confirmation by a majority of the members of the legislature in joint session. He shall appoint and commission all other officers.

This common constitutional provision places the governor in charge of the armed forces of the state (the Alaska Air National Guard and Alaska Army National Guard). Although it subordinates the military to civilian power (as in Article I, section 20), it does not give the governor significant military authority during normal times. The air and army national guard are more federal than state organizations, and were they to be used to enforce order, they would need to operate under civil law provisions, much as the police are constrained by statute.

---

[39] Harrison, *Alaska's Constitution*, 96.

SECTION 20

Martial law. The governor may proclaim martial law when the public safety requires it in case of rebellion or actual or imminent invasion. Martial law shall not continue for longer than twenty days without the approval of a majority of the members of the legislature in joint session.

The declaration of martial law is an inherent power of government. Section 20 authorizes martial law powers only to put down a rebellion or resist invasion. It would enable the governor to suspend the privilege of the writ of habeas corpus, making it possible for police and state troopers to arrest those suspected of criminal activity without warrants. The section limits martial law to a period of twenty days, unless a majority of legislators affirm it. The provision has not been used in state history.

SECTION 21

Executive clemency. Subject to procedure prescribed by law, the governor may grant pardons, commutations, and reprieves, and may suspend and remit fines and forfeitures. This power shall not extend to impeachment. A parole system shall be provided by law.

These clemency powers of the governor are considered to be exclusive executive powers, and they are commonly found in executive articles of state constitutions. They are brought into effect after a defendant has been sentenced by the judiciary. Although the first clause calls on the legislature to outline procedures to guide the governor in using the clemency powers, it has not yet done so. The governor may not pardon an impeached official, but the provision is silent regarding the even rarer case—those convicted of treason.

Placement of the parole system does not properly fit in the clemency section of the executive article because parole does not reduce or commute sentences. The issue at the constitutional convention was whether the governor's power should be shared with a parole board or council, which was then the practice in sixteen states, or simply issued "in accordance with law," as done in twenty states (*PACC*, 2190). The delegates decided to oblige the legislature to establish a parole system (but not to grant parole in any individual case), thus leaving it the details. In AS 33.16, the legislature established a parole system including a parole board.

SECTION 22

Executive branch. All executive and administrative offices, departments, and agencies of the state government and their respective functions, powers, and duties shall be allocated by law among and within not more than twenty principal departments, so as to group them as far as practicable according to major purposes. Regulatory, quasi-judicial, and temporary agencies may be established by law and need not be allocated within a principal department.

Section 22, when read together with sections 24 and 25 (making department heads subject to gubernatorial supervision), constitutes the basis for a modern, streamlined, and accountable executive branch. It is based on Article V, section IV.1, of the revised New Jersey Constitution and follows the *Model State Constitution*.[40] It permits the establishment of no more than twenty departments (the state has never had more than fifteen), grouping them by function to enhance their integration. The final sentence gives the legislature the flexibility to respond to particular problems without altering the permanent structure of the executive branch.

This article was interpreted by the supreme court in 1962 when the legislature's creation of the Alaska State Development Corporation, with a legal existence "independent of and separate from the state," was challenged (*De-Armond v. Alaska State Development Corporation*). The high court held that the corporation did not violate section 22 of the executive article because the commissioner of commerce sat on the board of directors and the other directors were all gubernatorial appointees. Annual auditing and reporting requirements and the temporary nature of the corporation indicated to the court that it was an instrumentality of the state within the department of commerce, and not fully independent.

This section was also applied in a case concerning the University of Alaska. When sued for damages, the university was denied a jury trial because it was an instrumentality of the state. In *University of Alaska v. National Aircraft Leasing, Ltd.* (1975), the supreme court acknowledged that the university was "an instrumentality of the sovereign which enjoys in some limited respects a status which is coequal rather than subordinate to that of the executive or the legislative arms of government" (p. 128). This did not stop the court from treating the university like any other public agency. The court held that lawsuits against the university fell within the scope of statutes governing the conditional waiver of sovereign immunity. In short, the university, too, was accountable *within* the confines of the executive branch.

SECTION 23

Reorganization. The governor may make changes in the organization of the executive branch or in the assignment of functions among its units which he considers necessary for efficient administration. Where these changes require the force of law,

[40] National Municipal League, *Model State Constitution*, 9–10, 32–33.

> they shall be set forth in executive orders. The legislature shall have sixty days of a regular session, or a full session if of shorter duration, to disapprove these executive orders. Unless disapproved by resolution concurred in by a majority of the members in joint session, these orders become effective at a date thereafter to be designated by the governor.

The legislature organizes the executive branch, and without specific constitutional authorization, the governor would face difficulty in arranging it to his or her liking. Section 23 gives the governor the power to create new departments from subdepartmental units, move divisions from one department to another, and merge departments. Unless organic legislation calls for legislative review, the governor may reorganize without legislative scrutiny; when the legislature has review powers, its review is limited to 60 days or less. (This is the first of two legislative vetoes in the Alaska Constitution; the second is in Article X, section 12.)

This section has been used by governors to create new departments, such as Governor Sheffield's creation of a department of corrections in 1983. Other governors have used it to merge departments, as when Governor Jay Hammond created the Department of Transportation and Public Facilities (DOTPF) from two existing departments.

SECTION 24

> **Supervision.** Each principal department shall be under the supervision of the governor.

This section along with section 25 pinpoints responsibility and control within the executive branch. No officer of an executive department lies outside the reach of the governor, which is unlike the pattern in those states (the majority) that lack unity in the executive (i.e., have elected department heads and commissioners).

SECTION 25

> **Department heads.** The head of each principal department shall be a single executive unless otherwise provided by law. He shall be appointed by the governor, subject to confirmation by a majority of the members of the legislature in joint session, and shall serve at the pleasure of the governor, except as otherwise provided in this article with respect to the secretary of state. The heads of all principal departments shall be citizens of the United States.

This section, together with section 24, establishes "unity in the executive" and its control over the administration of government in Alaska. It is based on Article V, section IV.2, of the revised New Jersey Constitution of 1947.

Heads of departments are to be individuals instead of boards or commissions unless the legislature decides otherwise. This terminated the power and proliferation of boards and commissions that had occurred during the territorial period. Nevertheless, the influence of territorial days survives in two departments. Both the departments of education and of fish and game have boards, and the board of education is the head of that department. Department heads fall under the supervision of the governor after being appointed by him or her.

The legislature's primary check on the executive branch is through confirmation of the governor's appointments. All department heads except the lieutenant governor may be removed, without cause, by the governor. The only unresolved issue between executive and legislative branches concerning appointments, noted Harrison, concerns interim appointments of exiting governors.[41] In the recent administrations of Walter J. Hickel (1990–1994) and Tony Knowles (1994–), the incoming governors have successfully blocked midnight appointments by their predecessors (by refusing to formally present them to the legislature).

Four substantive changes to the committee's proposed section on department heads were discussed at the constitutional convention. Delegate Victor Rivers moved that all appointments be approved in joint session, noting that this was the system used in the territorial era (*PACC*, 2178). The delegates agreed, by voice vote, to so amend section 25, and made this usage consistent throughout the constitution.

Second, the delegates discussed at length whether the attorney generalship should be appointed or elected. Delegate Frank Barr urged that the position be elective, remarking that many of his constituents had requested this. Further, he noted that the attorney general was called on to interpret the law, a semijudicial function that required impartiality (*PACC*, 2193). Delegate George McLaughlin countered by remarking, "His functions are not quasi-judicial. He is another attorney giving an opinion" (*PACC*, 2196). A second proposal sought to have the attorney general nominated by a judicial council, but this amendment also failed, largely because only one state (New Hampshire) had a similar selection process. A third unsuccessful proposal sought to mention the attorney general in section 25 because the position was listed elsewhere in the constitution. None of the proposals attracted support from more than one-third of the delegates; most wanted the attorney general subject to the governor, which makes the Alaska government one of only five with an appointed attorney general. (Nevertheless, electing the attorney general is a perennial issue in Alaska politics.)

Delegate Burke Riley proposed a third change to the committee draft by eliminating a requirement that the governor's appointees be "Alaska citizens." Several delegates spoke against the amendment, citing cases of officials brought to Alaska from Outside who had no experience and did not remain long enough

[41] Harrison, *Alaska's Constitution*, 103.

to acquire it. Delegate Herb Hilscher supported the amendment, however: "If we carry this [insistence on Alaska residence] to its logical conclusion we would not go to a doctor for medical attention unless he had been in the Territory for 50 years" (*PACC*, 2237). The adopted section contains no reference to Alaska residence, but it does require U.S. citizenship.

A final proposed amendment by delegate Jack Coghill sought to delete the requirement that officials appointed by boards, such as the commissioner of education, be approved by the governor (*PACC*, 2245). The convention resoundingly defeated this amendment, by a vote of 50 to 4, showing the opposition of almost all delegates to the power of virtually independent boards and commissions during territorial days.

The Alaska Supreme Court interpreted section 25 (and related provisions of section 26) in its decision, *Bradner v. Hammond* (1976). The legislature had sought by statute to require legislative confirmation of deputy heads of each principal executive department and nineteen specified directors of divisions; the governor declined to cooperate. The issue presented to the high court was whether section 25 set out the maximum or minimum number of gubernatorial appointments subject to legislative confirmation.

Justice Rabinowitz, writing for a unanimous court, found that the appointment of subordinate executive officers by the governor was an executive function. Legislative confirmation was a specific attribute (a power "super added" [p. 4]) of the appointment power of the executive delegated to the legislature. Thus, the court concluded that sections 25 and 26 marked the "full reach of the delegated, or shared, appointive function" (p. 7) to Alaska's legislature. It ruled unconstitutional the legislative statute claiming larger powers.

SECTION 26

Boards and commissions. When a board or commission is at the head of a principal department or a regulatory or quasi-judicial agency, its members shall be appointed by the governor, subject to confirmation by a majority of the members of the legislature in joint session, and may be removed as provided by law. They shall be citizens of the United States. The board or commission may appoint a principal executive officer when authorized by law, but the appointment shall be subject to the approval of the governor.

Section 26 continues the provisions of section 25 in situations where heads of departments or of regulatory or quasijudicial agencies are not single individuals but rather commissions or boards (called Section 26 boards). This has applied, since the 1960s, to the Department of Education, occupational licensing boards, and regulatory boards such as the Alaska Public Utility Commission.

This system gives the governor the same direct control over departments and agencies headed by boards as over those headed by individuals, with one important exception. The governor's ability to remove board or commission members is subject to conditions spelled out by the legislature. For some boards, such as the Board of Education, the governor's discretion is unimpeded, but for others, such as the Boards of Fish and Game, the governor may only remove members for cause. The governor also approves the executive officers of Section 26 boards and commissions: for example, the commissioner of education.

There was relatively little discussion of section 26 at the constitutional convention. Delegate Seaborn Buckalew sought to strike the phrase "quasijudicial" from the first sentence because, in his view, it would give the executive too much power (*PACC*, 2203); however, there was little support for this proposal. Delegate Ralph Rivers sought to amend the committee draft by exempting appointees of the board of education and the board of regents from the governor's approval (*PACC*, 2253), which would make their boards the de facto heads of the department of education and the University of Alaska, with authority greater than any of the principal departments. This proposal failed, indicating again the delegates' antipathy toward boards and commissions.

SECTION 27

Recess appointments. The governor may make appointments to fill vacancies occurring during a recess of the legislature, in offices requiring confirmation by the legislature. The duration of such appointments shall be prescribed by law.

This section was proposed as an amendment by constitutional convention delegate George Sundborg, who sought to give the governor greater flexibility in appointment powers. However, the legislature has sought to stop governors from avoiding the confirmation process by requiring the submission of the names of recess appointments within 30 days of the start of the session. Furthermore, individuals failing confirmation are proscribed from appointment to other interim positions.

Article IV

The Judiciary

The fourth article of the Alaska Constitution establishes the judicial power in a progressive court system, which has incorporated innovations from other states and is applauded by judicial reformers. The delegates to the constitutional convention aspired to have a court system equal in power to the other two branches of government. Using the same logic they had followed in designing the executive and legislative branches, they drew up a simple, unified, centralized blueprint for a judiciary that was unshackled by constitutional or statutory restrictions. Anticipating the need for changes in the future, they gave the legislature free rein to expand the court system.

The unity of the Alaska judicial branch resembles that of the federal court system, which has a limited number of courts of special jurisdiction. The unity of the judiciary in the revised New Jersey Constitution of 1947 impressed the framers of the constitution with its simplicity and centralization under the supreme court. Most other state court systems of that time had a variety of specialized courts (for example, traffic and family courts), each with its own functions, procedures, and finances, which made their judicial systems complex and inflexible.

Another model that impressed the framers was the Missouri Plan for judicial selection (see sections 5, 6, and 8). This provides for gubernatorial selection from a list of candidates prepared by a judicial council and retention elections after service of from one to three years. The effect of the plan is to remove the selection of judges from overt partisan influences and give the judiciary some independence from politics. The framers did not want aspirants for judicial positions to run against incumbents by attacking their decisions. (The Missouri Plan enables judges to decide cases without worrying about electoral consequences.) States using the Missouri Plan are far closer to the federal system than those following another design.

SECTION 1

Judicial power and jurisdiction. The judicial power of the State is vested in a supreme court, a superior court, and the courts established by the legislature. The jurisdiction of courts shall be prescribed by law. The courts shall constitute a unified judicial system for operation and administration. Judicial districts shall be established by law.

The first section of the article assigns the judicial power to the courts, as the first sections of the legislative and executive articles assigned those powers to, respectively, the legislative and executive branches. The inherent powers of the judiciary are not defined in the judicial article, but a number of cases have established their existence. For example, in *Citizens Coalition v. McAlpine* (1991), the supreme court remarked: "The court's rule-making authority under this section is inherent in the judicial power vested in it, as the supreme court of the state" (p. 165). In *Coghill v. Coghill* (1992), the supreme court reaffirmed this view.

Section 1 provides only for the supreme and superior courts (discussed further in sections 2 and 3), leaving the legislature to establish other courts as needed. The legislature also determines the jurisdiction of the various courts.

Upon statehood in 1959, the legislature established district magistrate courts as the sole subordinate court system of the state. Each district magistrate court had as court officers district magistrates with general trial power and deputy magistrates of limited trial power sufficient to meet immediate justice needs in less populated areas of the state. In 1966, district magistrates and deputy magistrates were renamed district judges and magistrates, respectively (*Buckalew v. Holloway*, 1979). The jurisdiction of district courts extends to all misdemeanor violations (ranging from drunk-driving infractions, shoplifting, and disorderly conduct to violations of city and borough ordinances) and civil cases where the recovery of property and damages is less than $50,000. The newest court is the court of appeals, which was established by the legislature in 1980 at the request of the supreme court in order to reduce its workload. The three-judge panel, which sits on the second rung of Alaska's judicial system, hears appeals of judgments from superior courts in criminal and certain quasicriminal cases. It handles juvenile delinquency cases, habeas corpus cases in which prisoners challenge the legality of their incarceration, and cases involving probation and parole decisions.

Misdemeanants have the option of appealing decisions to the superior court or directly to the court of appeals.[42]

Section 1 establishes a unified court system in Alaska. It is a judiciary with a single administrative head, a state court administrator who responds to the supreme court, and the same types of courts throughout the state. It follows uniform rules of procedure, and all its operations are financed by the same source (the state legislature).

Unlike Article III of the federal constitution, the judicial article does not contain a requirement of a "case or controversy." The Alaska courts do impose a requirement of standing to sue before the judicial power can be invoked by litigants; however, the requirement has been less stringent than that used in federal courts (*Alyeska Ski Corporation v. Holdsworth*, 1967).[43] As with the federal courts, advisory opinions are to be avoided (*Gieffels v. State*, 1976; *Earth Movers v. State, Department of Transportation*, 1992).

The supreme court has, on occasion, decided cases that have become "moot" (when there is no longer a live controversy) in light of "the recurring nature and importance of the issue" (*Central Construction Co. v. Home Indemnity Co.*, 1990, p. 597). As the court pointed out in *Hayes v. Charney* (1985), the determination of mootness is "ultimately left to the discretion of the courts" (p. 834).

At the constitutional convention, there was strong support for allowing the supreme court to establish judicial districts subject to change by the legislature, but this amendment failed by a vote of 23 to 21 (*PACC*, 675). The delegates left the design of judicial districts to the legislature, which preserved the four judicial districts used in territorial days, with one each in southeast, northwest, south-central, and interior Alaska.

SECTION 2

Supreme court. (a) The supreme court shall be the highest court of the State, with final appellate jurisdiction. It shall consist of three justices, one of whom is the chief justice. The number of justices may be increased by law upon the request of the supreme court.

(b) The chief justice shall be selected from among the justices of the supreme court by a majority vote of the justices. His term of office as chief justice is three years. A justice may serve more than one term as chief justice but he may not serve consecutive terms in that office.

---

[42] McBeath and Morehouse, *Alaska Politics and Government*, 194.

[43] In this case, the Alaska Supreme Court held that an appellant, as an aggrieved bidder on a state government contract, had standing to obtain a review of the determinations of the agency. Had the bidder operated under the federal Public Contracts Act, he would not have had litigable rights. See *Perkins v. Lukens Steel Co.* (1940).

The first paragraph outlines the jurisdiction and membership of the supreme court. As the highest court in the state, the supreme court is, in most cases, the court of last resort. As appellate court, it hears appeals of judgments rendered by superior courts on civil matters. It also has discretionary authority to review decisions by the court of appeals on criminal and quasicriminal matters, such as juvenile delinquency cases.[44]

The third sentence of the first paragraph allows the legislature to increase the court's membership, but only when the court requests it. This limitation restricts the legislature from enlarging the court in response to unpopular decisions. In 1967, the legislature increased the membership of the supreme court from three to five justices, one of whom is the chief justice.

Because the original section 2 said nothing about the selection of the chief justice, the second paragraph was added by amendment in 1970. Prior to that time, the governor had designated the chief justice, which reduced the office's accountability to the other justices.

The second paragraph makes the chief justice an officer of the court, who is not subject to the influence of the governor or legislature. Seniority in this leadership position is curtailed by the limitation on consecutive terms of office.

SECTION 3

Superior court. The superior court shall be the trial court of general jurisdiction and shall consist of five judges. The number of judges may be changed by law.

The superior court is the trial court that has original jurisdiction in all civil and criminal matters. The court hears appeals of final judgments by district courts. It retains authority over all cases involving domestic relations, juvenile delinquency, and child abuse and neglect, as well as probate, including sanity hearings, estates, guardianship, and adoptions. The superior court also hears high-interest criminal cases such as homicides, rapes, and assaults, as well as civil cases with a dollar value in excess of $50,000.[45]

This section establishes the membership at five judges, but it gives the legislature the authority to expand the court's membership. In 1996, 31 judges, divided among the four judicial districts established at statehood by the legislature, performed the work of the superior courts. Unlike the supreme court, each superior court judge holds court individually, under the overall supervision of a presiding judge for the judicial district.

[44] McBeath and Morehouse, *Alaska Politics and Government*, 194.

[45] Ibid.

SECTION 4

Qualifications of justices and judges. Supreme court justices and superior court judges shall be citizens of the United States and of the State, licensed to practice law in the State, and possessing any additional qualifications prescribed by law. Judges of other courts shall be selected in a manner, for terms, and with qualifications prescribed by law.

When delegates to the constitutional convention discussed qualifications of judges, parochial biases against Outsiders again appeared. Some delegates proposed that U.S. attorneys be prohibited from becoming eligible for state judgeships. This was opposed by delegate James Hurley as "discriminatory and unnecessary" (*PACC*, 618). Other delegates sought to have long residence requirements for members of the court system. A proposal to eliminate the five-year requirement outlined in the original version of the judiciary committee failed by a narrow margin, 24 to 28, with 3 absent. Revised to allow the legislature to set the minimum residency requirement, if it wished, the amendment passed by a 32-to-21 margin. Still, delegates spoke to the need for longer residency. Said delegate Irwin Metcalf: "We should have the five-year residence requirement so that we really know what people are under stress and under pressure" (*PACC*, 673).

The first sentence allows the legislature to increase the constitutional requirements for supreme court justices and superior court judges. The legislature has done so by requiring them to have been residents of the state for three years prior to appointment and to have practiced law for eight and five years, respectively. The legislature has required judges of the appeals and of district courts to be U.S. citizens and residents of the state for three years prior to appointment and to have practiced law for eight and three years, respectively.

In a case concerning the qualifications of magistrates, the supreme court clarified the meaning of section 4. The court held that section 4 directed the legislature to provide for the selection, terms, and qualifications of the judges of the courts it created. This directive, the court found, was "unqualified and would appear to vest absolute discretion in the legislature" (*Buckalew v. Holloway*, 1979, p. 244). The court continued by noting that the legislature was not even obliged to require state and federal citizenship or admission to the bar of judges for the courts it created. Magistrates are required only to be U.S. citizens and residents for six months prior to appointment. They are not required to be trained in the law.

SECTION 5

Nomination and appointment. The governor shall fill any vacancy in an office of supreme court justice or superior court judge by appointing one of two or more persons nominated by the judicial council.

Sections 5, 6, and 8 outline the elements of the Missouri Plan, which was adopted by the framers of the constitution for judicial selection and retention. Alaska entered the Union at a time when judicial reformers sought to limit gov' influence over the appointment of judges because of concerns about corruption. Reformers also lobbied to limit the partisanship of judges by making retention elections nonpartisan. The Missouri Plan (named after the state in which it originated) accomplished these objectives and was the choice of members of the judiciary committee at the constitutional convention.

A nominating body, called the judicial council, screens candidates for a vacancy on the bench (including the statutory appeals and district courts as well as the constitutional courts). It evaluates their standing based on hearings, interviews, a poll of bar association members, and background investigations. It then recommends two or more people to the governor, who appoints someone from the list. The new judge sits for three years or, in the case of district court judges, for only one year, after which he or she faces the voters in a nonpartisan retention election.[46] The interval between subsequent retention elections varies with the level of the court.

Discussion over the Missouri Plan at the constitutional convention distilled into a debate over elected versus appointed judges. Argument centered on which system would serve to remove judges the farthest from politics, and which would make them the most responsible, if not necessarily the most accountable, to the law.

Delegate Robert McNealy, an attorney, opposed an appointment system: "Being an Alaskan I feel I have lived under the appointment system so long that I feel I should have the right to vote for these judges. . . . In my opinion this appointment method will bring judges into politics more so than an election by the people" (*PACC*, 583). George McLaughlin, chairman of the judiciary committee and an elected magistrate for Anchorage, supported judicial appointments:

> One of the dangers of the elective system is the fact that a judge whenever he makes a decision, he has to keep peering over his shoulder to find out whether it is popular or unpopular. If we determine the validity of our laws in terms of popularity as the general acceptance, we are then not a government of laws on which we pride ourselves. . . . The way to keep them independent is to keep them out of politics. (*PACC*, 584)

This was the argument that prevailed.

Contrasting the elective and appointive systems, delegate Frank Barr called the Missouri Plan imperfect, but still the best system for the territory: "By election you have no guarantee of ability. You do have nearly 100 percent guarantee if appointed. In integrity you have no guarantee . . . in election. In appointment,

46 Ibid., 197.

you have some guarantee" (*PACC*, 602). By the end of the debate, the Missouri Plan of appointment was endorsed overwhelmingly, 51 to 2, with 2 absent.

SECTION 6

Approval or rejection. Each supreme court justice and superior court judge shall, in the manner provided by law, be subject to approval or rejection on a nonpartisan ballot at the first general election held more than three years after his appointment. Thereafter, each supreme court justice shall be subject to approval or rejection in a like manner every tenth year, and each superior court judge, every sixth year.

Section 6 provides for retention elections for all judicial officers except magistrates, because the legislature has extended its provisions to judges of statutory courts. It specifies when the first retention election for a newly appointed judge or justice will be held. The section describes the elections as nonpartisan, which, as determined by the legislature, means that voters are presented with this ballot question: "Do you favor or oppose the retention of Judge_____?" Following the first election, succeeding elections are staged by lengths related to the importance of the tribunal. Supreme court justices appear on the ballot every ten years; court of appeals judges, every eight years; superior court judges, every six years; and district court judges, every four years.

Retention elections provide a measure of accountability, but the record in Alaska, as elsewhere, shows that few judges fail to be retained. Of nearly 200 judges on the ballot from statehood to 1996, only three have lost retention elections, for reasons particular to them. Most judges are retained with from 60 to 75 percent of the vote.

Courts have clarified the meaning of this section in two respects. The phrase, "first general election held more than three years after his appointment," was interpreted by the supreme court to mean after the date of the individual's designation for office by the governor, and not the date of installation in office (*Division of Elections of State v. Johnstone*, 1983). In this case, a superior court judge who was appointed in October 1979 but did not take his seat until December claimed that his first retention election would be in 1984 and thus did not file for the 1982 general election. The court held that his first general election was November 1982, which was more than three years from the date on which the governor had appointed him.

A second case interpreted the applicability of section 6 to magistrates. The supreme court found that magistrates were judges within the meaning of the constitutional requirement that judges be selected for terms prescribed by law, but found that requiring them to serve "at the pleasure of the presiding judge of the superior court" did not violate the constitutional mandate (*Buckalew v. Holloway*, 1979, p. 243). Section 6 conveyed the intent of the framers that all judges be accountable. For judges such as district court judges and magistrates (not mentioned in section 6), the means of accountability could be either election or some other means, such as a review of performance by the presiding superior court judge.

SECTION 7

Vacancy. The office of any supreme court justice or superior court judge becomes vacant ninety days after the election at which he is rejected by a majority of those voting on the question, or for which he fails to file his declaration of candidacy to succeed himself.

Section 7 establishes a 90-day transition period for judges failing to win retention elections or file for reelection. This allows the judge time to conclude his or her affairs and for the process of appointing a successor to begin. The supreme court suspended the filing requirement in one case of a superior court judge who failed to file on a timely basis because he mistakenly believed that his retention election was in 1984 and not 1982, and who was encouraged in that belief by court officials (*Division of Elections of State v. Johnstone*, 1983).

SECTION 8

Judicial council. The judicial council shall consist of seven members. Three attorney members shall be appointed for six-year terms by the governing body of the organized state bar. Three non-attorney members shall be appointed for six-year terms by the governor subject to confirmation by a majority of the members of the legislature in joint session. Vacancies shall be filled for the unexpired term in like manner. Appointments shall be made with due consideration to area representation and without regard to political affiliation. The chief justice of the supreme court shall be ex-officio the seventh member and chairman of the judicial council. No member of the judicial council, except the chief justice, may hold any other office or position of profit under the United States or the State. The judicial council shall act by concurrence of four or more members and according to rules which it adopts.

The judicial council is an integral part of the Missouri Plan system of judicial selection. Its primary function is to screen applicants for court positions and prepare a list of two or more nominees for the governor. It is the only nominating council for trial court and appellate judges in Alaska. Section 8 describes the composition of the council. Three of its members are attorneys, who are appointed (without the necessity of legislative confirmation) by the Alaska State Bar Association, which has a quasiofficial status. The three lay members are selected by the governor; their confirmation follows the process used for executive officers of the state—by a majority of a joint session of the legislature. A geographical balance is preferred in the selection of members. Although appointments are to be made "without regard to political affiliation" in order to keep the council nonpartisan, there are no formal requirements for nonpartisan-ship or a balance of party loyalties, as are found in many state constitutions. The chief justice chairs the council. Other council members are not permitted to be employees of the federal or state government so as to avoid conflicts of interest. The council establishes its rules of procedure, but a majority of four is required for it to act.

The composition of the judicial council occasioned discussion at the constitutional convention. Delegate George McLaughlin reported his conversation with George M. Morris, president of the American Bar Association, who advised him that councils with laypersons on them obtained the best results. Quoting Morris, McLaughlin declared:

> Where either judges or lawyers serve alone they seem to lack energy for sustained attack. Where judges and lawyers serve together, each group seems to have a diffidence about imposing its views upon the other, which stultifies action. Where, however, laymen are included, their presence seems to act as an ice breaker and to stir activity among the professional members of the council. Laymen's criticisms are sharper. (*PACC*, 732)

The courts have not interpreted section 8 of the judicial article, other than to confirm the intent of the framers that its members are prohibited from holding any other salaried nontemporary employment under the United States or State of Alaska (*Begich v. Jefferson*, 1968).

Section 8 is the only part of the constitution that refers to an interest group—the Alaska Bar Association. In the early 1960s, the bar battled with the Alaska Supreme Court over the degree of autonomy it was to have in playing its quasi-official role.[47]

Under the integrated bar resolution of the Territorial Legislature in 1955, the bar association was to be placed in the judicial branch of government. Delegates to the constitutional convention recognized that the bar association was to play a judicial function when they made its representatives comprise half the judicial council. The establishment of the supreme court produced conflict, however. The new court and Chief Justice Buell Nesbett drafted rules for the bar that superseded previous actions of the Territorial Legislature and the board of governors of the bar association. The rules promised more direct control of the bar by the courts and threatened the autonomy of the association, which

---

[47] I am indebted to Fairbanks attorney Frederic E. Brown for sharing with me his unpublished manuscript, "Bench and Bar" (January 1968).

believed it was "entitled to have a group separate and apart from dominance by legislative, executive, or judicial influence."[48]

The association told the court that it preferred to follow the old bar act (similar to the situation in other states), and the court charged the bar with intransigence for failing to adhere to the new rules. Thereupon, the court ordered the removal of all members of the board of governors and seized the association's assets. The association sued in federal district court, alleging a violation of federal constitutional rights. The supreme court reinstalled the board members and returned the state bar funds. Meanwhile, the association enrolled the assistance of the American Bar Association in a mediation with the court, which produced a compromise: the supreme court "would approve new bar rules patterned after certain rules of the bars of Oregon and Washington, subject to the approval of the bar."[49]

The association dropped its suit and the court, with the association's participation, promulgated new rules in 1965. One casualty of this conflict was Supreme Court Justice Harry Arend, who lost a retention election in November 1964, probably due to negative publicity over the bar fight.

SECTION 9

Additional duties. The judicial council shall conduct studies for improvement of the administration of justice, and make reports and recommendations to the supreme court and to the legislature at intervals of not more than two years. The judicial council shall perform other duties assigned by law.

The judicial council's primary additional duty under this section is as a policy analyst for the judiciary. It has conducted and supervised a number of studies on the administration of justice in Alaska, including plea bargaining and the grand jury, among others. Perhaps the most noteworthy was a late-1970s report on disparity in the sentencing of offenders, showing that Native offenders received disproportionately long sentences. From this resulted the state's presumptive sentencing law, which reduced (but did not eliminate) judicial discretion in sentencing (see *Nell v. State*, 1982).[50]

The judicial council is staffed full time. In addition to its work in screening applicants for judicial offices (which by law also include the statutory courts and the public defender's office), the legislature has asked the council to review judges and justices facing retention elections. Before an upcoming election, the

---

[48] Ibid., 5.

[49] Ibid., 12.

[50] Some experienced critics in the judicial system thought presumptive sentencing was an attack on perceived or imagined judicial disparity and lenience, not race discrimination, in the sentencing of Native offenders.

judicial council solicits the opinions of members of the Alaska Bar Association as well as police and probation officers regarding the individuals standing for retention. It reviews court records and judicial decisions and also conducts hearings to gain public input. A summary of the results of its evaluation as well as the council's recommendations appears in newspapers and in a pamphlet provided to all registered voters two months before the election.[51]

SECTION 10

Commission on judicial conduct. The Commission on Judicial Conduct shall consist of nine members, as follows: three persons who are justices or judges of state courts, elected by the justices and judges of state courts; three members who have practiced law in this state for ten years, appointed by the governor from nominations made by the governing body of the organized bar and subject to confirmation by a majority of the members of the legislature in joint session; and three persons who are not judges, retired judges, or members of the state bar, appointed by the governor and subject to confirmation by a majority of the members of the legislature in joint session. In addition to being subject to impeachment under Section 12 of this article, a justice or judge may be disqualified from acting as such and may be suspended, removed from office, retired, or censured by the supreme court upon the recommendation of the commission. The powers and duties of the commission and the bases for judicial disqualification shall be established by law.

The commission on judicial conduct provides means short of impeachment for removing or disciplining judges. In its original version, the constitution assigned the judicial council the responsibility of certifying to the governor or the supreme court that justices or judges were incapacitated, leaving them to determine if the judicial officers should be retired. There were no procedures for remedying judicial misconduct.[52] The council recommended the establishment of a separate commission to investigate instances of misconduct as well as incapacitation, and to be modeled on California's commission of judicial performance. In 1968, the constitution was amended to establish a nine-member commission on judicial qualifications. The name was changed to the Commission on Judicial Conduct in a 1982 constitutional amendment designed to lessen confusion between the functions of the commission and the judicial council, and changes in composition were made, too.

The commission now consists of three judges elected by their colleagues, three lawyers appointed by the Alaska Bar Association, and three laypersons

[51] McBeath and Morehouse, *Alaska Politics and Government*, 198–199.

[52] Harrison, *Alaska's Constitution*, 117.

appointed by the governor. The attorney and lay appointees are confirmed by the state legislature sitting jointly.

The integrity of state court judges and justices falls under the purview of the commission. It makes recommendations to the supreme court regarding the disqualification, suspension, removal from office, retirement, and censure of judges. However, it does not review judicial decisions for quality or judges for their competence. Only a small number of cases have come before the commission since statehood.

The legislature specified the role of the commission by providing that, on its recommendation, the supreme court may

> censure or remove a judge for action occurring not more than six years before the commencement of his current term which constitutes willful misconduct in the office, willful and persistent failure to perform his duties, habitual intemperance, or conduct prejudicial to the administration of justice that brings the judicial office into disrepute. (AS 22.30.070 [c][2])

Alaska's supreme court has interpreted section 10 in three cases. In 1972, the supreme court further clarified its relationship to the commission in the case *In re Robson*. The high court held that the findings of the commission with respect to a judge's improper conduct—use of poor judgment, making inappropriate comments while presiding over court matters, and becoming too personally involved in the case—warranted public censure, and not a private reprimand as recommended by the commission.

In a second case, *Buckalew v. Holloway* (1979), the supreme court held that section 10 did not provide the only means for the removal of court officers. When a magistrate protested his removal by the superior court judge under whose pleasure he served, the court found that the removal provision, as crafted by the legislature, did not violate section 10 of the judiciary article.

The legislature passed legislation in 1981 further delineating the powers, duties, and procedures of the commission. Among the powers granted the commission was "to reprimand the judge publicly or privately" (AS 22.30.011 [d]). This power was ruled unconstitutional by the supreme court in the decision, *In re Inquiry Concerning a Judge* (1988). The high court held that the statute empowering the commission to publicly reprimand a judge violated section 10 by giving the commission self-effectuating sanctions. The court insisted that it must "exercise its independent judgment in determining an appropriate sanction," because failure to do so would result in the "abdication of its constitutional and statutory obligations" (p. 1296).

SECTION 11

Retirement. Justices and judges shall be retired at the age of seventy except as provided in this article. The basis and amount of retirement pay shall be prescribed by law. Retired judges shall render no further service on the bench except for special assignments as provided by court rule.

The Alaska judiciary article does not follow the federal model of a tenured, lifetime appointment. This subject was briefly discussed at the constitutional convention, and there was no support for an amendment to leave out a retirement age altogether. As in most state constitutions, retirement is at age 70. However, section 11 provides that retired judges and justices may perform special ad hoc assignments at the call of the supreme court.

SECTION 12

Impeachment. Impeachment of any justice or judge for malfeasance or misfeasance in the performance of his official duties shall be according to procedure prescribed for civil officers.

This section is read together with section 20 of Article II. It is somewhat more specific in that the reasons for impeachment—malfeasance or misfeasance in the performance of his official duties—are mentioned. Nevertheless, the procedure is complicated, which is why the constitutional convention delegates designed an alternative means in section 10. They did not, however, give the people a direct say through the recall process of Article XI, section 6. No Alaska judge had been impeached from office as of 1996.

SECTION 13

Compensation. Justices, judges, and members of the judicial council and the Commission on Judicial Conduct shall receive compensation as prescribed by law. Compensation of justices and judges shall not be diminished during their terms of office, unless by general law applying to all salaried officers of the State.

This section sets forth the requirement that the salaries of judicial officers and members of both the judicial council and commission on judicial conduct should be set by law. As in section 15 of Article III, the legislature is restricted from reducing judges'salaries during their terms unless salaries of all state employees are similarly reduced; this requirement is intended to protect the judiciary's independence.

SECTION 14

Restrictions. Supreme court justices and superior court judges while holding office may not practice law, hold office in a political party, or hold any other office or position of profit under the United States, the State, or its political subdivisions. Any supreme court justice or superior court judge filing for another elective public office forfeits his judicial position.

Section 14 completes the implementation in the Alaska Constitution of the separation of powers doctrine. It goes considerably further than the legislative and executive provisions, however, in order to assure the impartiality and non-partisanship of judicial officers. In addition to forbidding judges to hold other offices under the state or federal government, the provision disallows judges from practicing law or even holding party office. Moreover, at the minute when a judge indicates an intent to campaign for public office (by filing), he or she loses his or her judicial position. The supreme court referred to this section, as well as the restrictions on legislators and executives, in *Begich v. Jefferson* (1968).

SECTION 15

Rule-making power. The supreme court shall make and promulgate rules governing the administration of all courts. It shall make and promulgate rules governing practice and procedure in civil and criminal cases in all courts. These rules may be changed by the legislature by two-thirds vote of the members elected in each house.

This paragraph assigns very important powers to the supreme court outside the context of adjudicating cases. The high court has rule-making power over the areas of judicial administration and civil and criminal procedure in the courts. The supreme court's rules apply to all state courts and are used as a primary means to instill uniform procedures and integrate court operations. The legislature may change court rules only by a two-thirds vote in each house. By contrast, in the federal system, the Judicial Conference of the United States proposes rule changes to Congress, which then approves or (not uncommonly) rejects them. The Alaska system is unusual in the power given to the supreme court.

This section has been interpreted by the courts in several cases. An early supreme court case, *Leege v. Martin* (1963), concerned fishermen who had taken fish in a closed area and, under the prevailing statute, had lost their commercial fishing licenses without an opportunity to appeal. The high court acknowledged that the judicial power to make rules of practice and procedure was not absolute and that the legislature could change rules initiated by the judiciary. However, this required a two-thirds vote in order "to prevent unintentional, rash, ill-considered and too easy intervention by the legislature" (p. 450), which would frustrate the courts' primary authority and responsibility for regulating their own affairs. In the particular case, the supreme court held that in order to change court rules or procedures, the legislature needed to express the change specifically in bills. Because the statutes to change court procedures concerning fishing in closed areas had not done so, they were invalid.

In *State v. Browder* (1971) the supreme court held that its rules gave it a larger review jurisdiction than the law appeared to provide, especially when the rules—in this case, to allow the state to seek high court review on a criminal matter where appeal was barred by statute (AS 22.05.010)—agreed with the intent of the framers that the supreme court was the state's highest court with final appellate jurisdiction.

In a further refinement (*Galbraith v. State*) the court of appeals ruled, in 1985, that when the legislature attempted to change court rules as part of a substantive bill without that bill receiving a two-thirds approval in each house, the legislation remained effective only to the extent that it did not conflict with existing court rules or deal with subjects unrelated to court rules.

The supreme court reinforced its rule-making powers in *Coghill v. Coghill* (1992), a case in which the noncustodial parent challenged the authority of the superior court to determine his income for the purpose of assessing his child support obligation and also challenged the accuracy of the formula used. The high court held that a statute empowering the courts to set child support awards "as may be just and proper" (p. 927) did not violate the separation of powers doctrine by unconstitutionally allowing courts to exercise what were essentially legislative powers. The combination of sections 1 and 15 of the judiciary article, said the court, gave it both substantive and procedural rule-making authority, thus enabling the court to exercise a legislative function (see also *Citizens Coalition v. McAlpine*, 1991).

SECTION 16

Court administration. The chief justice of the supreme court shall be the administrative head of all courts. He may assign judges from one court or division thereof to another for temporary service. The chief justice shall, with the approval of the supreme court, appoint an administrative director to serve at the pleasure of the supreme court and to supervise the administrative operations of the judicial system.

Section 16 establishes the chief justice as the administrative head of the Alaska unified court system. It is modeled on the revised New Jersey Constitution of 1947, which created the nation's first modern, streamlined, unified court system. Further, the chief justice of the supreme court is authorized to assign and transfer judges from one court to another and to different locations, a power that further facilitates his or her authority over the courts and the efficient operation of the court system.

Finally, section 16 allows the chief justice to appoint an administrative director of the judicial system. Before this section was amended in 1970, the whole court approved the court administrator's hiring, but he or she served at the pleasure of the chief justice. Now the court administrator serves the whole court, which dilutes the chief justice's power. Section 16 completes the integration of the judicial system and its centralization under the supreme court.

Article V

Suffrage and Elections

The fifth article of the Alaska Constitution concerns voting and elections. It outlines the requirements, rules, and guarantees for voting in Alaska and for the democratic operation of elections. Article V is the second shortest article of the constitution, having only five sections. The details of electoral law are provided by the legislature.

Elections in Alaska, as in the other states, are largely governed by state law. However, civil and, particularly, voting rights legislation by Congress, as well as constitutional amendments, have sharply influenced the practice of voting. This is clearly seen in the record of four amendments to the voting qualification part (section 1) of Article V.

SECTION 1

Qualified voters. Every citizen of the United States who is at least eighteen years of age, who meets registration residency requirements which may be prescribed by law, and who is qualified to vote under this article, may vote in any state or local election. A voter shall have been, immediately preceding the election, a thirty day resident of the election district in which he seeks to vote, except that for purposes of voting for President and Vice President of the United States other residency requirements may be prescribed by law. Additional voting qualifications may be prescribed by law for bond issue elections of political subdivisions.

Section 1 governs the important matter of the qualifications for the vote. It requires U.S. citizenship of voters, establishes the voting age at eighteen years, and provides for a 30-day residency requirement to vote in state and local elections (but not in federal elections). It permits, but does not require, the legislature to set other "registration residency" standards. In the final sentence, it gives the legislature discretion to prescribe other qualifications for voting in bond elections at the local level, a provision now regarded as obsolete because it was designed to restrict nonresidents from voting in bond elections (a territorial practice carried into statehood but ruled illegal in the early 1960s).

Section 1 was broadly discussed at the constitutional convention, with attention focusing on both voting age and English-language requirements for the suffrage. The proposal of the judiciary committee required voters to be able to read or speak English. When it reached the floor, delegate Maurice Johnson Sought to change the language to "read, speak, and write" English, which would have made the provision consistent with then-current territorial law.

Most delegates spoke in opposition to this change. Frank Barr remarked that it was unnecessary to read in order to understand elections: "Up here, a person living in outlying communities, especially the Natives, they hear quite a bit over the radio[—] . . . all the campaign speeches." In his opinion, voters also should not have to be able to write anything more than their own name (*PACC*, 738).

Frank Peratrovich, the only Alaska Native delegate to the constitutional convention, was instrumental in retaining the original language, "to read *or* speak English":

> If we are going to be too restrictive . . . you are going to disqualify such people, citizens, from practicing the privilege of voting. . . . They can understand the English language, and they can go to the polls and vote intelligently on the grounds of what they heard. But if you were to ask them to sit down and write a letter from the constitution on certain sentences, they could not do it, (*PACC*, 740).

Delegate M.K. (Muktuk) Marston echoed these themes in his opposition to the amendment:

> I think these people who lived here and inherited this country might turn around and ask us some things about how we vote instead of our telling them how they can or can't vote. It is their country and I think every man should vote and we should not stop him. (*PACC*, 741)

Johnson's proposed amendment failed by a wide margin, and the adopted version of section 1 contained only a requirement to read or speak English. An extensive review of restrictive state voting requirements during and after the passage of the Voting Rights Act of 1965 brought critical scrutiny to this English-language prerequisite in Alaska. Simultaneously, the Native community was undergoing political mobilization related to land claims, and it objected to this discriminatory requirement, too. In 1970, the legislature proposed its elimination from the constitution, and voters approved.

The second area of controversy at the convention was the voting age requirement, which was set, in the committee proposal, at age twenty. Delegates Victor Fischer, George Sundborg, and Victor Rivers offered an amendment to lower it to age eighteen. Fischer's argument was that eighteen was the age at which men and women graduated from high school and finished their formal education. Delegate Marston supported the amendment on the typical grounds that if a person were old enough to fight, he was old enough to vote.

The doubters commanded the majority on this issue, however. Delegate Warren Taylor believed that lowering the voting age would open the doors to a lower drinking age as well: "Those people have the right to go into the bars and go into any place regardless of the moral atmosphere of it" (*PACC*, 746). Delegate Mildred Hermann doubted if 18-year-olds were qualified to serve on juries, and Irwin Metcalf doubted that Congress would approve such a low voting age when most other states had set it at 21. The need to please the Congress was a compelling argument in the debate over several sections of the constitution.

The motion to lower the voting age failed to attain a majority. However, a subsequent amendment, to lower the age from twenty to nineteen, passed by a narrow margin and became the constitutional age limit until 1970. Responding to national and state concerns about the fairness of a voting age of nineteen when in the Vietnam War men were being drafted at age eighteen, voters in Alaska lowered the voting age to eighteen. They did this about one year before the Twenty-Sixth Amendment to the U.S. Constitution was ratified (in 1971), establishing eighteen as the voting age in all federal, state, and local elections.

Two additional changes make section 1 the most amended part of the Alaska Constitution. In 1966, voters agreed to a proposed amendment that permitted the residency requirements for voting for president and vice president of the United States to be different from those established for state and local elections. This enabled the legislature to eliminate the residency requirement the following year-three years before Congress erased all residency requirements longer than 30 days for presidential elections. Finally, in 1972, voters amended section 1 by reducing residency requirements for voting in state and local elections from one year to 30 days. This was a direct reaction to the U.S. Supreme Court decision *Dunn v. Blumstein* (1972), in which the court stated that there was no reason for a residency of greater than 30 days in order to vote in state or local elections.

Section 1 has also been subject to two minor judicial interpretations. The supreme court clarified the significance of the franchise right in *Boucher v. Bomhoff* (1972). The prefatory language to a constitutional referendum ballot had been biased, giving voters to understand that the constitution required a convention to be held (when it requires only that the question be on the ballot every ten years); thus, the vote was invalidated. The court declared: "It is basic to our democratic society that the people be afforded the opportunity of expressing their will on the multitudinous issues which confront them" (p. 78), an opportunity that was forestalled them by the wording of the referendum.

Moreover, the supreme court supported the establishment by a local government of restrictions on the franchise, specifically, prohibitions on dual-position holding (disallowing a police officer from sitting on the North Pole City Council). These limitations, said the court, served compelling state interests of preventing public servants from accumulating many positions, avoiding direct or indirect pecuniary conflicts, and preventing employees from asserting control over their supervisors through their elected positions (*Acevedo v. City of North Pole*, 1983).

SECTION 2

Disqualifications. No person may vote who has been convicted of a felony involving moral turpitude unless his civil rights have been restored. No person may vote who has been judicially determined to be of unsound mind unless the disability has been removed.

These two sentences are exceptions to section 1. They are commonly placed in state constitutions to ensure that only morally and mentally fit citizens will vote. The first sentence permits the legislature to identify crimes of moral turpitude that cost perpetrators their voting rights. The list of crimes meeting this definition in Alaska include murder, sexual assault, incest, kidnapping, robbery, arson, burglary, theft, and forgery. Voting rights are restored to convicted felons when they are released unconditionally. The second sentence attempts to avoid the imprecision of statements stripping the mentally unstable of voting rights by vesting the authority in the judiciary.

SECTION 3

Methods of voting; election contests. Methods of voting, including absentee voting, shall be prescribed by law. Secrecy of voting shall be preserved. The procedure for determining election contests, with right of appeal to the courts, shall be prescribed by law.

This section follows provisions of the *Model State Constitution*[53] in allowing the legislature to determine voting methods, procedures, and contested outcomes. Unlike the practice in many states, it establishes as the constitutional rights of citizens absentee voting, the secret ballot, and judicial review of election challenges.

---

[53] National Municipal League, *Model State Constitution*, 3, 26.

Alaska's election laws did not encounter much judicial interpretation until the Republican party of Alaska (RPA) challenged the constitutionality of the state's primary system in the 1990s. Prior to 1967, Alaska had a traditional open primary, and voters could vote for a Republican or a Democratic slate of candidates, but not both. The leading party of the statehood era, the Democrats, resisted change, but when Republicans gained control of the legislature and executive in 1966, they made primary rules completely open (called the blanket or, disparagingly, the "free love" primary), allowing voters to select from any party's candidates in the primary.

For 25 years Alaskans, a majority of whom register as nonpartisan or undeclared voters, seemed satisfied with the system, but Republican party leaders became discontented. They claimed that supporters of other parties "raided" their primary races, supporting weaker candidates whom they hoped to defeat more easily in the general election. They also objected to Republican legislators who defied party rules by joining Democratic legislative coalitions, while election rules left them without means to punish traitors. In 1990 the RPA adopted a party rule allowing only those registered as Republicans, independents, and nonpartisans to vote in the Republican primary. Initially, the state (under a Democratic administration) declined to change rules for the 1990 primary, and the RPA filed suit in federal court. Their case was based on the U.S. Supreme Court decision in *Tashjian v. Republican Party of Connecticut* (1986), which endorsed the Connecticut Republican Party's attempt to open the closed primary to admit nonpartisan and undeclared voters.[54]

In 1992 U.S. District Court Judge James Singleton announced a tentative decision, agreeing that under the *Tashjian* interpretation, the blanket primary infringed on the RPA's associational rights.[55] Thereupon, the state, by then under a Republican administration, changed its position, and adopted administrative regulations to partially close the Alaska primary. For the 1992 and 1994 primaries, the state elections office prepared two ballots: a party rule ballot with names only of those who filed for the Republican nomination, available to those registered as Republicans, nonpartisan, or undeclared; and the statutory ballot, with names of candidates of all other political parties and available to all voters.

This change appeared to satisfy Republican leaders, who used it to punish errant Republican legislators.[56] However, the change was opposed in state court by several activists (including Green Party candidates) who called themselves Alaska Voters for an Open Primary. The superior court rejected their challenge,

[54] For a review of Alaska's primary election system, see Gerald A. McBeath, "Transformation of the Alaska Blanket Primary System," *Comparative State Politics* 15, no. 4 (1994): 25–42.

[55] *Zawacki v. State*, A92-414 CV (D. Alaska 1992), and cited on pp. 3–4 of the *O'Callaghan* decision.

[56] McBeath, "Transformation of the Alaska Blanket Primary System," 34–36.

but on appeal (by which time the state, under a new Democratic administration, had joined the appeal) the lower court decision was reversed.

In *O'Callaghan v. State of Alaska* (1996), the high court ruled that the Alaska blanket primary statute was constitutional. Writing for the court's majority, Chief Justice Allen Compton offered these justifications for the majority's decision:

> A state's election statute does not violate the first amendment associational rights of a political party solely by virtue of the fact that the statute conflicts with party rules pertaining to the primary. The blanket primary is nondiscriminatory. While the blanket primary may create some degree of interference with RPA's associational rights, this interference is minor and is justified by the State's interests.
>
> A blanket primary statute may harm the RPA in terms of creating a greater chance of raiding than under a partially-closed primary, though its real effect has not been shown and may not be as extreme as the party argues. Further, there is only a slightly greater loss of accountability of candidates to party principles under the blanket primary as compared to the partially-closed primary. The harm is not great and is justified by the State's interests.
>
> The State's interests in encouraging voter turnout, maximizing voters' choice among candidates, and ensuring that elected officials have relatively broad based constituencies are served by the blanket primary statute. These interests are important and are legitimate objectives for a state to seek to achieve when structuring election procedures.[57]

Following the decision, the state division of elections declared that only the statutory primary ballot would be prepared for the August 27, 1996, primary election. RPA leaders called for a write-in primary to determine their nominees, a plan which the lieutenant governor rejected because it would allow voters to have two primary election votes.

In a carefully argued dissent, Alaska's most experienced jurist, Justice Jay Rabinowitz, pointed out that the U.S. Supreme Court's position on state primary elections was unequivocal. Both the *Tashjian* decision and the earlier, 1981 *LaFollette* decision[58] (which held that the state of Wisconsin could not control the delegate selection process of a national party for its national convention) had defended association rights of political parties, basing them on guarantees of the First and Fourteenth Amendments of the federal constitution. These rights, argued Rabinowitz, had to be given strict scrutiny. "The state of Alaska has failed to demonstrate compelling state interests which outweigh the harms to the Republican Party of Alaska's constitutional protected associational rights."[59]

---

[57] *O'Callaghan v. State of Alaska*, Supreme Court No. S-6249, April 12, 1996, p. 30.

[58] *Democratic Party of United States v. Wisconsin ex rel. LaFollette* (1981).

[59] *O'Callaghan v. State of Alaska*, 40–41.

The different visions of democracy which this controversy over Alaska's primary rules has evoked will not be reconciled until the U.S. Supreme Court engages the issue of state election rules again.

SECTION 4

Voting precincts; registration. The legislature may provide a system of permanent registration of voters, and may establish voting precincts within election districts.

At the time of statehood, Alaska had no system of voter registration. Voters were organized into precincts, but the small population of the territory and prevalence of small communities did not seem to make necessary a formal system of voter identification. Delegates to the constitutional convention toyed with the idea of continuing this practice but decided to assign to the legislature the authority to establish procedures for registering voters when this became necessary.

SECTION 5

General elections. General elections shall be held on the second Tuesday in October of every even-numbered year, but the month and day may be changed by law.

Section 5 continued the territorial practice of conducting elections in October. Within a year of statehood, however, the legislature changed the date of general elections to correspond to the date for federal elections—the first Tuesday after the first Monday in November. This saved the new state the expense of conducting within a single month elections for state and federal officials.

Article VI

Legislative Apportionment

The sixth article of the Alaska Constitution sets forth the procedure for reapportioning the legislature, following decennial censuses. It is unique among the American states because it assigns the power of reapportionment to the executive and not to the legislative branch or a commission, as typically is the case in the American states.

Much of Article VI has been nullified by actions of the U.S. Supreme Court. In *Baker v. Carr* (1962) and *Reynolds v. Sims* (1964), the court established the "one person, one vote" rule of apportionment. It required that the houses of state legislatures be apportioned on population alone, with legislative seats representing approximately the same number of voters. These changes invalidated the area-based organizing principle of the Alaska State Senate, which, like most state upper houses, overrepresented rural areas at the expense of cities.

In 1964, Governor Egan used sections 8–10 of Article VI to reapportion the senate, a plan that the Alaska Supreme Court upheld (*Wade v. Nolan*, 1966). Each of the succeeding gubernatorial reapportionment plans, however, has been declared unconstitutional by the supreme court (recorded in *Egan v. Hammond*, 1972; *Groh v. Egan*, 1974; *Carpenter v. Hammond*, 1983; *Kenai Peninsula Borough v. State*, 1987; and *Hickel v. Southeast Conference et al.*, 1993).[60]

---

[60] See also Gerald A. McBeath, "Alaska," in Leroy Hardy, Alan Heslop, and George Blair, eds., *Redistricting in the 1980s* (Claremont, CA: Rose Institute, 1993), 17–20.

The equal representation requirements of the federal and state courts have been especially difficult to satisfy in Alaska. As the state's population increases in urban areas without a change in the size of the legislature, fewer seats are available to rural areas. It becomes necessary to combine rural regions spanning the size of entire American states to form districts equal to the concentrated population of urban districts.

Because the constitution allows any citizen to take a reapportionment issue to court, the Alaska superior and supreme courts have been deeply involved in apportionment policy making.

SECTION 1

Election districts. Members of the house of representatives shall be elected by the qualified voters of the respective election districts. Until reapportionment, election districts and the number of representatives to be elected from each district shall be set forth in Section 1 of Article XIV.

Article VI was designed to be read with sections 1 and 2 of Article XIV, which set out the initial election districts for the House of Representatives and the Senate and distributed seats to each district. The provisions of Article XIV are now obsolete. Current election districts and the allocation of seats to districts are detailed in the April 20, 1993, report and proposed permanent plan of the Governor's Advisory Reapportionment Board and the May 27, 1993, proclamation of permanent reapportionment and redistricting and accompanying statement.

The constitutional convention committee had divided Alaska into 24 election districts. District lines were drawn primarily on the basis of watershed boundaries, following the recording districts of territorial administration. Because the convention fell in the middle of the decade, the 1950 census figures were out of date. Committee members updated the census with 1954 school attendance figures to arrive at a population estimate of 203,000. That number led the committee to set the House size at 40, which meant that each seat would represent about 5,000 people. Committee chair John Hellenthal called a house of 40 a wieldy, economical figure and noted that it was in line with the size of other state houses (*PACC*, 1839).

SECTION 2

Senate districts. Members of the senate shall be elected by the qualified voters of the respective senate districts. Senate districts shall be as set forth in Section 2 of Article XIV, subject to changes authorized in this article.

Originally, section 2 was linked with Article XIV, section 2, in which the outlines of the senate districts were established. It is now obsolete.

At the constitutional convention, committee chair John Hellenthal said that twenty senators would be chosen from combinations of election districts. He reported that the committee had endeavored to develop a plan that treated rural residents fairly:

> The Committee . . . believed that the major criticism . . . of the judicial divisions [of the territory] was that it permitted a situation to develop where tundra [the rural areas] could elect senators . . . and frequently . . . the senators were chosen from the urban areas of Alaska, and the Committee felt definitely that that situation should be avoided. (*PACC*, 1840)

Delegate George Cooper, who was also a committee member, reminded delegates that the House apportionment plan was "based on population, and that the senatorial plan . . . [was] based primarily on geographical representation" (*PACC*, 1843).

Section 2 was nullified by the federal judicial decisions on legislative apportionment. The historic decision of *Baker v. Carr* (1962) was a response to gross inequities in the worth of citizens' votes, which abounded throughout the U.S. political system. It held that the apportionment of a state legislature was subject to review by the courts for violation of the equal protection clause of the Fourteenth Amendment of the federal constitution.

Two years later, in *Reynolds v. Sims* (1964), the U.S. Supreme Court ruled that the equal protection clause required that seats in both houses of bicameral state legislatures were to be apportioned on a population basis, which focused attention on upper houses of legislatures nationwide. Section 2 of Article XIV, the apportionment schedule, had established Senate districts based on area and defined by combining various House districts. The Alaska Supreme Court held that such an areal apportionment was unconstitutional under federal constitutional provisions (*Wade v. Nolan*, 1966), and it upheld Governor Egan's reapportionment of the Senate in 1964.

SECTION 3

> **Reapportionment of house.** The governor shall reapportion the house of representatives immediately following the official reporting of each decennial census of the United States. Reapportionment shall be based upon civilian population within each election district as reported by the census.

The first sentence of section 3 follows the national pattern of reapportionment following decennial censuses. It refers to reapportionment of the House only, but since 1964 the Senate has also fallen under this and related provisions (sections 8–10). The second sentence, which bases redistricting on civilian, and not combined civilian and military, populations, was a controversial issue in several of the judiciary's reapportionment decisions; it is now obsolete. The minutes of the proceedings of the constitutional convention do not provide a clear explanation of this sentence, but discussion at the convention referred to the highly transient nature of the military population, which did not call Alaska its home, and the desire of delegates to base election districts on the resident population.

Following the 1971 reapportionment of the Alaska legislature, thirteen of its members challenged the validity of the plan. One of their complaints was that excluding the military from the population base was a denial of equal protection of the laws under both the U.S. and Alaska Constitutions. The effect of including all military personnel, the complainants said, would be to give greater political power to communities adjoining major military installations (such as Anchorage and Fairbanks).

In 1972, the Alaska Supreme Court applied provisions of *Davis v. Mann* (1964) to Alaska, and ruled that it was constitutionally impermissible to discriminate against a class of individuals merely because of the nature of their employment (*Egan v. Hammond*, 1972). Although finding the second sentence of section 3 unconstitutional, the court continued, "[T]hat is not to say that some military cannot be excluded as a permissible device for limiting the impact of transients and nonresidents on legislative districting."

The state chose to exclude nonresident military personnel from the reapportionment count in the 1970s and 1980s. In the 1970s, resident military numbers were estimated from voter registration data. In the 1980s, surveys were made of the military population to determine those who were considered residents, and this was factored into redistricting equations. Neither practice used population data "as reported by the census," but both methods were approved by the court (*Groh v. Egan*, 1974; *Carpenter v. Hammond*, 1983). The Hickel reapportionment board decided to include all military personnel in its plan, and the supreme court supported it (*Hickel v. Southeast Conference et al*, 1993).

SECTION 4

Method. Reapportionment shall be by the method of equal proportions, except that each election district having the major fraction of the quotient obtained by dividing total civilian population by forty shall have one representative.

Section 4 provides that reapportionment be accomplished by the method of equal proportions, meaning that election districts should be of relatively equal size. It is read together with section 5 to offer guidance on the amount of acceptable variation in election district populations after reapportionment. Although population is still the basis for the reapportionment of the House and Senate, both section 4 and section 5 are now obsolete.

SECTION 5

Combining districts. Should the total civilian population within any election district fall below one-half of the quotient, the district shall be attached to an election district within its senate district, and the reapportionment for the new district shall be determined as provided in Section 4 of this article.

Section 5 provided for the representation of districts that lost population between censuses, by linking them with other election districts within Senate districts. The constitutional sections on Senate districts essentially froze representation by area, as a counter to the change of House districts as population shifted. Two months after the U.S. Supreme Court declared such upper-house representation schemes unconstitutional (*Reynolds v. Sims*, 1964), the attorney general of Alaska issued an opinion advising that the governor had the authority to reapportion the Alaska Senate. When the governor proclaimed his reapportionment plan for the Senate, his authority was challenged. The supreme court held that the frozen apportionment of the Senate had resulted in gross malapportionment and that the governor's action was justified (*Wade v. Nolan*, 1966).

SECTION 6

Redistricting. The governor may further redistrict by changing the size and area of election districts, subject to the limitations of this article. Each new district so created shall be formed of contiguous and compact territory containing as nearly as practicable a relatively integrated socioeconomic area. Each shall contain a population at least equal to the quotient obtained by dividing the total civilian population by forty. Consideration may be given to local government boundaries. Drainage and other geographic features shall be used in describing boundaries wherever possible.

This section expresses the reform principle of legislative redistricting—that newly created election districts should be compact, contiguous, and integrated socioeconomic units. It is read in connection with section 5 on the combination of districts. The intent of the framers of the constitution was to avoid the excesses of legislative gerrymandering found in many of the American states. (They were not wholly successful.) Further, section 6 pays attention to local government jurisdictional lines and to other geographic features, such as transportation and drainage patterns.

Section 6 has been involved in each of the challenges to reapportionment plans in the 1970s, 1980s, and 1990s. In a first challenge to Governor Egan's 1971 proclamation of reapportionment and redistricting, thirteen legislators contended that percentage variations from the population norms for legislative districting violated the equal protection clauses of both the U.S. and Alaska Constitutions. The supreme court held that the plan was invalid and that there was no adequate justification for variances ranging from +23.35 to –45.93 percent in house districts and from +26.14 to –7.20 percent in Senate districts (*Egan v. Hammond*, 1972). The court noted the difficulty, given Alaska's sparse and widely scattered population and the relative inaccessibility of some areas in the state, of drawing districts of equal population; moreover, the court remarked that surprisingly small changes in district boundaries created large percentage variances from the ideal number. Nevertheless, it found the variances in the 1971 plan unfair; it ordered two court masters to redraw district lines for interim use in the 1971 elections and requested the governor to develop a permanent reapportionment plan.

This plan of December 1972 was challenged in early 1974 for, among other reasons, excessive population variances between districts and the division of the greater Anchorage area into six districts, which contradicted the spirit of section 6. One of the reasons advanced by the reapportionment board for disparities in district size was the need to preserve boundaries of regional Native corporations established under the Alaska Native Claims Settlement Act of 1971 (ANCSA). The high court found the maximum deviation in the house to be 29 percent (through underrepresentation of the Juneau district by 14 percent and over-representation of the Nome district by 15 percent). In the Senate, the maximum deviation was 22.4 percent. Total deviations between several pairs of districts was in excess of 10 percent, which did not meet standards of close scrutiny enunciated by the U.S. Supreme Court (*Groh v. Egan*, 1974). The federal high court had prohibited population disparities greater than 16.4 percent.

However, the Alaska Supreme Court did not invalidate the division of the greater Anchorage area into six legislative districts, and it refused to substitute its judgment for that of the reapportionment board in the design of the districts. The smaller districts, said the court, still conformed to the constitutional standard, and the reapportionment board's decision was based on rational grounds.

One of the challenges to the 1981 Hammond administration reapportionment plan also involved the interpretation of section 6. The plan had included Cordova, in southcentral Alaska, along with southeast coastal communities in what was jocularly called the "ice worm" district. (It extended 700 miles in a jagged line from its southeasternmost to its northeasternmost points.) The state argued that even though the communities were neither compact nor contiguous, they were coastal communities with common interests in fisheries. In *Carpenter v. Hammond* (1983), the supreme court found that in this respect, the plan violated section 6, and ordered that the district be redrawn.

The most recent challenge to a reapportionment plan occurred in 1991, when the Hickel administration issued its proclamation of reapportionment and redistricting, which significantly changed the alignment of legislative districts in the state. Seven lawsuits were filed in superior court challenging the governor's plan, five of which were consolidated for trial before Anchorage Superior Court Judge Larry R. Weeks. Judge Weeks concluded that the plan was unconstitutional because it lacked compliance with section 6 and the equal protection provisions of the state constitution. His findings were largely sustained by the supreme court.

The high court emphasized the reapportionment plan's violation of antigerrymandering provisions (*Hickel v. Southeast Conference*, 1993). It pointed to districts that overlooked several local municipal boundaries. The plan ignored natural geographic boundaries by splitting several major islands. One district mixed small, rural, Native communities with urban areas of Ketchikan and Sitka, which had different social concerns and political needs. Another city in an agricultural area (Palmer) that was more socioeconomically integrated with nearby cities was included in a district with small fishing communities. Further, organized and unorganized boroughs were included in the same district. Three cities that had been placed in separate districts in fact shared most of their public facilities. The North Slope was combined with sparsely populated river drainages of the state's interior. Finally, two areas were populated with culturally distinct groups of Natives who were historically, physically, linguistically, and economically disparate and had little or no present-day socioeconomic integration.

SECTION 7

Modification of senate districts. The senate districts, described in Section 2 of Article XIV, may be modified to reflect changes in election districts. A district, although modified, shall retain its total number of senators and its approximate perimeter.

In the mid-1950s, upper houses of state legislatures followed the U.S. Senate in using principles of area representation, and the Alaska Constitution mirrored this practice. In an interchange at the constitutional convention, delegate Robert McNealy inquired of committee chairman John Hellenthal what would happen if the population of one judicial district grew to be twice as large as that of all other judicial districts. Delegate James Nolan added that it would seem "that the senatorial districts are fixed permanently without a constitutional amendment" (*PACC*, 1881), which Hellenthal confirmed.

Although now obsolete, section 7 (read together with section 2 of Article XIV) attempted to create some flexibility in Senate districts as election district boundaries for House seats changed, without compromising the representation of Alaska's regions. However, under the reapportionment plan of 1965, which followed section 7 of this article and section 2 of Article XIV, 30.7 percent of the voters still resided in districts that could elect a majority of the senate. The state supreme court declared that for the plan to freeze representation without a reapportionment of the Senate was invalid and justified the governor's reapportionment of the Senate on an interim basis (*Wade v. Nolan*, 1966). Because the reapportionment article of the constitution has not been amended, successive reapportionments have been done on an "interim basis," too.

SECTION 8

Reapportionment board. The governor shall appoint a reapportionment board to act in an advisory capacity to him. It shall consist of five members, none of whom may be public employees or officials. At least one member each shall be appointed from the Southeastern, Southcentral, Central, and Northwestern Senate Districts. Appointments shall be made without regard to political affiliation. Board members shall be compensated.

This section implements the governor's reapportionment powers. The board it establishes is advisory to the governor, leaving him or her in charge of the final shape of electoral districts—a power unrivaled in any of the other American states.

The reapportionment board is designed to represent Alaska's major regions and traditional judicial districts, which are featured in the constitutional language. The board is a lay body, a feature that occasioned questions during the constitutional convention. Delegate James Hurley asked committee chair John Hellenthal why the board excluded "public employees or officials," remarking that "it relegates all public employees to second-class citizens" (*PACC*, 1953). Several delegates indicated that public employees were too "politically inclined" (p. 1956), and would lack objectivity. Delegate George Cooper, who was also a committee member, responded that the exclusion was intended to ensure that reapportionment would not end up in the hands of the legislature—which was then the practice in the American states.

The clause calling for appointments "without regard to political affiliation" was designed to remove the board as far as possible from partisan influence and increase its objectivity. At the constitutional convention, committee chair John Hellenthal explicitly rejected an alternative phrasing: "chosen from each of the major parties." He said "That alternative was specifically rejected because [the committee] felt it placed emphasis upon political considerations on this board which . . . it is hoped to keep as objective as possible" (*PACC*, 1958). The constitutional language has not reduced complaints about the political nature of reapportionment boards, however.

The constitutional status of the reapportionment board has been reinforced as well as challenged in several court cases. In *Wade v. Nolan* (1966), the high court affirmed the governor's authority and responsibility, and in turn his use of an advisory apportionment board, as the obvious intent of the framers of the state constitution because "over the years it had been forcefully demonstrated on a nationwide scale that state legislatures would not reapportion themselves" (p. 699). Although the constitution made no explicit reference to reapportionment of the state Senate, when this was required by U.S. constitutional rulings of 1962 and 1964, the Alaska Supreme Court held that the power to reapportion implicitly fell to the governor and his reapportionment board.

The board's composition was first challenged in *Egan v. Hammond* (1972). Democratic governor Bill Egan had appointed no Republican members to the board, which legislative challengers to the 1971 reapportionment plan believed was in violation of section 8. Because the high court found the plan unconstitutional on other grounds, the question was moot. Nevertheless, the court opined that the governor had not acted from political considerations or in bad faith. Having ordered the governor and his board to prepare a new plan, the court spelled out some criteria it thought applicable in deciding whether a board had been appointed "without regard to political affiliation" (p. 872), so as to withstand challenge. The germane considerations for its review included: political affiliation of members of the board; nature of their activities in partisan politics, particularly if from one political party only; and the expertise and general qualifications that they bring to the board.

Finally, in *Groh v. Egan* (1974), the supreme court specified the standard of review it would use in reapportionment cases. The court declined to arrogate to itself the power to decide what was preferable between alternative rational plans. It held that "[t]he constitutional authority to reapportion resides in the executive, not the courts" (p. 866). The court said that its view of a reapportionment plan was analogous to its review of regulations adopted under delegation of authority from the legislature to an administrative agency to formulate policy and promulgate regulations. The court reviewed regulations to ensure that the agency had not exceeded the power delegated to it. Second, it determined whether each regulation was reasonable and not arbitrary. It did not, in other words, substitute its judgment for that of the executive.

SECTION 9

Organization. The board shall elect one of its members chairman and may employ temporary assistants. Concurrence of three members is required for a ruling or determination, but a lesser number may conduct hearings or otherwise act for the board.

Section 9 sets out elementary operating procedures for the reapportionment board, including its leadership and quorum requirements. This section has not been subject to judicial interpretation.

SECTION 10

Reapportionment plan and proclamation. Within ninety days following the official reporting of each decennial census, the board shall submit to the governor a plan for reapportionment and redistricting as provided in this article. Within ninety days after receipt of the plan, the governor shall issue a proclamation of reapportionment and redistricting. An accompanying statement shall explain any change from the plan of the board. The reapportionment and redistricting shall be effective for the election of members of the legislature until after the official reporting of the next decennial census.

Section 10 establishes the timelines for actions of the reapportionment board and the governor, and is self-executing. Upon receiving official census results (which may be delayed by challenges), the governor and board have six months to complete the reapportionment plan. The objective was to complete reapportionment so that the new electoral districts could be used in the first legislative elections following the census. This objective has been frustrated by litigation, and the state has used interim plans for at least the first election following censuses in 1970, 1980, and 1990.

By their negative commentary on legislative reapportionments in other states, which were at best done tardily, the framers indicated concerns in bringing the legislature into accord with shifts in the population of the state. However, they did not allow the governor to deal with population shifts between censuses or make any other adjustments. Once the governor's plan was proclaimed, no re-districting could be done until after the next census.

In *Wade v. Nolan* (1966), the Alaska Supreme Court held that the governor and the reapportionment board were merely delegated the duty of determining a plan for application of the constitutional formula for apportionment. Once a valid plan had been established and proclaimed, it became law or "effective" by the force of the constitution.

SECTION 11

Enforcement. Any qualified voter may apply to the superior court to compel the governor, by mandamus or otherwise, to perform his reapportionment duties or to correct any error in redistricting or reapportionment. Application to compel the governor to perform his reapportionment duties must be filed within thirty days of the expiration of either of the two ninety-day periods specified in this article. Application to compel correction of any error in redistricting or reapportionment must be filed within thirty days following the proclamation. Original jurisdiction in these matters is hereby vested in the superior court. On appeal, the cause shall be reviewed by the supreme court upon the law and the facts.

Before courts became extensively involved in the reapportionment of state legislatures in the 1960s, the Alaska Constitution gave any voter the right to challenge an action of the reapportionment board or the governor in court. Section 11 gives citizens the same time to respond and seek remedies—90 days—that the governor and the reapportionment board have. Moreover, it vests trial power in the state's superior courts, with review by the supreme court. At the constitutional convention, the committee had given original jurisdiction to the supreme court, borrowing its language from the Hawaii Constitution. Delegate Warren Taylor sought an amendment to decide redistricting disputes in superior court, which would give a "local" judge jurisdiction (*PACC*, 1944).

In *Groh v. Egan* (1974), the supreme court clarified this provision by stating that appellate review would be in the nature of a *de novo* proceeding, but without additional evidence being presented. In reviewing the reapportionment board's use of 1970 census data for its 1973 plan, instead of more recent demographic data, the court held that this was not an arbitrary process but reflected a rational decision.

In a second clarification, the high court held that one did not need to reside and vote in the area whose redistricting one challenged in order to have standing (*Carpenter v. Hammond*, 1983). Status as a registered voter of Alaska was sufficient to establish the standing to attack any reapportionment plan.

Article VII

Health, Education, and Welfare

Article VII is the shortest article in the Alaska Constitution and initially was the least controversial. It requires the legislature to establish a unified K through 12 public school system and establishes the University of Alaska. It also makes general statements pertaining to public health and welfare.

SECTION 1

Public education. The legislature shall by general law establish and maintain a system of public schools open to all children of the State, and may provide for other public educational institutions. Schools and institutions so established shall be free from sectarian control. No money shall be paid from public funds for the direct benefit of any religious or other private educational institution.

Section 1 is the framework for Alaska's K through 12 public school system. This system must be "open to all," which has been defined as accessible to all school-age children throughout the state. The second and third sentences attempt to erect a constitutional wall between public schools and those under sectarian or other private control. Delegate Warren Taylor of Fairbanks (a Masonic lodge member) proposed the section, which is probably the strongest *public* school constitutional provision.

Most of the discussion on education at the constitutional convention concerned relations between the state and private educational institutions. One question concerned the third sentence—"No money shall be paid from public funds for the direct benefit [of private education]"—and whether such a reference to finance was appropriate. Delegate Victor Fischer noted that section 7 of Article IX included the statement: "No tax shall be levied or appropriation of public money made or public property transferred, nor shall the public credit be used, except for a public purpose." In his view, this section would cover education as well as all other state expenditures (*PACC*, 1515). Delegate Rolland Armstrong, who sat on the Health, Education, and Welfare committee, noted that the committee wanted the statement included as part of Article VII "so that it could always be clarified in relationship to this subject" (*PACC*, 1516).

The second question concerned the support of nonpublic schools. Delegate Jack Coghill sought an amendment to section 1 that would replace the word *direct* with *indirect*. He argued, "I believe we should take direct steps to maintain a free public education not encroached upon by any quarter" (*PACC*, 1516). Other delegates, however, thought that the effect of the word *indirect* would be radical. They noted, for example, that it might be construed to prevent children at private schools from receiving welfare benefits typically administered through the schools (*PACC*, 1521). The amendment was defeated by a nearly 2-to-1 vote.

An early supreme court case tested the meaning of section 1 in the context of providing public bus transportation to private school students. Such busing had been provided to Catholic school students in Fairbanks under a 1955 territorial statute. When challenged by the Fairbanks school district, the supreme court held that the statute had been unconstitutional under the territory's Organic Act. Moreover, the new state constitution's prohibitions on providing direct benefits to religious schools precluded the busing of these students at public expense (*Matthews v. Quinton*, 1961). Although attorneys' general opinions consistently support this finding that the public funding of private school students' transportation is illegal, the state continued to provide it to Fairbanks parochial school students in 1996.

A more recent case tested the same part of section 1. During the 1970s a state grant program gave students attending private colleges the difference between their schools' tuition and that charged by the state university. When challenged, supporters sought to amend the constitution to allow such tuition grants. Voters rejected the amendment, and the high court later invalidated the grant program (*Sheldon Jackson College v. State*, 1979). Although the grants were made to students, the supreme court found that the students were merely a "conduit" (p. 132) for a direct benefit to the private institutions.

The high court established the relative independence of public schools from local governments in a 1971 interpretation of section 1 (*Macauley v. Hilde-brand;* see also Article X). The court ruled that the legislative delegation of educational functions to local school boards for the purpose of adapting schools to different localities did not diminish constitutionally mandated state control over education. Such control at the state level prohibited home rule boroughs and other local governments from controlling the accounting of school districts.

Although the state legislature, under the terms of section 1, has established a compulsory attendance law and regulations that support student disciplinary codes, the supreme court has followed a standard of vigilance in matters of the protection of individual constitutional liberties. For this reason, the court has rejected the expulsion of students who differ from the majority, such as by having their own hairstyle, without some compelling interest of safety and order for other students (*Breese v. Smith*, 1972).

When that interest in an orderly school environment is paramount, however, the supreme court has condoned infringements of students' liberties. In the first Alaska case on school searches of minor students, the high court upheld the search of a Kenai High School student who was suspected of theft. It acknowledged the constitutional question under the federal constitution's Fourth and Fourteenth Amendments. Nevertheless, it ruled that "searches of school children on school premises during school hours by school teachers and administrators" were analogous to the warantless searches upheld in federal and state courts (*D.R.C. v. State*, 1982).[61]

Perhaps the major constitutional issue concerning section 1 has been the access of Native Alaskan children to high school programs in their own villages. Prior to statehood, Alaska had a dual school system. Territorial schools operated in urban areas; most of their students were Caucasians. In most rural areas of the state, the greater population of which was Alaska Native, schooling was provided by the federal Bureau of Indian Affairs (BIA). The objective of the framers was to integrate educational services in one statewide system of public education.

The limited resources of the new state, however, delayed the state's expansion of schools in rural Alaska. The new state government established the Alaska State-Operated School System (ASOSS) for unincorporated villages in rural Alaska and gradually assumed control of the BIA schools. By the early 1970s, about half of rural school children still attended BIA schools. Moreover, these were K through 8 day schools. Only one high school was available solely for students of small villages: Mt. Edgecumbe boarding school in Sitka. (Some village youth attended regional boarding schools.) Many Native students were sent out of state for secondary training. While the prospect of oil revenues allowed the state to phase out the BIA day schools, the problem of secondary education was not addressed.

[61] In *United States v. Biswell* (1972), the U.S. Supreme Court upheld a warrantless search of a pawnshop where guns were sold; in *Nathanson v. State* (1976), the Alaska high court upheld a warrantless search of a boat used for crab fishing. Both cases were analogous because those who were subject to search were traditionally under close supervision.

In 1972, a suit was instituted on behalf of 28 Native secondary school youth against the state-operated school system, which sought to compel the state to provide secondary schools in their communities of residence (*Hootch v. Alaska State-Operated School System*, 1975). The supreme court held that the statutes did not require secondary schools for as few as eight students and that the constitutional right to education did not include the right to attend school in one's own community.

Justice Rabinowitz issued a dissent in this case, noting: "I fail to see how a public school system can be truly 'open' to its students where school is not reasonably accessible to them. The word 'open' must be construed not only as meaning free of charge, but also as encompassing a right of reasonable access."

Trial continued on the equal protection and racial discrimination claims, and after extensive negotiations—and with promises of oil riches on the horizon—the state signed a consent degree, *Tobeluk v. Lind* (1979). This led to the development of secondary school programs in Native villages having both a grade school and at least one high school-aged student. Questions about the cost and effectiveness of these school programs have kept the issue of educational access alive into the 1990s.[62]

SECTION 2

State university. The University of Alaska is hereby established as the state university and constituted a body corporate. It shall have title to all real and personal property now or hereafter set aside for or conveyed to it. Its property shall be administered and disposed of according to law.

This section establishes the state university as the sole system of public higher education in the state. One central statewide administration administers its campuses throughout the state, and it receives public funding through appropriations from the legislature. Further, the university's autonomy is provided for by designation as a corporate institution with title to property, and is hedged only by the legislature's involvement through the final clause of the last sentence, "according to law." This seeming autonomy, however, has been tempered by a series of court interpretations.

In 1974, the supreme court held that a university employee who was tenured but not holding a faculty position was entitled to a hearing before the termination of employment. This judgment was reached even though university regulations did not allow hearings for nonfaculty employees (*University of Alaska v. Chau-vin*, 1974).

[62] See *Fairbanks Daily News-Miner*, January 21–26, 1996.

When action was brought against the university for damage to an aircraft that attempted to land on an experimental floating ice strip maintained by the university, the supreme court treated the university as an arm of state government. The court held that despite the degree of constitutional as well as statutory autonomy that the university possessed, and despite its unique corporate character and its power to sue and be sued, it fell within the ambit of the language of statutes governing suits against the state. Trial by jury was not allowed in actions against the university (*University of Alaska v. National Aircraft Leasing, Ltd.*, 1975).

Legislative actions in 1977 compromised the university's fiscal autonomy and brought it under the purview of Alaska's fiscal procedures and executive budget acts, much as though it were another state agency. When the university protested, the attorney general opined: "The University of Alaska is similar in all or most respects to other state executive agencies for purposes of budgeting and accounting."[63]

The clearest evidence of corporate status—the university's property right to lands—has not been supported by judicial interpretation. When the university sued the state because the legislature allowed the sale of a land parcel held in trust for the university and did not provide compensation to it, the supreme court was equivocal. It permitted the land transaction but required compensation for the university (*State v. University of Alaska*, 1981). Only after extensive negotiations did the state agree to restore the land trust for the university.

SECTION 3

Board of regents of university. The University of Alaska shall be governed by a board of regents. The regents shall be appointed by the governor, subject to confirmation by a majority of the members of the legislature in joint session. The board shall, in accordance with law, formulate policy and appoint the president of the university. He shall be the executive officer of the board.

Section 3 is read together with section 2, as it further expresses provisions providing for the university's autonomy and self-regulation. The governor appoints, and the legislature confirms, the governing body of the university, which is its board of regents. It is the board that sets university policy and hires its chief executive officer, the president. Unlike departments of state government with boards, the university regents do not require the approval of the governor when they hire a president.

Even this degree of detail has not provided independence for the state university system. When the university refused to provide the Alaska Public Employees Association with a list of university employees and their locations to

[63] Harrison, *Alaska 's Constitution*, 146.

be used in a union-organizing campaign, the courts declined to support the university's autonomy. The supreme court held that the university was not immune from compliance with statutes on the disclosure of public records, as it was an "agency" within the meaning of that statute. Further, the university president, although appointed, was a "public officer" under the terms of the disclosure statute and thus was obliged to follow its provisions (*Carter v. Alaska Public Employees Associations*, 1983).

SECTION 4

Public health. The legislature shall provide for the promotion and protection of public health.

This statement expresses the policy intent of the framers to enhance public health through agencies of the state. Unusual in state constitutions, section 4 expresses in constitutional language what is an inherent police power of the state—to safeguard the public health of its citizenry. It has not been subject to judicial interpretation.

SECTION 5

Public welfare. The legislature shall provide for public welfare.

Section 5 is a statement of objectives, without definition, which is read together with section 4. Several delegates to the constitutional convention emphasized the state's responsibilities to the less fortunate. They were impressed with provisions of the Hawaii Constitution that made both health and welfare the fundamental, constitutional obligations of the state. It has not been interpreted by the judiciary.

Article VIII

Natural Resources

Alaska was the first state to have a constitutional article on natural resources. This was natural, of course, given the resource bounty of the new state and its extreme dependence on a few resources, such as fisheries, mining, logging, oil, and gas.

In fact, the territory's delegate to Congress, Bob Bartlett, said in his keynote address to the constitutional convention that the careful husbandry of Alaska's natural resources was the most important work before the delegates:

> [T]he people of Alaska may very well judge the product of this convention not by the decisions taken upon issues like local government, apportionment, and the structure and powers of the three branches of government, but rather by the decision taken upon the vital issue of resources policy. (*PACC*, appendix II, p. 3)

Often, the discussion concerning the natural resource article at the constitutional convention waxed historical and philosophical. Delegates were sharply critical of the lackluster management of Alaska's resources by federal agencies, which had not promoted development for the benefit of all. Thus, Article VIII committed the new state to development in the public interest, which was expressed in several places through the concepts of " sustained yield" and "multiple use." Resource development was intended to avoid the creation of special privileges and exclusive rights; instead, the constitution guaranteed common use and access to the public. The process for making allocation decisions among competing users was to occur in full public view.

The two major areas of contention concerning the article pertained to fish and game management and Native land claims. In *Alaska's Constitutional Convention*, Victor Fischer described the debate over management of fisheries and wildlife resources as "one of the deepest controversies of the convention."[64] The debate centered on whether these resources should be managed by a single commission, by two separate commissions—as in the territory—or left up to the legislature.

At the outset, the constitutional Committee on Resources proposed: "Regulation and administration of the commercial fisheries and of the wildlife including game fish, shall be delegated to a commission, or to separate commissions, under such terms as the legislature shall prescribe" (*PACC*, appendix V, p. 93). Some delegates questioned why two commissions or any commission at all was necessary when other natural resources, such as minerals, were not proposed for commission control. Delegate Leonard King explained the reason as resulting from "a difference of opinion between the sportsmen organizations and the Fish and Wildlife Service as to the separation of the departments into a commercial fisheries department and into fish and game departments" (*PACC*, 2501).

Delegate George Sundborg remarked that the delegates had heard from as many as 10,000 people across the territory on this issue and he believed the committee's proposed language would satisfy them. Other delegates demurred, however. Several objected to boards and commissions as heads of departments, which was the territorial practice. Ultimately, by a 3-to-2 vote, the delegates decided to strike the committee's proposal; they instead left it to the legislature to decide how fish and game resources should be managed.

Delegate Muktuk Marston sparked another debate by his attempt to secure land rights for Alaska Natives. Marston was a land developer from Anchorage and had been an organizer of the Alaska Territorial Guard. He proposed: "The Legislature shall provide for translating the traditional rights of Alaskans of Indian, Aleut or Eskimo ancestry to the use of land, fishing, hunting and trapping areas in approximately equivalent homestead or other property rights" (*PACC*, 2525).

There was some support for Marston's proposal. Delegate Jack Coghill, for example, said that the delegates needed to give "the Native people, who were here long before us, at least their legal right to holding the lands that they are on" (*PACC*, 2544).

Two strong objections were made to this proposal. Delegate and resources committee member Burke Riley reported that the committee felt the matter was beyond the scope of the constitution; decisions about who received which land

---

[64] Victor Fischer, *Alaska's Constitutional Convention* (Fairbanks: University of Alaska Press, 1975), 134.

would be determined by the federal government. The more persuasive objection from other members of the convention was that they did not want to treat one class of people unequally in the constitution. In the end, Marston's proposed amendment became tangled in a parliamentary snarl. Delegate and author Victor Fischer made this observation about the Native land rights issue: "Thus, . . . the proposal for granting land rights to Alaska Natives went down to defeat without ever coming to a vote on the basic issues involved. However, the action expressed the delegates' belief that this was a subject for federal rather than state disposition."[65] Indeed, the land rights issue was only resolved in 1971, when Prudhoe Bay oil, which had been discovered in large quantities in 1968, could only be developed for an energy-hungry America provided Native land claims were settled.

SECTION 1

Statement of policy. It is the policy of the State to encourage the settlement of its land and the development of its resources by making them available for maximum use consistent with the public interest.

Delegates to the constitutional convention were uniform in their belief that Alaska's natural resources had been "locked up" and devalued by the negligent actions of the federal government and absentee owners. Alaskans depended on a small number of natural resources, whose careful development spelled the difference between a future of plenty or of poverty. Thus, the delegates were committed to the maximum development of Alaska's resources. However, they hedged their need to exploit resources with the requirement that resource use was a public trust. They were influenced by the modern principles of resource conservation and use, such as sustained yield and multiple use, which they made the constitutional objectives for all resource policy decisions, as expressed in the phrase, "maximum use consistent with the public interest."

Several judicial decisions have discussed the meanings and definitions of "public interest," as noted in the commentary below. One definition is found in the supreme court's finding in *Alyeska Ski Corporation v. Holdsworth* (1967), where it stated that the constitution recognizes the importance of providing legal safeguards in the disposal of state resources: "[Article VIII] of our constitution reflects the framers' recognition of the importance of our land resources and of the concomitant necessity for observance of legal safeguards in the disposal or leasing of state lands" (p. 104). A second meaning emerges from court decisions stressing the need for public notification when public land and resources are leased or sold. Thus, the supreme court held that to terminate a

[65] Ibid., 139.

state grazing lease without affording the lessee notice and a hearing undermined Article VIII (*McCarrey v. Commissioner of Natural Resources*, 1974). Other definitions have emphasized equal treatment of all in the allocation and conservation of resources, so that they will be available for use by future generations.

SECTION 2

General authority. The legislature shall provide for the utilization, development, and conservation of all natural resources belonging to the State, including land and waters, for the maximum benefit of its people.

Section 2 gives the state legislature the authority to direct the ways in which natural resources will be used and conserved. The development of these resources is an obligation of the state. However, the constitution instructs the legislature to adhere to the policy of maximum benefit for the people. The judiciary has elaborated this section in several cases.

When the commissioner of the Department of Natural Resources and the director of the Division of Lands planned to award a 55-year lease (under the Alaska Land Act) to a bidder who had failed to file proof of his authority to act for the leasing corporation, had not prefiled a development plan, and had paid with a check that did not conform to regulations, the supreme court entertained a complaint from the unsuccessful bidder (*Alyeska Ski Corporation v. Holdsworth*, 1967). In the opinion of the court, the agency had not followed the grant of authority it received from the legislature.

Section 2 figured prominently in federal/state contention over the Alaska Hire Act. The Alaska Supreme Court objected to the law's one-year residency requirement but saw no offense in its preference for residents over nonresidents, commenting that "a state may prefer its residents in dealing with natural resources that it owns" (*Hicklin v. Orbeck*, 1977, p. 169). However, the U.S. Supreme Court reversed this decision, finding Alaska's resource ownership an inadequate reason for discriminating against nonresidents (*Hicklin v. Orbeck*, 1978).

A clear test of section 2 occurred when the Kenai Peninsula Fisherman's Cooperative Association challenged the state Board of Fisheries' regulation of recreational and commercial fisheries of salmon in Cook Inlet. The association contended that the board was charged by the legislature only with development and conservation of fisheries resources, and not with utilization; thus, its attempts to establish priorities among beneficial users fell within the ambit of "utilization," which appeared to have been reserved by the legislature for itself. The supreme court supported the board's regulatory authority, arguing that "conserving" and "developing" both treated the use of resources (*Kenai Peninsula Fisherman's Cooperative Association, Inc. v. State*, 1981).

When the state seized the Permanent Fund dividends of incarcerated felons, they protested to the supreme court, alleging that the dividend represented a constitutionally protected interest in the natural resources of the state. The high court found that the existence of the Permanent Fund was protected under section 1 but stated that this provision did not entitle each resident of the state to a *dividend* from the fund (*State v. Anthony*, 1991).

The Alaska Supreme Court invoked sections 2 through 4 of the natural resources article when deciding the case *Shepherd v. State, Department of Fish & Game* (1995). Hunters had challenged the constitutionality of a statute under which residents had preference over nonresidents for taking moose, deer, elk, and caribou for personal use. The high court acknowledged that fish and game were resources of the state and that the state was required to prefer residents to nonresidents in making allocation decisions, except when such preferences were in conflict with a paramount federal interest.

SECTION 3

Common use. Wherever occurring in their natural state, fish, wildlife, and waters are reserved to the people for their common use.

Section 3 of Article VIII, together with sections 15 and 17, restricts the state from establishing exclusive privileges for resource use. Its purpose is opposition to monopoly, to be achieved by incorporating within the constitution principles of the common law that impose on the state a public trust duty with regard to the management of fish, wildlife, and waters.

A paper prepared for the Committee on Resources at the constitutional convention explained the section's origin:

> Ancient traditions in property rights have never recognized that a private right and title can be acquired by a private person to wildlife in their natural state or to water in general. The title remained with the sovereign, and in the American system of government with its concept of popular sovereignty this title is reserved to the people or the state on behalf of the people. The expression "for common use" implies that these resources are not to be subject to exclusive grants or special privilege as was so frequently the case in ancient royal tradition.[66]

The way in which the state has regulated the harvesting of fish and game has often brought cases to the courts to test whether the regulation legitimately implements the state's power to conservatively manage resources or establishes a special privilege that violates the common use provision.

Commercial fishermen sought to use section 3 to avoid regulations that had established two "superexclusive" use fisheries, prohibiting fishermen who operated in one from participating in any other herring sac roe fishery. The supreme

[66] Public Administration Service (PAS), *Constitutional Studies*, 3 vols. (Chicago: PAS, 1955).

court held that the authority to make allocation decisions "does not imply a power to limit admission to a user group," but the regulations in question did not violate any of the Article VIII clauses (*State v. Hebert*, 1990, p. 866).

When fish spotters objected to a ban on the aerial spotting of salmon in a particular bay during the commercial salmon season, the supreme court held that this regulation did not violate the common use clause of the constitution. The court ruled that it was a permissible limitation, which has traditionally been imposed by states on the means and methods citizens may employ as they utilize fishery resources. The common use clause, said the court, did not guarantee access to a natural resource by a person's preferred means or method (*Alaska Fish Spotters Association v. State, Department of Fish and Game*, 1992; *see also Meier v. State Board of Fisheries*, 1987).

In six cases, the supreme court indicated its intent to apply the common use clause in a way that strongly protects public access to natural resources. With respect to Article VIII generally, the court has held that "A careful reading of the constitutional minutes establishes that the provisions in article VIII were intended to permit the broadest possible access to and use of state waters by the general public" (*Wernberg v. State*, 1973, pp. 1198–1199).

In *State v. Ostrosky* (1983), the court addressed the constitutionality of limited entry fishing:

> [W]e have difficulty squaring the section 3 reservation of fish to the people for common use with a system which grants an exclusive right to fish to a select few who may continue to exercise that right season after season. . . . [L]imited entry is inconsistent with the command of Article VIII, section 3. (p. 1189)

However, the court ruled that the Limited Entry Act was not unconstitutional because of a 1972 constitutional amendment explicitly permitting limited entry to fisheries, notwithstanding section 3 (see section 15).

In *CWC Fisheries v. Bunker* (1988), the supreme court addressed the question of whether a state tidelands grant included an exclusive right of fishery or was subject to a public trust easement. It held for the latter interpretation without determining whether the common use clause imposed a higher duty than that required by the public trust principles of common law. It assumed that the legislature intended to act in ways consistent with "the plain wording of the constitutional [common use] mandate" (p. 1120).

In another limited entry case, *Johns v. Commercial Fisheries Entry Commission* (1988), the court noted the tension between the limited entry clause of the state constitution and the clauses that guarantee open fisheries (sections 3 and 15 of this article). It held that a limited entry system needed to impinge on the open fishery clauses as lightly as possible and consistent with its purposes: the prevention of economic distress and resource conservation.

The court addressed a comparable situation when a hunting guide challenged the Guide Licensing and Control Board's assignment of exclusive guide areas in which only the designated guide could lead hunts. The supreme court held that statutes and regulations of the board permitting exclusive guide areas were in contravention of section 3 because they resembled "the types of royal grants the common use clause expressly intended to prevent" (*Owsichek v. State, Guide Licensing and Control Board,* 1988, pp. 497–498). Following this decision, the attorney general advised the Department of Natural Resources that its proposal to issue permits in order to limit the number of commercial fishing guides on the Kenai River violated the common use clause.[67]

In its most controversial decision on the natural resources article, the supreme court declared that the subsistence preference laws of the state were in violation of sections 3, 15, and 17 of the constitution (*McDowell v. State,* 1989). In crafting the state's subsistence laws, the legislature attempted to provide special protection for rural hunters and fishers—most of whom are Alaska Natives—that would satisfy the federal government's interest in protecting Native subsistence under the special relationship between the federal government and Native American peoples.[68] The first statute, in 1978 (chapter 151, section 4 SLA), gave subsistence hunting and fishing priority over other uses of fish and game stocks. It established two tiers of subsistence users: (1) those who could take fish or game for subsistence purposes when populations were adequate to satisfy all subsistence needs; and (2) those who could take fish and game for subsistence purposes when populations were inadequate to supply all subsistence needs. Second-tier users were distinguished from those in the first tier based on customary and direct dependence, local residency, and the availability of alternative resources.

Barely two years after passage of the legislature's first subsistence act, the U.S. Congress passed the Alaska National Interest Lands Conservation Act (AN-ELCA). Section 3114 of ANILCA required that on federal public lands in Alaska, subsistence uses were to be given priority over the taking of fish and wildlife for other purposes; only rural Alaska residents were entitled to a subsistence priority. Federal management could be supplanted by the state only if it enacted and implemented subsistence laws " which are consistent with, and which provide for the definition, preference, and participation specified in," **ANILCA.**

Unlike the 1978 statute, the 1986 subsistence statute imposed a rural residency requirement as a condition to becoming a first-tier subsistence user. At its

---

[67] Harrison, *Alaska's Constitution,* 154.

[68] The subsistence issue in Alaska involves conflict between the state and federal government because the chief beneficiaries of rural subsistence provisions are Alaska Natives who, as aboriginal residents of the state, are a "dependent sovereignty" specially protected by the federal constitution. Two fine studies by David Stanway Case, an Anchorage attorney who specializes in Native Alaska law, describe the special relationship and current legal status of Alaska Natives: *The Special Relationship of Alaska Natives to the Federal Government* (Anchorage: Alaska Native Foundation, 1978) and *Alaska Natives and American Laws* (Fairbanks: University of Alaska Press, 1984).

passage, the U.S. Interior Department stated that Alaska was in compliance with **ANILCA**, and therefore could manage federal lands. The challenge addressed by the Alaska Supreme Court was that the 1986 act crudely excluded from eligibility as subsistence users all urban dwellers; by including all rural dwellers, the act unfairly excluded some urban residents who had lived a subsistence lifestyle and desired to continue to do so, while needlessly including numerous rural residents who had not engaged in subsistence hunting and fishing. A divided high court agreed with the protesters and declared the 1986 subsistence law in violation of the Alaska Constitution, because it violated provisions prohibiting exclusive or special privileges in the taking of fish and wildlife. After this decision, the federal government found the state out of compliance with **ANILCA** and resumed control of fish and game management on federal lands in Alaska.

The six high court opinions on the equal access provisions of the Alaska Constitution since 1987 prompted this observation from Stephen White: "One fundamental, consistently applied principle, has emerged: limitations on admission to fish and wildlife 'user groups' are subject to strong judicial scrutiny under the equal access clauses."[69] In the judgment of most participants, to resolve the controversy requires an amendment to the Alaska Constitution, providing preferential access to fish and wildlife for rural (predominantly Native) users, or amendment to **ANILCA**, eliminating the rural subsistence priority.

Neither resolution was likely as of 1996. In fact, the fragile state and federal government accommodation over this conflict splintered, and the issue escalated with the conclusion of federal judicial involvement in the *Katie John* case. John, an Ahtna Native elder, had appealed to federal courts for protection of her subsistence rights, including preferential access on state waterways. In a landmark ruling of 1995, the Ninth U.S. Circuit Court of Appeals gave the federal government power to manage subsistence hunting and fishing on Alaska's navigable waterways. The ruling required Interior Department officials to develop a plan to manage wildlife on federal land selected but not yet conveyed to the state or to Alaska Native corporations. It further stipulated that wildlife outside federal boundaries fell under federal jurisdiction whenever users on federal land faced an emergency shortage.

The state of Alaska appealed this ruling to the U.S. Supreme Court and was supported in friend-of-the-court briefs by eleven other Western states—Arizona, California, Colorado, Hawaii, Idaho, Montana, Nevada, North Dakota, South Dakota, Utah, and Wyoming. However, the federal high court let the circuit court ruling stand in 1996 without comment.[70]

---

[69] Stephen White, "'Equal Access' to Alaska's Fish and Wildlife," *Alaska Law Review* 11, no. 2 (1994): 299.

[70] *Fairbanks Daily News-Miner*, May 14, 1996.

SECTION 4

Sustained yield. Fish, forests, wildlife, grasslands, and all other replenishable resources belonging to the State shall be utilized, developed, and maintained on the sustained yield principle, subject to preferences among beneficial uses.

This provision states the model principle of fish and wildlife management—sustained yield. This fundamental premise of conservation means that the harvesting of the renewable resource should not endanger its survival. The state is given the latitude to establish priorities among competing uses for the maximum benefit of the public. The state's regulation of harvesting is based on this section and section 3.

SECTION 5

Facilities and improvements. The legislature may provide for facilities, improvements, and services to assure greater utilization, development, reclamation, and settlement of lands, and to assure fuller utilization and development of the fisheries, wildlife, and waters.

Section 5 is read together with section 2. It allows the legislature to authorize agencies, such as Fish and Game or the Department of Natural Resources, to stock lakes and streams with fish and to create parks for the public. The state possesses the inherent power to build facilities and make improvements to achieve public purposes, and thus the statement expresses the hopes of the framers that the state's resources will be developed.

The high court has held that this section does not allow the legislature to authorize private aquaculture associations to collect mandatory assessments on the sale of salmon by commercial fishermen (*State v. Alex*, 1982). Nothing in Article VIII, said the court, could be construed to grant the legislature the power to ignore other express constitutional limitations on its taxing power.

SECTION 6

State public domain. Lands and interests therein, including submerged and tidal lands, possessed or acquired by the State, and not used or intended exclusively for governmental purposes, constitute the state public domain. The legislature shall provide for the selection of lands granted to the State by the United States, and for the administration of the state public domain.

Section 6 defines the public domain of the state as all those government-owned lands and interests in lands that are not set aside for the special purposes of government. The legislature has the inherent authority to determine how public lands will be administered, which is reinforced in the second sentence. The legislature, and no other party, decides which lands from the federal public domain that were transferred pursuant to the statehood act will be selected for Alaska.

Upon attaining statehood, Alaska received 103.5 million acres of federal lands in the state, over 30 percent of the total lands. Among the early selections by the state were North Slope lands, which were the site of the enormous Prudhoe Bay oil fields. By the end of 1995, 89 million acres had been surveyed and conveyed to the state.

SECTION 7

Special purpose sites. The legislature may provide for the acquisition of sites, objects, and areas of natural beauty or of historic, cultural, recreational, or scientific value. It may reserve them from the public domain and provide for their administration and preservation for the use, enjoyment, and welfare of the people.

This provision, like sections 5 and 6, restates an inherent state power. It authorizes the legislature to expand the properties of the state by acquiring those with aesthetic and other nonmaterial values, for uses such as state parks, forests, trails, and wildlife reserves. Further, the section allows the state to restrict access to these properties but also mandates it to administer them for the benefit of the public.

This section was tested by the supreme court in a case concerning federal trust lands for the support of the University of Alaska, which the state had included in a park. The court found that section 7 did not preclude the legislature from disposing of university land without obtaining the university's approval (*State v. University of Alaska*, 1981). The lands "belonged" to the state and were being reserved because of their recreational value.

SECTION 8

Leases. The legislature may provide for the leasing of, and the issuance of permits for exploration of, any part of the public domain or interest therein, subject to reasonable concurrent uses. Leases and permits shall provide, among other conditions, for payment by the party at fault for damage or injury arising from noncompliance with terms governing concurrent use, and for forfeiture in the event of breach of conditions.

This provision gives the legislature authority to rent state lands and interests in lands, including submerged and tidal lands. Importantly, the first sentence enjoins the leaseholder to provide for concurrent uses. The section also includes default, injury, and damage provisions for use of the state's public domain.

The supreme court in *Alyeska Ski Corporation v. Holdsworth* (1967) referred to this section when it found the commissioner of Natural Resources and the director of the Division of Lands negligent in their leasing of state lands for development purposes.

SECTION 9

Sales and grants. Subject to the provisions of this section, the legislature may provide for the sale or grant of state lands, or interests therein, and establish sales procedures. All sales or grants shall contain such reservations to the State of all resources as may be required by Congress or the State and shall provide for access to these resources. Reservation of access shall not necessarily impair the owners' use, prevent the control of trespass, or preclude compensation for damages.

Section 9 is read with section 8 in delineating the state's management authority concerning the disposition of the public domain. It applies to the state's sale or grant of lands for the purpose of homesteading or agricultural development, for example. The second sentence refers to the state's ownership interest in subsurface mineral deposits (primarily oil), which are reserved to the state in perpetuity unless specifically allowed for transfer by action of the U.S. Congress (which prohibited the state from selling or giving away mineral rights in the Alaska Statehood Act). While the state is not obliged to provide access to the lands it sells or grants, it must develop access to subsurface (mineral) deposits that does not vitiate the owners' use and control of the property. The Alaska Land Act implements this section and the preceding one.

The need to protect the resources of the state against exploitation and the pressure of special interest groups figured prominently during discussions of Article VIII at the constitutional convention. A suggested provision on natural resources drafted by the Public Administration Service would have required a reservation to the state of all the minerals in lands sold, granted, deeded, or patented by the state.[71] In drafting the provision, however, the delegates rejected the view that the constitution should spell out absolute restraints on the alienation of mineral rights.

Section 9 of Article VIII was applied in a difficult constitutional issue involving a three-way exchange of land between the state of Alaska, the U.S. government, and the Cook Inlet Region, Inc., a regional Native corporation chartered under the Alaska Native Claims Settlement Act. The question raised by challengers was whether the exchange violated state constitutional prohibitions against the alienation of mineral rights in state lands. In *State v. Lewis* (1977), the supreme

[71] Public Administration Service, *Constitutional Studies.*

court held that section 9 did not contain constitutional restraints on the alienation of mineral rights. It remarked that the provision left the decision to Congress and the state legislature. Thus, the state could engage in exchanges with Native corporations and the federal government of parts of the public domain.

SECTION 10

Public notice. No disposals or leases of state lands, or interests therein, shall be made without prior public notice and other safeguards of the public interest as may be prescribed by law.

This straightforward public notice and safeguards requirement is the strongest means in Article VIII for the protection of the public interest in land and resources. It is designed to prevent fraudulent disposals or those that might grant special benefits, thereby violating the common use provision of section 3. The legislature enacted the Alaska Land Act in accordance with this constitutional provision. One part of this act provided: "The leasing shall be made at public auction to the highest qualified bidder by the director. An aggrieved bidder may appeal to the commissioner within five days for a review of the director's determination." When an aggrieved bidder challenged the director and commissioner's acceptance of a bid which did not follow procedures, the supreme court gave it standing and reversed the action of the agency (*Alyeska Ski Corporation v. Holdsworth,* 1967).

SECTION 11

Mineral rights. Discovery and appropriation shall be the basis for establishing a right in those minerals reserved to the State which, upon the date of ratification of this constitution by the people of Alaska, were subject to location under the federal mining laws. Prior discovery, location, and filing, as prescribed by law, shall establish a prior right to these minerals and also a prior right to permits, leases, and transferable licenses for their extraction. Continuation of these rights shall depend upon the performance of annual labor, or the payment of fees, rents, or royalties, or upon other requirements as may be prescribed by law. Surface uses of land by a mineral claimant shall be limited to those necessary for the extraction or basic processing of the mineral deposits, or for both. Discovery and appropriation shall initiate a right, subject to further requirements of law, to patent of mineral lands if authorized by the State and not prohibited by Congress. The provisions of this section shall apply to all other minerals reserved to the State which by law are declared subject to appropriation.

This section describes the process through which citizens can gain the right to explore for, and exploit, minerals found in state lands. It was crafted at a time of transition in federal land policies, which later were to influence the provisions on mineral disposition in the Alaska Statehood Act of 1958. In the mid-1950s, there were two methods for the disposition of minerals located on federal lands—location and lease. The location system was the oldest method of mineral disposition. It originated on the public domain as a matter of custom and is found in the federal Mining Law of 1872. Under its terms, the first claimant discovering valuable mineral deposits (silver, gold, and other metallic minerals) on unappropriated public domain staked and filed a mining claim, which gave him or her a legally protected interest. The locator was entitled to produce minerals from the deposit without paying rent or royalties and had the right to obtain title by means of a patent issued by the U.S. government.

The primary alternative to the location system is mineral leasing. It was initiated by the Congress because of its belief that revenues were being lost under the location system. Leasing usually requires competitive bids for leases on lands known to contain valuable mineral deposits (initially oil and coal, but later, metallic minerals, too). The leaseholder pays a fee to the government and shares income (royalties) with it from the sale of the minerals produced.

At the time of the Alaska constitutional convention, the relevant mining law was the School Lands Act of 1927. It enlarged the original statehood land grants to embrace lands mineral in character. Such grants, however, were subject to a mineral alienation condition that prohibited state disposal of land without a reservation of minerals; it did permit a forfeiture action on behalf of the United States.

These school land restrictions were incorporated into Alaska statehood bills pending in Congress when the Alaska Constitution was written. The restrictions signaled a change from the location system to a leasing system. Because of the anticipated benefits of statehood, the framers adopted a provision (Article XII, section 13) that expressly consented to the mineral rights restrictions.

However, the framers also sought to preserve key elements of the existing location system should Congress permit. Thus, they adopted section 11 of the natural resources article. According to delegate Victor Fischer:

> In part, this provision was inserted in the hope that Congress might recede from its restrictions. On the other hand, delegates who concurred in the policy limiting permanent disposal of minerals went along with the proposal because they assumed Congress would stand firm. Most also saw the provision as a demonstration to miners, who might otherwise object to the constitution, that any restrictions applicable to alienation of mineral lands were being imposed from outside and were not the convention's doing.[72]

[72] Fischer, *Alaska's Constitutional Convention*, 134.

In the statehood act, Congress did prohibit the state from giving away the title to its minerals. It further required that "mineral deposits in such lands shall be subject to lease by the state" (Alaska Statehood Act, section 6[i]). The state's first mining law used a system that was called leasing but actually was closer to the location system, because it required no payments to the state.

Section 11 was tested in a challenge to the state's disposition of mineral rights by a coalition of fishing, environmental, and Native groups. In *Trustees for Alaska v. State* (1987), the supreme court held that the state's leasing law violated mineral leasing requirements of the Alaska Statehood Act because the state did not require the payment of either rent or royalties in leases of lands. Effectively, it obliged the state to collect rent or royalties for all leases of lands, including those known to contain minerals at the time of state selection.

SECTION 12

Mineral leases and permits. The legislature shall provide for the issuance, types and terms of leases for coal, oil, gas, oil shale, sodium, phosphate, potash, sulfur, pumice, and other minerals as may be prescribed by law. Leases and permits giving the exclusive right of exploration for these minerals for specific periods and areas, subject to reasonable concurrent exploration as to different classes of minerals, may be authorized by law. Like leases and permits giving the exclusive right of prospecting by geophysical, geochemical, and similar methods for all minerals may also be authorized by law.

Section 12 confers on the legislature broad powers to lease lands for mineral exploration and development. The first sentence spells out examples of the types of nonmetallic minerals that may be acquired through a leasing system. The second and third sentences specify that leases may provide exclusive rights of exploration and prospecting. The legislature has implemented this section in a statute providing for competitive oil and gas leases—AS 38.05.135–180. Oil companies compete either at auctions or in sealed bids for leases. Royalties from these leases and severance taxes have been the mainstay of government operations in Alaska.

SECTION 13

Water rights. All surface and subsurface waters reserved to the people for common use, except mineral and medicinal waters, are subject to appropriation. Priority of appropriation shall give prior right. Except for public water supply, an appropriation of water shall be limited to stated purposes and subject to preferences among beneficial uses, concurrent or otherwise, as prescribed by law, and to the general reservation of fish and wildlife.

Section 13 allows the state to sell rights to water, except for mineral and medicinal waters, and is comparable to water rights provisions in the other western states. Water rights are to be sold on a priority basis, with those appropriating them first having the established title. The sale of water rights must observe other principles of the natural resources article, specifically, higher ranking for more beneficial uses and common use provisions concerning fish and wildlife (meaning that rights to water do not include the fish and other wildlife using it).

SECTION 14

Access to navigable waters. Free access to the navigable or public waters of the State, as defined by the legislature, shall not be denied any citizen of the United States or resident of the State, except that the legislature may by general law regulate and limit such access for other beneficial uses or public purposes.

This section guarantees public access to the state's navigable waterways, rivers, and publicly owned streams and lakes. It disallows any discrimination against nonresident users, and it makes the use of navigable waters subject to regulation and limitations on access, in the presence of other public purposes. This section requires the state to reserve easements allowing access by the public when it sells or leases public lands adjacent to navigable waters. The court interpreted this section in *CWC Fisheries Incorporated v. Bunker* (1988), where it ruled that the sale of tidelands implicitly required the provision of an easement for public access.

SECTION 15

No exclusive right of fishery. No exclusive right or special privilege of fishery shall be created or authorized in the natural waters of the State. This section does not restrict the power of the State to limit entry into any fishery for purposes of resource conservation, to prevent economic distress among fishermen and those dependent upon them for a livelihood and to promote the efficient development of aquaculture in the State.

Section 15 originally contained only the first sentence, which prohibited special use fisheries in the state, consistent with the common use provisions of sections 3 and 17. Within a decade of statehood, however, pressure developed to limit entry into the state's salmon fisheries, which were overfished. In 1968, the legislature adopted a limited entry statute, but it was nullified by both federal and state courts.

In 1972, voters amended the constitution to add the second sentence, which established the limited entry system, which has been used from that time to the present. Individuals wishing to fish in restricted areas must obtain a limited entry permit, which is issued by the Commercial Fisheries Entry Commission. The provision permits limited entry only for three purposes—conserving the fisheries resource, preventing hardship for fishermen and their families, and developing aquaculture.

A number of court cases have further defined the meaning of section 15. In general, the judiciary has upheld regulations if it finds a reasonable basis for treating people differently and if the regulations do not grossly infringe on common use. One example is of a group of commercial fishermen who challenged the validity of action taken by the Board of Fisheries and Commissioner of Fish and Game that affected recreational and commercial fisheries of salmon stock in Cook Inlet. In *Kenai Pen. Fisherman's Co-op Ass'n v. State* (1981), the supreme court held that section 15 was not meant to "prohibit differential treatment of such diverse user groups as commercial, sports, and subsistence fishermen" (p. 904).

Similarly, in *State v. Hebert* (1990), the supreme court found constitutional regulations establishing two "superexclusive" use fisheries and prohibiting fishermen who operated in one from participating in any other. The fisheries zones did not create an exclusive right of fishery, as those who chose to fish were treated equally: they could fish in either one zone or the other. Finally, in *Alaska Fish Spotters v. State, Department of Fish and Game* (1992), the high court found that a regulation prohibiting the aerial spotting of salmon during commercial salmon-fishing periods did not violate the exclusive rights clause. The regulation did not exclude fish spotters from other uses of the resource, nor did it grant a special monopolistic privilege to a limited number of individuals.

The courts have expressly prohibited the establishment of monopolistic rights to fisheries. When the Metlakatla Indian community sought to continue the use of fish traps, the court enjoined this use. The law prohibiting the use of fish traps was consistent with the section 15 provisions that there should be no exclusive right or special privilege of fisheries (*Metlakatla Indian Community, Annette Island Reserve v. Egan*, 1961). Moreover, one of the bases by which the supreme court held the 1986 rural preference law unconstitutional was its infringement of the prohibition on exclusive rights of fisheries (*McDowell v. State*, 1989).

The judiciary has upheld limited entry statutes based on the 1972 constitutional amendment. In one interpretation, however, the supreme court ruled that private aquaculture associations that collected mandatory assessments on the sale of salmon by commercial fishermen were unconstitutional, notwithstanding language in section 15 to "promote the efficient development of aquaculture" because they violated the Article IX, section 7, prohibition of dedicated taxes (*State v. Alex*, 1982). When the transferability of limited entry permits was challenged, the supreme court found that the provisions did not violate section 15 by creating a special privilege for the fishery (*State v. Ostrosky*, 1983).

SECTION 16

Protection of rights. No person shall be involuntarily divested of his right to the use of waters, his interests in lands, or improvements affecting either, except for a superior beneficial use or public purpose and then only with just compensation and by operation of law.

Section 16 further protects citizens' rights of public access to state-owned waters and lands against appropriation by others. Only two circumstances permit the infringement of these rights—a more beneficial use or a public purpose. In that event, the section calls for equitable compensation.

The chief interpretation of section 16 is found in *Wernberg v. State* (1973), where the supreme court held that under this section, an Anchorage property owner might recover for the loss of his accustomed access to navigable waters. This decision was largely based on the potential adverse effects on land values if the court had not agreed to compensation:

> We are concerned that the uncompensated taking of such a littoral access right may effectively render abutting land valueless or greatly reduce its value. Alaska has a sea-coast longer than that of the entire United States. A large number of Alaskan communities are located on the shores of bays and inlets, (p. 1200).

However, when a landowner named Classen complained to the courts that the state's construction of a highway bridge was a taking of his riparian rights (because he could no longer take off safely from the river in his floatplane with a heavy load), the supreme court held that he was not entitled to compensation (*Classen v. State, Department of Highways*, 1980). The court found that the state's action did not prevent Classen's use of the river; it simply made it less convenient.

SECTION 17

Uniform application. Laws and regulations governing the use or disposal of natural resources shall apply equally to all persons similarly situated with reference to the subject matter and purpose to be served by the law or regulation.

The uniform application section of the natural resources article is read in combination with sections 3 and 15. Like them, its purpose is to prohibit exclusive grants or special privileges. It emphasizes equal protection of the laws in the citizenry's use of natural resources. The Committee on Resources' commentary with respect to section 17 states: "This section is intended to exclude any especially privileged status for any person in the use of natural resources subject to the disposition of the state" (*PACC*, 84).

Although section 17 is part of Article VIII, the supreme court has identified it as a "more stringent . . . equal protection clause [for] . . . cases involving natural resources" (*McDowell v. State,* 1989, p. 18). In this decision, the court found that the 1986 rural preference statute violated equal protection clauses as well as prohibitions on exclusive fisheries, as it had declared exclusive guide areas unconstitutional in the 1988 *Owishek v. State, Guide Licensing and Control Board* decision.

As noted in commentary on section 15 of Article VIII, the high court has not invalidated regulations of natural resource use. It has held that state fish and game regulations that create nonuniform classifications must have a legitimate purpose. However, it has defended regulations that limited the total harvest of salmon in one particular interceptor fishery, while allowing a larger harvest in neighboring fisheries. The court pointed out that the different fisheries were not similarly situated in terms of being terminal or interceptor fisheries, spawning patterns, and historical catch levels and participation (*Gilbert v. State, Department of Fish and Game,* 1990). It upheld superexclusive use fisheries in *State v. Hebert* (1990), and prohibitions of aerial spotting of salmon in *Alaska Fish Spotters v. State* (1992).

The uniform application section was one basis for the supreme court's support of an aggrieved bidder in *Alyeska Ski Corporation v. Holdsworth* (1967). In *Commercial Fisheries Entry Commission v. Apokedak* (1980), the high court upheld a statute limiting the eligible pool of applicants for entry permits to gear license holders, stating, "Equal protection, even under Alaska's stricter standard, does not demand perfection in classification" (p. 1267). Additionally, in *State v. Anthony* (1991), the supreme court held that denying Permanent Fund dividends to certain felons did not deny them uniform application.

The supreme court also applied this section in addressing a challenge to Alaska's fish and game regulations, which give preferences to residents over nonresidents (*Shepherd v. State, Department of Fish & Game,* 1995). The high court upheld a statute that required the Alaska Board of Game to adopt regulations preferring residents over nonresidents in the taking of moose, deer, elk, and caribou for personal consumption. It held that Alaska residents and nonresidents were not similarly situated with respect to their rights of access as recreational users of fish and game.

SECTION 18

Private ways of necessity. Proceedings in eminent domain may be undertaken for private ways of necessity to permit essential access for extraction or utilization

> of resources. Just compensation shall be made for property taken or for resultant damages to other property rights.

The final section of Article VIII is based on a provision of the Wyoming Constitution. It allows the use of the state's power of eminent domain to create access for the development of natural resources, such as for an oil or gas pipeline. Any such taking of property or damage to it must, however, be equitably compensated. This section has not been elaborated by the judiciary.

Article IX

Finance and Taxation

Article IX of the Alaska Constitution provides for the financing of state government and authorizes its powers of taxation. This article is unlike those of older state constitutions, which place limits on taxing power and public debt. It does restrict the debt of the state and local governments to capital projects, which voters must approve. However, it gives the legislature broad authority to tax without limit. A significant example of this authority is the prohibition on dedicated funds in section 7.

With the exception of section 7 (on dedicated funds), the review by delegates at the constitutional convention was noncontroversial. Most of the recommendations of the Committee on Finance and Taxation proposed were accepted by the convention.

Three significant amendments have been made to Article IX. In 1976 voters added section 15, which established the Alaska Permanent Fund, the only public savings account in any state's constitution. In 1982, voters approved section 16, which established an appropriation limit, and they upheld it four years later. Finally, in 1990, voters agreed to the establishment of a constitutional Budget Reserve Fund (section 17). These actions by voters corresponded to times of oil wealth in Alaska and demonstrated increased concern by political leaders and citizens with cushioning the state fiscally when oil revenues declined because of depletion of Prudhoe Bay reserves.

SECTION 1

Taxing power. The power of taxation shall never be surrendered. This power shall not be suspended or contracted away, except as provided in this article.

Section 1 prohibits the surrender, suspension, or permanent contracting away of the state's taxation power, to indicate that any tax exemptions given by the legislature would not become contractual obligations. Such language was recommended in the *Model State Constitution*.[73] The second sentence provides flexibility for making tax exemptions (for industrial development, for example). The state has delegated its taxing power only to local governments.

SECTION 2

Nondiscrimination. The lands and other property belonging to citizens of the United States residing without the State shall never be taxed at a higher rate than the lands and other property belonging to the residents of the State.

Section 2 prohibits the state from taxing nonresident land and other property at a higher rate than that paid by state residents. The nondiscrimination clause is technically unnecessary because of the equal protection language of both the Alaska and the federal constitutions. It did signal, however, that commercial property of nonresidents would not be taxed at a different rate than that of residents by the state or local governments.

SECTION 3

Assessment standards. Standards for appraisal of all property assessed by the State or its political subdivisions shall be prescribed by law.

Section 3 leaves to the legislature the development of a common set of appraisal standards for all property in the state. Two questions arose over the committee's proposal at the constitutional convention. Delegate Les Nerland, committee chairman, read a letter to delegates from Wood, King, and Dawson, a firm of bond attorneys in New York who had reviewed the committee proposal. They recommended adding a debt limit provision, which was generally specified as a particular percentage of assessed valuation of taxable property. Nerland said the committee did not include the debt limit provision because they thought it provided little protection; also, they had little information available about assessed valuation (*PACC*, 2303).

---

[73] National Municipal League, *Model State Constitution*, 13, 40.

Delegate Maurice Johnson asked why the committee had not used the word *uniform* with respect to assessment, as such language had been used in the enabling act and as many state constitutions required that taxation be "uniform and equal" (*PACC*, 2304). Delegate Barrie White responded that the committee had declined to adopt "any uniformity provisions because that leads you into a lot of other difficulties that we wanted to avoid" (*PACC*, 2305). Specifically, delegates wanted the legislature and local governments to have fiscal discretion to establish reasonable differences in taxes, for example tax exemptions for the elderly. White also said that the intent of the section was to suggest to the legislature that it should establish common standards, but not uniformity.

The only legislative implementation of section 3 has been through a statute calling for assessment to be based on the "full and true value" of property—AS 29.45.110. A 1962 attorney general's opinion has discussed standards.[74] Based on this, the state objected to a differential tax rate levied by the Kenai borough assembly, which taxed real property at a lower rate than personal property (including oil and gas transportation property). The supreme court supported the state's position that the same rate should be applied to both kinds of property (*Kenai Peninsula Borough v. Department of Community and Regional Affairs*, 1988).

SECTION 4

Exemptions. The real and personal property of the State or its political subdivisions shall be exempt from taxation under conditions and exceptions which may be provided by law. All, or any portion of, property used exclusively for non-profit religious, charitable, cemetery, or educational purposes, as defined by law, shall be exempt from taxation. Other exemptions of like or different kind may be granted by general law. All valid existing exemptions shall be retained until otherwise provided by law.

Section 4 contains important language on those properties and interests that are exempt from state taxation. Here, the framers of Article IX were guided by other state constitutions. They exempted property of state and local governments when used for governmental purposes, but allowed taxation under certain circumstances (for example, property used for commercial purposes). They also exempted property used entirely for nonprofit religious, charitable, cemetery, or educational purposes. The key focus in evaluating tax exemptions was to be the use to which the property was put, and not the status of the owner. They grandfathered existing exemptions, while allowing the legislature to rescind them or add yet other exemptions (which it has done by exempting hospitals and enabling local governments to give additional tax exemptions).

[74] Harrison, *Alaska's Constitution*, 172.

Some discussion at the constitutional convention concerned the exemptions clause. Delegates questioned why cemeteries were exempt from taxation when during the territorial years, they had not been. The subject of cemeteries, once broached, seemed to illuminate the weariness of the delegates, who could not pass up the opportunity for a few bad jokes. Delegate John Hellenthal said: "We've gotten along in Alaska for 50 years, cemetery property never being exempt, and I know of no crying demand for exemption of cemetery property" (*PACC*, 2327). To this, committee chair Nerland responded: "I'd say it's a 'dead' issue." Hellenthal then moved to strike the word *cemetery* from the article, saying:

> Mr. President, to make it perfectly clear, the only reason that I made the amendment is that Alaska law—and I have it here—for many years has exempted property used exclusively for religious . . ., educational, and charitable purposes, and then the veterans, and that's all. We have omitted the veterans and thrown in the cemeteries. I think the cemeteries should go. (*PACC*, 2328)

To this, delegate Thomas Harris responded: "I don't know, but I kind of like to think that when I die, I'm free from taxation" (*PACC*, 2329). Most delegates were reluctant to amend the committee's version, and they left it intact.

Section 4 has been subject to several judicial elaborations, focusing primarily on the justifiability of exemptions for nonprofit religious and educational institutions. When the city of Nome assessed taxes on property of the Evangelical Covenant Church that was used as a parsonage for the assistant pastor, the supreme court invalidated its action. The court ruled that the property was tax-exempt under section 4 and the state statute, which defined the term "used for religious purposes" as including the residence of a pastor (*Evangelical Covenant Church of America v. City of Nome*, 1964).

In 1968, the high court reversed the tax assessment on a camp in the Matanuska-Susitna borough that was run by a charitable organization and collected modest user fees to support the camp's operation. Because the property was used exclusively for a nonprofit, charitable purpose and the user fees were not the result of profit-making activity, the court supported the continuation of the charity's tax-exempt status (*Matanuska-Susitna Borough v. King's Lake Camp*, 1968).

Then, in 1971, the supreme court supported the tax-exempt status of property owned by a nonprofit management trust and occupied by school facilities for apprenticeship programs for journeymen electricians (*McKee v. Evans*, 1971). The court found that the nontraditional educational program, while not parallel to that offered in publicly supported educational institutions, still fit the constitutional and statutory provisions exempting such property from taxation.

The high court held in 1972 that the tax-exempt status could be applied to the Alaska State Development Corporation, a development agency within the Department of Commerce. When the corporation foreclosed on a loan, it obtained title and continued to operate a hotel-restaurant-bar in Nome in order to keep the property salable. The city of Nome was disallowed from assessing property taxes because the use of the property while in the hands of the corporation "was in consonance with its powers and in furtherance of its valid public purpose" (*City of Nome v. Block No. H, Lots 5, 6 & 7*, 1972, p. 127).

Finally, the high court further defined exclusivity of use in a case concerning office space rented by the Sisters of Charity, a longtime health care provider in Alaska. The court found that where a portion of the building was rented for use as private office space for doctors (who had staff privileges at the hospital but were not employed by it), the building was not being used "exclusively for nonprofit hospital purposes" and could be taxed by the municipality (*Greater Anchorage Area Borough v. Sisters of Charity*, 1976, p. 472).

SECTION 5

Interests in government property. Private leaseholds, contracts, or interests in land or property owned or held by the United States, the State, or its political subdivisions, shall be taxable to the extent of the interests.

Although section 4 exempts the real and personal property of governments from taxation, this does not apply to private leases, contracts, and other interests. Section 5 provides for the taxability of these largely commercial interests in government property (primarily leases of, and improvements to, land).

SECTION 6

Public purpose. No tax shall be levied, or appropriation of public money made, or public property transferred, nor shall the public credit be used, except for a public purpose.

In section 6, the framers incorporated into the Alaska Constitution the "public purpose doctrine," which is commonly found in state basic laws. Although the concept of public purpose is quite vague, the intent is to pledge government involvement toward activities that benefit the community and state as a whole instead of some private interest. Typically (as in several state constitutions), the public purpose doctrine expands when necessary to encompass changing public needs. The Alaska Supreme Court has interpreted the doctrine in several issue areas.

When a parochial school student was denied transportation to her school on a public school bus—which had been granted parochial students in Fairbanks under territorial law—she protested. The supreme court held that the practice violated section 6 (as well as Article VII, section 1) of the constitution.

Protesters claimed that the territorial law served a valuable public purpose by encouraging compliance with the state's compulsory education law and enhanced health and safety through eliminating hazards of the highway and meliorating climatic conditions for nonpublic school children, but the high court disagreed. It said that only nonpublic school children fortunate enough to live along a public school bus route were given transportation (*Matthews v. Quinton*, 1961).

In *DeArmond v. Alaska State Development Corporation* (1962), the high court ruminated on the meaning of "public purpose." The particular context was a challenge to the constitutionality of an act creating the Alaska State Development Corporation, which was established by the legislature as "an instrumentality of the state to develop, stimulate, and advance business prosperity and economic welfare of Alaska and its citizens" (p. 719). Chief Justice Nesbett observed:

> [T]he phrase "public purpose" represents a concept which is not capable of precise definition. We believe that it would be a disservice to future generations for this court to attempt to define it. It is a concept which will change as changing conditions create changing public needs. Whether a public purpose is being served must be decided as each case arises and in the light of the particular facts and circumstances of each case.
>
> In determining the question presented this court adopts for its guidance the general rule, supported by the great weight of authority, that where the legislature has found that a public purpose will be served by the expenditure or transfer of public funds or the use of the public credit, this court will not set aside the finding of the legislature unless it clearly appears that such finding is arbitrary and without any reasonable basis in fact. (p. 721)

Following this logic, the supreme court held that the Alaska State Development Corporation was constitutional. In a similar case, the court upheld the constitutionality of the Alaska State Mortgage Association, finding that the corporation's purpose—to provide additional financing for those unable to obtain it in the general market—was in the public purpose (*Walker v. Alaska State Mortgage Association*, 1966).

The supreme court upheld the city of Ketchikan when it leased a hospital built with federal, state, and local funds to a religious corporation for operation. The court stated that the hospital had been built for a public purpose and that its purpose did not become nonpublic as a result of being turned over to a charitable, nonprofit corporation (*Lien v. City of Ketchikan*, 1963).

The high court allowed the state to retire mortgages of those who lost property in the 1964 earthquake, even though a small part of the public was benefited (*Suber v. Alaska State Bond Committee*, 1966). Speaking for the court, Justice Dimond said the fact that some private purpose might be derived from the program would not alone invalidate it. The earthquake had impaired the general welfare of a segment of the citizenry and the state was obligated to relieve their economic distress. He paraphrased the New Jersey high court's commentary in *Roe v. Kervick* (1964):

> The basic objective of government is to protect and promote the health, safety, and general welfare of the people. When a condition of affairs appears in the state which presents a threat to the accomplishment of that objective, the government has the right, and the obligation, to cope with such threat by whatever measures, within constitutional limits, that are necessary or appropriate, (pp. 551–552).

Moreover, the supreme court held that the city of Palmer's issuance of general obligation bonds to finance a twenty-year improvement program was not a violation of the public purpose requirement. The bonds provided for the purchase of a site and the construction of a manufacturing and processing facility that would be leased to a private corporation, which the court found likely to benefit residents of the greater community (*Wright v. City of Palmer*, 1970).

The supreme court held that the Anchorage municipal utility did not appropriate public funds to nonpublic purposes when it leased, rented, and sold customer phone equipment. Moreover, the utility's actions promoted access to consumers, increased their convenience, and provided the public an identifiable, reputable, and dependable alternative to other service (*Comtec, Inc. v. Municipality of Anchorage*, 1985).

The supreme court did, however, balk at the state's tuition grant program, which awarded state residents attending private colleges in-state an amount generally equal to the difference between the tuition charged by the student's private college and that of the state university. It found that this was an expenditure of public funds for private and not public purposes, for only private colleges and their students benefited (*Sheldon Jackson College v. State*, 1979).

SECTION 7

> **Dedicated funds.** The proceeds of any state tax or license shall not be dedicated to any special purpose, except as provided in Section 15 of this article or when required by the federal government for state participation in federal programs. This provision shall not prohibit the continuance of any dedication for special purposes existing upon the date of ratification of this section by the people of Alaska.

Until amended in 1976, section 7 forbade all but two forms of earmarking of funds by the legislature, which was one of the objectives of the *Model State Constitution*.[75] The committee proposed a prohibition on dedicated funds in response both to territorial practices and conditions found in other states. Delegate Barrie White said the committee wanted to avoid a situation like that in

[75] National Municipal League, *Model State Constitution*, 13, 14, 41.

Texas, which earmarked 90 percent of all state funds, leaving the legislature only 10 percent with which to work (*PACC*, 2364). The delegates referred to a study that noted, "The most severe obstacle to the scope and flexibility of budgeting results from the earmarking or dedication of certain revenue for specified purposes or funds."[76]

Delegate Muktuk Marston mentioned one good example of earmarking in the territory—the tobacco tax, whose proceeds financed the building and repair of schools. Delegate Dorothy Awes, however, disagreed: "The reason for this section is that earmarking is one of those things that grows and grows and never dies" (*PACC*, 2374). In fact, earmarked funds composed 27 percent of territorial funds, and the number was growing.

Delegates also discussed the continuation of special purpose funds, and delegate Maurice Johnson sought to amend the article to protect them. In a 3-to-1 vote, delegates defeated this amendment in favor of the milder language that their continuance would not be prohibited. The general sense seemed to be that the need for presently earmarked funds would decline (*PACC*, 2383).

The third clause of the first sentence expresses the first exception: special funds required for participation in federal programs, such as the fish and game fund. The second exception is found in the continuation of the school fund, as authorized by the second sentence.

An ambiguity in this section was whether revenues from sources other than a "tax or license" could be dedicated. This became an issue when Alaska began receiving bonuses from oil leases and royalties and policy makers sought to establish a state savings account. An attorney general's opinion in 1975 held that all state revenues fell under the restrictions of section 7. Thus, it was necessary to take the issue to the voters. In the 1976 elections, by a large majority, voters approved section 15 of Article IX, establishing the Alaska Permanent Fund and the corresponding change in section 7.

The chief case in which the supreme court has interpreted section 7 is *State v. Alex* (1982). Commercial fishermen protested a statute authorizing private aquaculture associations to collect mandatory assessments on the sale of salmon. The high court found that the assessment provision was a tax or license to a special purpose, in contravention of section 7, and invalidated it.

SECTION 8

State debt. No state debt shall be contracted unless authorized by law for capital improvements or unless authorized by law for housing loans for veterans, and ratified by a majority of the qualified voters of the State who vote on the question. The State may, as provided by law and without ratification, contract debt for the purpose of

[76] Public Administration Service, *Constitutional Studies*, part IX, 27.

> repelling invasion, suppressing insurrection, defending the State in war, meeting natural disasters, or redeeming indebtedness outstanding at the time the constitution becomes effective.

Section 8 spells out the conditions under which the state may contract debt, which are considerably more liberal than those found in many state constitutions. The second sentence allows the state to borrow money without voter approval in order to respond to military and natural emergencies—war, invasion, insurrection, or natural disasters. It also permits the state to contract debt to repay territorial debts outstanding at the time of statehood.

The first sentence provides strict limits on nonemergency borrowing of the state in order to protect the state's credit, among other reasons. The original language of the first sentence permitted contracting debt only for "capital improvements," an imprecise phrase that the framers did not elect to define. Voters amended the first sentence in 1982 to allow the state to incur indebtedness to construct housing for veterans by taking advantage of a 1980 federal law allowing the sale of veteran housing bonds in the tax-exempt market.[77] Both uses require legislative authorization and voter approval.

The Committee on Finance and Taxation had proposed one section to cover both state and local debt. On the floor of the convention, delegate Burke Riley moved an amendment splitting the issues into two sections, the first placing a safeguard on the legislature and the second safeguarding political subdivisions of the state. Although some delegates supported imposing stringent requirements before the legislature could authorize debt (at the time, Massachusetts and South Dakota required a two-thirds vote in each house and Delaware required approval from three-fourths of the legislators), most thought a majority vote was sufficient (*PACC*, 2421).

The supreme court has elaborated section 8 in several cases. In *Suber v. Alaska State Bond Committee* (1966), a taxpayer asked the court to invalidate a mortgage adjustment plan that the legislature had passed in conjunction with federal government legislation to assist recovery from the 1964 earthquake. The plan, alleged the protester, did not meet a natural disaster as mentioned in section 8 because it did not entail necessary and immediate expenditures for emergency measures such as temporary shelter and medical services. The high court admitted that "meeting natural disasters" was a concept that could not be precisely defined or described, and legislative judgment and discretion were involved. It ruled that the legislation was a reasonable response to the effects of the disaster and met constitutional tests.

In challenging the constitutionality of the Alaska State Mortgage Association, protesting taxpayers said that its authorization to issue bonds, notes, and debentures constituted incurring "state debt" and that the association thus needed

[77] Harrison, *Alaska's Constitution*, 179.

explicit authorization by law and ratification by the voters for required capital improvements. The supreme court held that the mortgage association's activities neither imposed nor created a legal or moral obligation on the part of the state to meet the association's indebtedness; thus, it was not in violation of section 8 (*Walker v. Alaska State Mortgage Association*, 1966).

SECTION 9

Local debts. No debt shall be contracted by any political subdivision of the State, unless authorized for capital improvements by its governing body and ratified by a majority vote of those qualified to vote and voting on the question.

Section 9 applies even greater limits to political subdivisions than to the state, restricting their bonding authority to capital improvements only, which the local governing body must authorize and voters must approve. The delegates to the constitutional convention were clearly intent on protecting the financial integrity of political subdivisions. The limitation on the purposes for which they could incur indebtedness to capital improvements was the means they selected.

The supreme court has scrutinized carefully challenges to local bonding authority. In *City of Juneau v. Hixson* (1962), the court held that a proposed bond issue to purchase land that would be conveyed to the state for expansion of the state capitol was not for a "capital improvement" within the meaning of section 9. The high court hesitated to define "capital improvements," but specified some of their characteristics: they are associated with assets in the form of real or personal property and intended to connote a degree of permanency, such as streets, bridges, wharves, sewers, municipal buildings, schools, libraries, and public utilities. Land given to the state for its use met none of these characteristics.

When the city of Palmer sought to issue bonds to finance a twenty-year improvement program providing for the purchase of a site and construction of a manufacturing and processing facility that would be leased to a private corporation, the supreme court found the issuance consistent with the intent of section 9. The city's real ownership of the structure, the court held, would increase as years of rental payment went by, constituting "capital improvement" within the meaning of section 9 (*Wright v. City of Palmer*, 1979).

The village of Chefornak sought to use section 9 to protect itself against the necessity of paying a settlement in a suit against it by Hooper Bay. Its argument was that to pay the settlement was to "contract a debt" (p. 1268) in violation of this section. The supreme court held that constitutional restrictions on debts which political subdivisions contracted were inapplicable to judgment debt (*Village of Chefornak v. Hooper Bay Construction Company*, 1988).

SECTION 10

Interim borrowing. The State and its political subdivisions may borrow money to meet appropriations for any fiscal year in anticipation of the collection of the revenues for that year, but all debt so contracted shall be paid before the end of the next fiscal year.

Section 10 gives flexibility to local governments by allowing them to engage in short-term borrowing to balance their budgets. Customarily, the municipality issues revenue anticipation notes, based on expected revenues. The local governments are obliged under this provision to repay the notes before the end of the next fiscal year. The courts have not interpreted this section.

SECTION 11

Exceptions. The restrictions on contracting debt do not apply to debt incurred through the issuance of revenue bonds by a public enterprise or public corporation of the State or a political subdivision, when the only security is the revenues of the enterprise or corporation. The restrictions do not apply to indebtedness to be paid from special assessments on the benefited property, nor do they apply to refunding indebtedness of the State or its political subdivisions.

Section 11 creates additional flexibility for the state, its chartered enterprises or corporations, or its political subdivisions by authorizing the issuance of revenue bonds. Unlike general obligation bonds, which pledge the "full faith and credit" of the state or municipality to lenders (meaning they are backed by the government's full taxing authority), revenue bonds are secured only by the revenue from products of their operations. They do not require voter approval. The state has sold revenue bonds to finance improvements to its major airports in Anchorage and Fairbanks; the bonds are retired through airport fees. Similarly, the Alaska Housing Finance Corporation has sold revenue bonds to enable it to finance housing construction; these bonds are retired by mortgage payments. This section also permits borrowing to be repaid from special assessments, such as those in service areas.

SECTION 12

Budget. The governor shall submit to the legislature, at a time fixed by law, a budget for the next fiscal year setting forth all proposed expenditures and anticipated income of all departments, offices, and agencies of the State. The governor, at the same time, shall submit a general appropriation bill to authorize the proposed expenditures, and a bill or bills covering recommendations in the budget for new or additional revenues.

Section 12 outlines the governor's budgetary powers and responsibilities, and is a standard part of state constitutions. It is the governor's obligation to submit a comprehensive budget of proposed expenditures and income to the state legislature. The date set by statute (AS 37.07) is December 15, one month before the legislature meets. Simultaneously, the governor is obliged to submit a general appropriations bill to cover all proposed expenditures for the next fiscal year and bills to provide for new or additional revenues for the same period.

SECTION 13

Expenditures. No money shall be withdrawn from the treasury except in accordance with appropriations made by law. No obligation for the payment of money shall be incurred except as authorized by law. Unobligated appropriations outstanding at the end of the period of time specified by law shall be void.

Section 13 is taken from the *Model State Constitution;*[78] it is found in most state constitutions as a guard against fiscal mismanagement. The first sentence recognizes that the power to appropriate money is a legislative power matching the governor's budgetary authority, and the legislature must appropriate before money is spent. The second sentence expands the scope by covering obligations as well as actual moneys. The third sentence provides for the lapsing of unspent and unobligated appropriations at the end of fiscal periods. For the operating budget, this is the end of the fiscal year—June 30. For capital programs, it is usually at the completion of the project.

SECTION 14

Legislative post-audit. The legislature shall appoint an auditor to serve at its pleasure. He shall be a certified public accountant. The auditor shall conduct post-audits as prescribed by law and shall report to the legislature and to the governor.

Section 14 provides for the state auditor, who is the only state official appointed constitutionally by the legislature. He is answerable to the legislature and not the governor in order to avoid conflicts of interest. The state auditor reviews and monitors the expenditure of public funds to ensure that they have been spent in accordance with law and regulations.

SECTION 15

Alaska permanent fund. At least twenty-five per cent of all mineral lease rentals, royalties, royalty sale proceeds, federal mineral revenue sharing payments and

[78] National Municipal League, *Model State Constitution,* section 706, p. 300.

> bonuses received by the State shall be placed in a permanent fund, the principal of which shall be used only for those income-producing investments specifically designated by law as eligible for permanent fund investments. All income from the permanent fund shall be deposited in the general fund unless otherwise provided by law.

Section 7 prohibited the creation of any dedicated (or "earmarked") funds, but soon after the discovery of oil at Prudhoe Bay in 1968, Alaskans began to think about preserving the state's anticipated oil wealth for future generations. The Alaska Permanent Fund was the most constructive fiscal innovation since statehood. At the urging of Governor Hammond and legislative leaders, in 1976 voters adopted this section as an amendment to the state constitution. It requires that one-quarter of petroleum lease bonuses, royalties, and rentals be directly deposited into the fund, thus bypassing the legislature; they may be used only for "income-producing investments." The exclusion of severance taxes from the fund meant that only about 10 percent of oil revenues had to be deposited.

The fund management policy was left up to the legislature, which established a Permanent Fund Corporation. Subsequent legislation determined that the fund should be conservatively managed as a savings account and that only the earnings could be spent, not the principal.

By 1996, sound investments by the Permanent Fund Corporation had propelled the principal to more than $18 billion. Savings required by law account for 40 percent of the total, and "inflation proofing" (via redeposited earnings) accounts for 25 percent. Surprisingly, 35 percent of the savings stems from special deposits of surplus funds by the legislature during the boom years.[79]

Dedicated funds in other states specify the purpose for which the fund may be spent. This section says that Permanent Fund earnings are deposited in the general fund "unless otherwise provided by law." The legislature has dedicated earnings to only one purpose, the dividend program. The legislature created the program in 1980 for two reasons. First, dividends were considered the most efficient way to deliver the benefits of petroleum development equally to all state citizens, and second, dividends would create a popular constituency with a vested interest in protecting the fund from raids on its principal. The supreme court has declined to hold, however, that the dividend is a constitutional right. When incarcerated felons protested the statute, which prohibited some felons from collecting dividends, the high court ruled that the existence of the permanent fund was constitutionally protected but that no resident of the state was necessarily *entitled* to a dividend from the fund (*State v. Anthony*, 1991).

---

[79] McBeath and Morehouse, *Alaska Politics and Government*, 63–64.

SECTION 16

Appropriation limit. Except for appropriations for Alaska permanent fund dividends, appropriations of revenue bond proceeds, appropriations required to pay the principal and interest on general obligation bonds, and appropriations of money received from a nonstate source in trust for a specific purpose, including revenues of a public enterprise or public corporation of the State that issues revenue bonds, appropriations from the treasury made for a fiscal year shall not exceed $2,500,000,000 by more than the cumulative change, derived from federal indices as prescribed by law, in population and inflation since July 1, 1981. Within this limit, at least one-third shall be reserved for capital projects and loan appropriations. The legislature may exceed this limit in bills for appropriations to the Alaska permanent fund and in bills for appropriations for capital projects, whether of bond proceeds or otherwise, if each bill is approved by the governor, or passed by affirmative vote of three-fourths of the membership of the legislature over a veto or item veto, or becomes law without signature, and is also approved by the voters as prescribed by law. Each bill for appropriations for capital projects in excess of the limit shall be confined to capital projects of the same type, and the voters shall, as provided by law, be informed of the cost of operations and maintenance of the capital projects. No other appropriation in excess of this limit may be made except to meet a state of disaster declared by the governor as prescribed by law. The governor shall cause any unexpended and unappropriated balance to be invested so as to yield competitive market rates to the treasury.

In an effort to reduce state spending toward the end of Alaska's oil-rich years, the state legislature, in a 1981 special session, approved a spending limit. Voters adopted this in 1982 as an amendment to the Alaska Constitution. Governor Jay Hammond pushed the legislature to pass the spending limit law. In exchange for lawmakers' approval of the limit, he agreed to the legislature's $1.8 billion capital budget that year. In the 1982 election, he told voters that the limit "may be our last chance to control the juggernaut which otherwise will likely crush us into bankruptcy."[80]

The appropriation limit in section 16 has had virtually no effect in limiting spending. Drafters in the legislature and governor's office set a ceiling of $2.5 billion on appropriations, which was near the 1981 level—then the high point of state spending. They also provided for raising the ceiling in response to population growth and inflation. By the time the limit was to go into effect in 1984, however, revenues had already fallen nearly to the level of the ceiling; soon, they dropped below it.

Section 16 also provides for a series of exceptions to the appropriation limit. It does not apply to appropriations for permanent fund dividends (nearly a half billion dollars in 1996), payments of general obligation bonds, revenue bond

[80] Ibid., 65.

proceeds, and enterprise or public corporation revenues. Under several conditions, the legislature may exceed the appropriations limit—to increase appropriations to the permanent fund or for capital projects—although special majorities and voter approval are required for these special appropriations. Finally, appropriations in excess of the spending limit may be made in the event of natural disasters.

The constitutional amendment of 1982 gave voters the opportunity to repeal it in a 1986 referendum (Article XV, section 27). They supported it strongly, by a vote of 119,775 to 48,909.

SECTION 17

Budget reserve fund. (a) There is established as a separate fund in the State treasury the budget reserve fund. Except for money deposited into the permanent fund under Section 15 of this article, all money received by the State after July 1, 1990, as a result of the termination, through settlement or otherwise, of an administrative proceeding or of litigation in a State or federal court involving mineral lease bonuses, rentals, royalties, royalty sale proceeds, federal mineral revenue sharing payments or bonuses, or involving taxes imposed on mineral income, production, or property, shall be deposited in the budget reserve fund. Money in the budget reserve fund shall be invested so as to yield competitive market rates to the fund. Income of the fund shall be retained in the fund. Section 7 of this article does not apply to deposits made to the fund under this subsection. Money may be appropriated from the fund only as authorized under (b) or (c) of this section.
(b) If the amount available for appropriation for a fiscal year is less than the amount appropriated for the previous fiscal year, an appropriation may be made from the budget reserve fund. However, the amount appropriated from the fund under this subsection may not exceed the amount necessary, when added to other funds available for appropriation, to provide for total appropriations equal to the amount of appropriations made in the previous calendar year for the previous fiscal year.
(c) An appropriation from the budget reserve fund may be made for any public purpose upon affirmative vote of three-fourths of the members of each house of the legislature.
(d) If an appropriation is made from the budget reserve fund, until the amount appropriated is repaid, the amount of money in the general fund available for appropriation at the end of each succeeding fiscal year shall be deposited in the budget reserve fund. The legislature shall implement this subsection by law.

The second dedicated fund created under Article IX was the constitutional budget reserve. Governor Steve Cowper proposed and strongly advocated this second "rainy day" fund for the state, to be used when oil revenues declined in the 1990s. Moreover, extensive litigation in which the state had been engaged with oil companies over back taxes, transportation charges, and other issues was beginning to bear fruit. Many policy makers, seeing that the appropriation limit had failed to limit spending as intended, feared that if one-time oil tax and other litigation settlements were deposited directly into the general fund, they would be as quickly spent. Thus, in 1990, the legislature passed a proposed constitutional amendment, which voters approved in the November 1990 election.

Aggressive litigation by the Hickel Administration (1990–1994) brought billions of dollars into the constitutional budget reserve and also increased pressure to spend it as oil revenues continued to decline. Subsection (b) provides that moneys may be spent from the budget reserve only when revenues of the current fiscal year are lower than the previous year, and then no more may be spent totally than had been spent in the previous fiscal year. Subsection (c) provides for an extraordinary legislative majority—three-fourths—before moneys can be appropriated.

When British Petroleum announced a nearly three-quarter billion dollar settlement with the state in 1993, a pattern of activity began that led to the judicial interpretation of section 17. Instead of depositing the settlement proceeds into the budget reserve fund, Attorney General Charles Cole directed that these funds resulted from "pre-termination" not the "termination" of litigation.[81] Thus, they could be deposited into the general fund and be available for appropriation by the legislature with only a simple majority, bypassing the supermajority necessary if the funds were in the Constitutional Budget Reserve. The legislature quickly appropriated the tax settlement in a capital spending spree totaling over $800 million. Former Governor Cowper and Republican leaders of the state Senate challenged the action of the legislature and governor in court.

In 1994, the superior court ruled that the tax settlement proceeds had been illegally deposited in the general fund and unconstitutionally appropriated. The court required the legislature to correct its action by redepositing funds into the budget reserve and drawing them out following the terms of subsection (c), which required the majority to gain the cooperation of the minority.

In 1995, the legislature tapped the constitutional budget reserve again, on this occasion to cover a budget deficit of nearly a half billion dollars, which required cooperation across party lines. To avoid that necessity in the future, Republican legislators creatively applied subsection (b). They attempted to reduce the amount available for appropriation in fiscal year (FY) 1996 by depositing earnings from the Permanent Fund back into its principal. This action would have made it impossible to use the budget reserve in the next fiscal year. New Governor Tony Knowles exercised his line item veto on this action, reducing the amount deposited into the Permanent Fund so that the administration (and legislature) would have access to the budget reserve in the future.

---

[81] *Anchorage Daily News*, February 4, 1993.

The three amendments to Article IX were responses of Alaskans to a sharp rise and then decline in state revenues from oil and gas production. The establishment of the Permanent Fund technically violated the framers' intent but is today widely supported by the public and policy makers. The more recent amendments, establishing an appropriation limit and constitutional budget reserve, also were departures from the original design of this article. Additionally, their lengthy, detailed, and poorly crafted exposition of procedures (which were an invitation to political manipulation and litigation of section 17) diverged from the spare statements and general principles favored by the framers.

Article X

Local Government

Victor Fischer, a delegate to the constitutional convention and member of the Local Government Committee, found little that was controversial in deliberation over the local government article:

> Local government was a subject for which there was little Alaska experience to provide a useful point of departure and which provided few useful models. The local government committee, therefore, determined early that innovation was the key to structuring a local government system for Alaska. Study of the PAS [Public Administration Service] staff paper and a review of local government experiences throughout the United States, Canada, Scandinavia, Latin America, and other parts of the world convinced committee members that they could look outside Alaska primarily for the purpose of evaluating basic principles and determining what not to do.[82]

What "not to do" was a topic of local government reform throughout the United States in the 1950s: overlapping jurisdictional lines, multiple taxing authorities, rigid government institutions, and urban/suburban conflicts. The some 3,000 counties, which formed the cornerstone of local government in the United States, were then called "forgotten" governments. They derived their powers from states and could not flexibly address problems as they arose.

[82] Fischer, *Alaska's Constitutional Convention*, 116–117.

Alaska suffered less from these problems, although special purpose districts were burgeoning in the early 1950s, than it did from powerlessness of local government units—limited in the amount they could tax and in their territorial reach.

The chief innovation of the constitutional convention, upon the advice of PAS consultants, was to create in Alaska an integrated and unified system of local government and to place at its center the borough as the mid-level, general-purpose governmental unit between the state and cities. Boroughs would provide a framework within which city governments, school districts, and other local responsibilities could be administered.

The concept of "borough" was discussed extensively, beginning with the comments of the sometimes-cranky delegate Frank Barr (who spoke for several delegates who had problems with the term): "I am trying to get rid of the word "borough" because I want to be able to walk down the streets without people throwing rocks at me. I am not the only one who does not want to live in a borough" (*PACC*, 3623).

Alternatives to *borough* included county, canton, province, and division, each with some adherents. Definitely, however, the delegates wanted to avoid any tint of the problems of local government outside Alaska. Said delegate Warren Taylor about county: "It brings to mind mismanagement, political mismanagement" (*PACC*, 2781). When all terms were put to a poll, *borough* received the highest vote.

John Bebout, an expert on American local government, made these observations on the new borough system at the time of statehood:

> There has probably been more speculation and less consensus on the future of the borough system under the Alaska Constitution than on any other one subject connected with local government. This is natural since the borough would be something new not only in Alaska but in America. As an intermediate level between city and state, the borough will correspond in some respects to county government in most of the older states. However, the determination of the members of the Convention to avoid reproducing many of the typical features of the county on the Alaska scene points in the direction of a system which has no precise counterpart anywhere else.[83]

Indeed, in three urban parts of the state with concentrated populations—Juneau, Anchorage, and Sitka—unified city/boroughs have developed, and these have admirably achieved the ambitious hopes of the framers.

The only other concern of the convention was the relationship of school districts and boroughs. Committee members explained repeatedly that the

[83] John Bebout, *Local Government Under the Alaska Constitution* (Chicago: Public Administration Service, 1959), 44.

borough would not replace school districts or cities, but would be a framework for them, and would eliminate overlapping taxing authority.

Still delegates, such as Maurice Johnson, worried that schools might be slighted under the new regime, and he moved to give school districts equal taxing power with cities and boroughs (*PACC*, 2696). This amendment failed, however, on a 4-to-1 vote.

SECTION 1

Purpose and construction. The purpose of this article is to provide for maximum local self-government with a minimum of local government units, and to prevent duplication of tax levying jurisdictions. A liberal construction shall be given to the powers of local government units.

The first sentence of section 1 states the innovative principle of local government organization in Alaska. The people will have the greatest powers of self-government at the local level, but within the smallest number of governmental units. Moreover, units of local government shall be integrated, to reduce the number of taxing jurisdictions. The second sentence states the principle of liberal construction, which was designed to reduce court challenge to and restrictive judicial interpretation of local government authority that occurred in most of the other states, based on Dillon's Rule (the precedential ruling of an administrative law judge in 1868 to the effect that local government powers would be narrowly construed).

Several court cases have applied both the integration and liberal construction aspects of section 1. In 1962, the supreme court supported the annexation of a public utility district by the city of Anchorage, notwithstanding the lack of a vote on the annexation (*Fairview Public Utility District No. 1 v. City of Anchorage*), arguing that this action fell within the authorization of section 1 among other sections of Article X. Similarly, the supreme court upheld the unification of the cities of Douglas and Juneau in the city and borough of Juneau, even though the majority of voters in Douglas opposed unification (but were outvoted by Juneau voters) (*City of Douglas v. City and Borough of Juneau*, 1971).

In a controversial case, which was resolved in 1974, the supreme court upheld the incorporation of the North Slope Borough, which was America's largest local government (containing about 15 percent of Alaska's territory), and also its richest. Mobil Oil Corporation and other oil companies, whose assets at Prudhoe Bay would fall under borough taxation, protested the incorporation, but the high court found that the statement of purpose in the local government article upheld incorporation when the requirements for forming local governments had been minimally met (*Mobil Oil Corporation v. Local Boundary Commission*).

When, however, private aquaculture associations attempted to collect assessments on salmon sales by commercial fishermen, the supreme court ruled the action unconstitutional and stated that the private associations were not part of a unified local government, among other disqualifying reasons (*State v. Alex*, 1982). With a high degree of consistency, the judiciary has supported the integration of local government units.

In another series of decisions, the high court has supported more expansive powers for local governments than challengers have found proper. In *Brayton v. City of Anchorage* (1963), the court rejected the appeal of a candidate for office who objected to the city's ordinance prohibiting placement of campaign posters on telephone utility poles. The court held that Anchorage was then a home rule city and was "clothed with considerably broader powers" than most municipalities in Alaska (p. 833).

When commercial fishermen in Bristol Bay objected to the borough's tax on raw fish, the supreme court upheld it. In part, the court found this an appropriate unification of taxing jurisdictions, as provided for in the first sentence of section 1, and in part, it found the broad grant of taxing authority consistent with the second sentence of section 1. The court ruled that the action of the Bristol Bay Borough supported the framers' intention "to overrule a common law rule of interpretation which required a narrow reading of local government powers" (*Liberati v. Bristol Bay Borough*, 1978, p. 1120).

In a not dissimilar case, the supreme court held that the Kenai Peninsula Borough had the power to impose a civil penalty for a resident's failure to remit sales taxes, because "our state constitution requires that a liberal construction be given to the powers of municipalities" (*Bookey v. Kenai Peninsula Borough*, 1980, p. 569). The court also used this section of Article X to defend the Municipality of Anchorage's code provision that provided for final and binding interest arbitration with regard to some municipal employees (*Municipality of Anchorage v. Anchorage Police Department Employees Association*, 1992).

SECTION 2

Local government powers. All local government powers shall be vested in boroughs and cities. The State may delegate taxing powers to organized boroughs and cities only.

Section 2 of Article X is read together with section 1. The first sentence gives local government authority only to boroughs and cities. This means that school and public utility districts, which had taxing powers before statehood, lost them under the constitution. This sentence further implements the integration principle of Article X. The second sentence denies taxing powers to institutions that are not boroughs or cities, or to institutions not formally incorporated within them as service areas. It implements the first sentence of section 1, which sought to prevent the "duplication of tax levying jurisdictions." This sentence denies taxing powers to school districts, which have them in most parts of the United States.

The judiciary has interpreted section 2, usually in connection with section 1, on a number of occasions. As mentioned, *Fairview Public Utility District Number One v. City of Anchorage* (1962) allowed the elimination of a public utility district because it was not a local government unit as defined under the constitution. When the state legislature incorporated eight specifically designated and defined areas of the state as organized boroughs, the supreme court supported the action (*Walters v. Cease*, 1964) because it followed the provisions of section 2.

When asked to permit a state legislator to continue to serve as a teacher under the State-Operated School District, the high court demurred, as that institution was neither a city nor a borough but rather an instrumentality of the state (*Begich v. Jefferson*, 1968). Residents of Douglas protested that section 2 implied that their city not be dissolved in favor of the unified borough of Juneau but the supreme court disagreed. It held that section 2 "merely authorizes but does not require the coexistence of cities and boroughs" (*City of Douglas v. City and Borough of Juneau*, 1971, p. 1044).

The delegation of taxing authority only to cities and boroughs has been carefully reviewed by the high court. *Liberati v. Bristol Bay Borough* (1978) established that the borough's raw fish tax was a sales tax, something commonly delegated to local governments, and not a severance tax, which was reserved for the state.

The court's ruling in *State v. Alex* (1982) voided the collection of mandatory assessments by private aquaculture associations on grounds that this was an impermissible delegation of the legislature's taxing powers to entities other than boroughs or cities. However, in *Municipality of Anchorage v. Anchorage Police Department Employees Association* (1992), the high court found that the city's provision for binding interest arbitration was not an unconstitutional delegation of the legislature's taxing authority.

SECTION 3

Boroughs. The entire State shall be divided into boroughs, organized or unorganized. They shall be established in a manner and according to standards provided by law. The standards shall include population, geography, economy, transportation, and other factors. Each borough shall embrace an area and population with common interests to the maximum degree possible. The legislature shall classify boroughs and prescribe their powers and functions. Methods by which boroughs may be organized, incorporated, merged, consolidated, reclassified, or dissolved shall be prescribed by law.

Section 3 continues, and further specifies, section 2. It divides the entire state into boroughs but allows the designation "unorganized" for those areas unready for local government. The legislature has not created unorganized boroughs in different rural areas of the state. Instead, it has treated all areas outside organized boroughs as one vast, unorganized borough. Gradually, the legislature has created service districts, such as the Rural Educational Attendance Areas (REAAs), rural school districts established in the unorganized borough by the legislature in 1976.

Section 3 provides important integration standards for the formation of boroughs, and requires boroughs to contain areas and populations that are compact to the greatest extent possible. It leaves the state legislature large powers with respect to specifying further standards for borough incorporation, classifying boroughs, and specifying their powers, functions, and changes thereto.

The legislature established standards in statute which closely follow the constitutional principles (in AS 29.05.031). It also classified boroughs as first, second, and third class, with a descending range of powers (third-class boroughs may no longer be formed). Today, all first-class boroughs are unified municipalities—Anchorage, Juneau, and Sitka. They are relatively compact areas with a dominant city at the core and offer the largest amount of authority and self-government to citizens. The rest of Alaska's boroughs, with one exception, are second class, which means that their powers are limited and their assemblies cannot expand services without a vote of the people. The exception is Haines, which had only an independent school district until the legislature amended the borough act in 1968 to authorize third-class "school boroughs," thereby legalizing Haines's local government.[84]

The supreme court has clarified the meaning of section 3 in several cases concerning borough incorporation and borough powers. When Inupiat Eskimos formed a borough covering the entire North Slope, and included within it both the Naval Petroleum Reserve and the Prudhoe Bay oil fields, the major lease-holding oil companies protested. One of their arguments was that the petroleum reserve was included unconstitutionally and that the borough did not meet either geography or transportation standards for incorporation. The supreme court supported the formation of the borough. It found that the borough boundaries did "conform generally to the natural geography of the area" (*Mobil Oil Corporation v. Local Boundary Commission*, 1974, p. 99), and that inclusion of the petroleum reserve (under federal jurisdiction) was necessary for integrated local government. Further, the court held that although surface transportation was limited to dog teams and snowmobiles, the ability to travel by charter aircraft was adequate in the Alaska context.

[84] Thomas A. Morehouse, Gerald A. McBeath, and Linda Leask, *Alaska's Urban and Rural Governments* (Lanham, MD: University Press of America, 1984), 66.

However, the court disapproved the incorporation of a new borough from within the confines of an existing one. In *Abrams v. State* (1975), the high court held that the legislature's establishment of an Eagle River–Chugiak borough went well beyond what section 3 provided regarding changing boroughs. Moreover, the court found it violated section 19 of Article II, which prohibits special and local legislation.

SECTION 4

Assembly. The governing body of the organized borough shall be the assembly, and its composition shall be established by law or charter.

This section identifies the borough assembly as the government of the borough, but statutes and charters in most Alaska boroughs now also provide for elected mayors. The original version of section 4 called for the representation of cities on borough assemblies as a means to facilitate integration and cooperation. This proved an unworkable experience, however, and it also contradicted new apportionment rules laid down by the federal courts in the early 1960s. The voters approved an amendment to the constitution in 1972 to remove the requirement.

SECTION 5

Service areas. Service areas to provide special services within an organized borough may be established, altered, or abolished by the assembly, subject to the provisions of law or charter. A new service area shall not be established if, consistent with the purposes of this article, the new service can be provided by an existing service area, by incorporation as a city, or by annexation to a city. The assembly may authorize the levying of taxes, charges, or assessments within a service area to finance the special services.

A service area is a jurisdiction in which a service such as fire protection or road maintenance and improvement is provided and the property receiving the service is taxed to pay for it. Section 5 gives borough assemblies broad powers over the formation, elimination, and change of service areas. It discourages the proliferation of service areas by the requirement that new ones may not be created if the service can be provided through other means. The section also gives assemblies the power to authorize the assessment of taxes and fees within the service area to support provision of special services.

The court considered the section on service areas in *State v. Alex* (1982), which tested the constitutionality of private aquaculture associations that collected mandatory assessments on the sale of salmon by commercial fishermen.

It found that the aquaculture associations were not service areas, because they spanned the entire Alaska panhandle—an area including several organized boroughs and cities.

The supreme court defined the last sentence of section 5 in 1990 when it invalidated a tax by the city of Valdez on oil and gas property. The court precluded the city from imposing a higher property-tax mill rate on oil and gas property than on other property in the city by establishing a service area that included only oil and gas property (*City of Valdez v. State, Department of Community & Regional Affairs*, 1990). Although the city justified the special tax based on provision of berthing for disabled tankers at the city's public dock, the amounts spent on this service were minute in comparison to the taxes paid by the companies.

In another decision, *North Kenai Peninsula Road Maintenance Service Area v. Kenai Peninsula Borough* (1993), the court approved the consolidation by the Kenai Peninsula Borough of four of its service areas into one, without votes of affected residents, affirming the power given borough assemblies over service areas.

SECTION 6

Unorganized boroughs. The legislature shall provide for the performance of services it deems necessary or advisable in unorganized boroughs, allowing for maximum local participation and responsibility. It may exercise any power or function in an unorganized borough which the assembly may exercise in an organized borough.

The framers designed the unorganized borough for those areas of the state lacking requisites for self-government, especially populations of a sufficient size and a tax base (initially, most of the territory of Alaska outside a dozen cities). Section 6 gives the legislature plenary power over unorganized boroughs, enabling it to act very much as would a borough assembly. The section also allows the creation of unorganized boroughs to perform any service the legislature finds appropriate, but it charges that they must encourage local participation and responsibility.

Although it was the intent of the framers that plural unorganized boroughs be created, the legislature has not done so. Instead, it has used provisions of section 5 to establish several kinds of service areas, each with its own governing board, which contributes to a proliferation of governmental entities in rural Alaska.

When the legislature authorized private aquaculture associations to collect mandatory assessments from fishermen, however, the supreme court found the action to contravene section 6. It held that the associations were completely independent of any government control (*State v. Alex*, 1982). Further, there was no representative relationship between the associations' directors and the commercial fishermen to whom they were to provide services. Thus, the court held that the "entity has no political responsibility and cannot be granted unfettered discretion in governing a 'service area'" (p. 213).

SECTION 7

Cities. Cities shall be incorporated in a manner prescribed by law, and shall be part of the borough in which they are located. Cities shall have the powers and functions conferred by law or charter. They may be merged, consolidated, classified, reclassified, or dissolved in the manner provided by law.

Section 7 parallels section 3 in setting out authority for establishing and changing cities. Importantly, cities are not independent of organized boroughs if any surrounds them; they are part of the borough, which implements the integration objectives of the local government article. However, cities are independent regarding their statutory powers. This section authorizes cities to develop their own charters, which outline their powers over internal affairs and functions. However, the manner by which cities are incorporated and changed structurally is left for the legislature to determine. Initially, the legislature created four classes of cities. Now it allows the incorporation of first- and second-class cities in addition to home rule cities. (See sections 9 and 10.)

The supreme court examined the authority of charters in two cases involving cities. In *Lien v. City of Ketchikan* (1963), the high court looked at the conflict between a legislative act that restricted a city's lease of its property, and a charter provision permitting it. It ruled that the charter of a home rule city, and not a legislative act, was superior when determining whether a particular power had been conferred upon the city.

In another case of conflict between charter provisions (concerning consolidation) and state law, the supreme court held that the state statute was constitutional. This issue concerned the unification of the city of Douglas with the city and borough of Juneau (*City of Douglas v. City and Borough of Juneau,* 1971), without a majority vote in Douglas, as required by its charter. The court held that section 7 gave powers of dissolution of cities as well as merger and consolidation to the legislature, because its responsibility was broader: ["T]his cleavage is reflective of a policy which has as its objective the placement of decisional responsibility for local problems within local control and decisional responsibility for broader problems in control of a broader community" (p. 1043).

SECTION 8

Council. The governing body of a city shall be the council.

Section 8 establishes the source of authority in the city as the council, as section 4 provides that the governing body of the borough will be called the "assembly."

SECTION 9

Charters. The qualified voters of any borough of the first class or city of the first class may adopt, amend, or repeal a home rule charter in a manner provided by law. In the absence of such legislation, the governing body of a borough or city of the first class shall provide the procedure for the preparation and adoption or rejection of the charter. All charters, or parts or amendments of charters, shall be submitted to the qualified voters of the borough or city, and shall become effective if approved by a majority of those who vote on the specific question.

Section 9 is a continuation of section 1, in that it provides for the "liberal construction" of local government powers through the home rule charter. Such a charter becomes the basic law for the city, allowing it to assume all powers that it is not specifically prohibited from exercising by the state legislature. If the legislature does not implement this section, the second sentence allows all first-class cities and boroughs to prepare for, and vote to adopt, charters. The adoption, revision, or elimination of the charters is done by a majority of qualified voters in the municipality.

Whether the charter prevails over state statute is an issue the judiciary has addressed several times, as seen in the commentary on section 7. The high court ruled in *Lien v. City of Ketchikan* (1963) that a statute permitting municipalities to lease out property that was no longer required for municipal purposes did not apply to home rule cities; the city was not required to make a determination that the property was unnecessary for municipal purposes before leasing it.

Similarly, the court ruled in *Brayton v. City of Anchorage* (1963) that the city's campaign ordinance under its charter was constitutional. In this case, the court did not define the extent of the power of a home rule city, but it opined that as a home rule city, the municipality was "therefore clothed with considerably broader powers than the usual municipal corporation in Alaska" (p. 833).

However, the court has not supported charter powers in all cases (see section 11). The court held that although section 9 empowered first-class cities to determine whether to have home rule without interference by others, it is the role of the legislature to decide the broader and different question of whether a home rule city should be dissolved, as well as the method or manner of dissolution (*City of Douglas v. City and Borough of Juneau*, 1971).

SECTION 10

Extended home rule. The legislature may extend home rule to other boroughs and cities.

This sentence allows the legislature to give home rule powers to boroughs and cities which are not of the first class, following procedures laid out by the legislature. In statute (AS 29.10.010), the legislature has provided that secondclass cities may adopt a home rule charter if it meets area and population size criteria.

SECTION 11

Home rule powers. A home rule borough or city may exercise all legislative powers not prohibited by law or by charter.

Section 11 is read together with section 9, as specifying one of the meanings of "liberal construction" found in section 1 of Article X. The meanings of home rule, as partially indicated in previous sections, are not precise, and this section has been subject to significant judicial interpretation.

Over three decades the high court has specified limits to municipal home rule powers. In *City of Juneau v. Hixson* (1962), the court held that the possession of greater legislative powers under home rule status did not permit the city of Juneau to purchase land with bond proceeds when the project was not a "capital improvement" (p. 748), as expressly required by section 9 of Article IX. In *Chugach Electric Association v. City of Anchorage* (1970), the supreme court ruled against the city's attempt to deny Chugach permission to run electricity to a bowling alley within limits served by the city's utility, when that service was permitted by the state regulatory agency. The state legislature, said the court, had invested in the Public Service Commission the power to regulate the transmission of electric current, which preempted the power of home rule municipalities.

The high court ruled against the home rule municipality of Juneau when it attempted to require its school system to participate in centralized accounting without the statutorily required approval of the school board (*Macauley v. Hildebrand*, 1971). In *Johnson v. City of Fairbanks* (1978), the court reversed the city's denial of a negligence claim because it had not been filed within 120 days of the injury. The court found conflict between the action of the home rule municipality and the state's two-year statute of limitations, which prevailed.

Finally, in *Simpson v. Municipality of Anchorage* (1981), the court overturned the city's drunk-driving ordinance because it substantially conflicted with the state law relating to operating a motor vehicle under the influence of intoxicating liquor. The court recognized that charters were adopted in order to abrogate traditional restrictions on the exercise of local legislative authorities. However, it held that section 11 was not meant to "render boundless" the legislative powers of home rule municipalities (p. 1198).

Perhaps the clearest statement of the judiciary's interpretation of home rule powers is found in *Jefferson v. State* (1974):

> To say that home rule powers are intended to be broadly applied in Alaska is not to say that they are intended to be pre-eminent. The constitution's authors did not

> intend to create 'city states with mini-legislatures.' They wrote into article X, section 11 the limitation of municipal authority 'not prohibited by law or charter.' The test we derive from Alaska's constitutional provisions is one of prohibition, rather than traditional tests such as statewide versus local concern. A municipal ordinance is not necessarily invalid in Alaska because it is inconsistent or in conflict with a state statute. The question rests on whether the exercise of authority has been prohibited to municipalities. The prohibition must be either by express terms or by implication such as where the statute and ordinance are so substantially irreconcilable that one cannot be given its substantive effect if the other is to be accorded the weight of law. (p. 43)

The supreme court has, in another series of decisions, supported home rule charters granting powers that appeared to conflict with statutes. For example, in *Lien v. City of Ketchikan* (1963), the high court declared a statute on leasing to be irrelevant when the powers of a home rule city were being considered. In this case, the court found that the city's power to lease its hospital to the Sisters of Charity was properly based in its charter. Similarly, in *Brayton v. City of Anchorage* (1963), the court endorsed the city's campaign ordinance. In another Anchorage case, the high court agreed with the city administration that its charter's lack of express requirements that appropriations be made by ordinance allowed it to spend money by memo as well as by ordinance (*Municipality of Anchorage v. Frohne*, 1977).

In *Liberati v. Bristol Bay Borough* (1978), the court ruled that the borough's raw fish tax was constitutional, even though the state managed the harvesting of fish to a detailed extent. The court helped clarify by noting:

> Merely because the state has enacted legislation concerning a particular subject does not mean that all municipal power to act on the same subject is lost. . . . An appropriate accommodation can be made between the state and general law municipalities by a rule which determines preemption to exist, in the absence of an express legislative direction or a direct conflict with a statute, only where an ordinance substantially interferes with the effective functioning of a state statue or regulation or its underlying purpose, (pp. 1121–1122)

In a final case, the supreme court held in *Municipality of Anchorage v. Anchorage Police Department Employees Association* (1992) that the municipality could provide for final and binding "interest" arbitration (the financial part of the contract) for some municipal employees constitutionally. The court pointed out that "the right of the Assembly to delegate powers to govern the affairs of the municipality will not be strictly construed" (p. 1084).

The best summary of the status of home rule in Alaska is provided by Gerald Sharp. In 1973 he wrote:

> (A) home rule municipality in Alaska may act in areas of mixed state and local concern so long as the acts are not inconsistent with state statutes. If it can find an area of

purely local concerns, it may exercise broad governmental powers by acting in conflict with those statutes which are not intended to apply to home rule municipalities.[85]

SECTION 12

Boundaries. A local boundary commission or board shall be established by law in the executive branch of the state government. The commission or board may consider any proposed local government boundary change. It may present proposed changes to the legislature during the first ten days of any regular session. The change shall become effective forty-five days after presentation or at the end of the session, whichever is earlier, unless disapproved by a resolution concurred in by a majority of the members of each house. The commission or board, subject to law, may establish procedures whereby boundaries may be adjusted by local action.

Section 12 establishes in the constitution the Local Boundary Commission, which is a testament to its significance. (It is one of five boards and commissions created by the constitution; the others are the Board of Regents, the Judicial Council, the Commission on Judicial Conduct, and the Reapportionment Board.) The section gives the commission power to approve any boundary change (such as annexations or detachments) of local government bodies. (Sections 3 and 7 of this article give the legislature power to incorporate cities and boroughs, and to merge, classify, and dissolve them.) The legislature may reject the proposed change by a simple majority vote in each house. This is the second legislative veto in the constitution; unlike the veto over executive reorganization (Article III, section 23), this is not done in joint session. The commission also has the authority to develop procedures for change of boundaries at the local level, subject to legislative review.

Minutes of the Committee on Local Government at the constitutional convention show the concept considered when section 12 was written. Committee members thought that local political decisions did not usually create proper boundaries and that boundaries should be established at the state level: "[The advantage] lies in placing the process at a level where area-wide or state-wide needs can be taken into account. By placing authority in this third-party, arguments for and against boundary change can be analyzed objectively."[86] Moreover, delegates thought the need for a commission was immediate because of rapid

---

[85] Gerald L. Sharp, "Home Rule in Alaska: Clash between the Constitution and the Court," *UCLA: Alaska Law Review* 3, no. 1 (1973): 53; see also Linda Duvall, "Delimitation of the Powers of the Alaska Home Rule City," *Alaska Law Journal* 8, no. 10 (October 1970): 232–244.

[86] Minutes of Committee on Local Government, November 28 and December 4, 1995; *PACC*, appendix V, pp. 48–50, 58–59.

growth in urban areas, such as Anchorage, after World War II, and the existence of many overlapping jurisdictions.

Opponents of boundary changes have challenged the authority of the Local Boundary Commission (established by the legislature in 1959) in several court cases. In 1960, the Fairview Public Utility District challenged its absorption into the city of Anchorage. The supreme court upheld the annexation, pointing out that although one house of the legislature had opposed it, the other had not (*Fairview Public Utility District Number One v. City of Anchorage*, 1962). Moreover, the court held that the commission's authority began at the moment of its establishment and that it could propose changes without public comment. (See also *Oesau v. City of Dillingham*, 1968.)

When oil producers challenged the constitutionality of the incorporation of the North Slope Borough in 1972, the court held that the incorporation did not deny due process to corporations and individuals holding surface leases and owners of interests in oil and gas wells and other property in the Prudhoe Bay area, notwithstanding the ability of property owners to supply many of the services which the borough was empowered to provide (*Mobil Oil Corporation v. Local Boundary Commission*, 1974 A). The court also affirmed the right of the commission to accept petitions of incorporation without subjecting them to legislative veto, because its authority to review incorporations was conferred on it by the legislature.

In an interesting ruling in 1980, the supreme court held that the legislative action on the proposed changes of the Local Boundary Commission did not constitute an illegal "legislative veto," analogous to its attempted use in overturning administrative regulations (see Article II, section 14). The court held that presentation of changes to the legislature, with a time limit for action, was not the exercise of rule-making power but instead the power to change statutes. The expression of this power in the constitution did not carry any implication that general administrative rule making was meant to be forbidden (*State v. A.L.I.V.E. Voluntary*, 1990).

SECTION 13

Agreements; transfer of powers. Agreements, including those for cooperative or joint administration of any functions or powers, may be made by any local government with any other local government, with the State, or with the United States, unless otherwise provided by law or charter. A city may transfer to the borough in which it is located any of its powers or functions unless prohibited by law or charter, and may in like manner revoke the transfer.

The first sentence of section 13 adds flexibility to the powers of local governments by allowing them to enter intergovernmental agreements—with other local governments, with the state, or with the federal government. The second sentence permits cities to transfer powers to boroughs, which facilitates the objectives of the framers in integrating and unifying local government services.

The city of Juneau referred to the first sentence of section 13 when it sought to sell bonds to purchase land that would make Juneau a more attractive site as the state capitol. The supreme court agreed that the city was free to choose the means by which it attained a bargaining position with the state, which might result in acceptance of the offer it made to the state. However, the court pointed out that the means the city chose could not be prohibited, as was the case of Juneau's plan (*City of Juneau v. Hixson*, 1962).

SECTION 14

Local government agency. An agency shall be established by law in the executive branch of the state government to advise and assist local governments. It shall review their activities, collect and publish local government information, and perform other duties prescribed by law.

Section 14 is the only mention in the constitution of an executive agency of government, attesting to the significance framers placed on assisting the formation of local governments. Although the agency is given a regulatory mission, through "review [of] their activities," its primary functions are facilitative. The legislature established the agency first as the Local Affairs Agency and later as the Department of Community and Regional Affairs.

SECTION 15

Special service districts. Special service districts existing at the time a borough is organized shall be integrated with the government of the borough as provided by law.

Section 15 is a further and more specific continuation of sections 1 and 2. With the creation of boroughs as areawide local governments, all other governmental units are to be absorbed within them. At the time of statehood this applied primarily to school districts and a few public utility districts.

One indirect challenge to section 15 was made shortly after statehood, when the city of Anchorage annexed the Fairview Public Utility District. The utility district, surrounded by the city of Anchorage, challenged the constitutionality of the action, but the supreme court supported it (*Fairview Public Utility District No. 1 v. City of Anchorage*, 1962).

Article XI

The Initiative, Referendum, and Recall

Like most of the western states, Alaska's constitution has some populist features, chief among which are provisions in Article XI for the initiative, referendum, and recall. These measures give the people the right to originate law, to respond to—including to repeal—laws passed by the legislature, and to remove officials from office.

Whether the constitution should include such provisions was an issue of debate in the Alaska constitutional convention. Some delegates had a healthy distrust of the legislature and lobbyists and wanted to secure the rights of the people. Other delegates wanted to safeguard the republican form of government. Concern also was expressed about the potential for unreasonable expenditures on special elections.

Delegate Victor Fischer wrote of the opposing views:

> Those supporting inclusion of direct legislative authority cited: (1) successful use of the initiative in other states to enact laws upon which the legislature refused to act, (2) the value of additional checks and balances, and (3) the importance of the legislature's awareness that such power exists with the people. They argued that the initiative and referendum represent progressive government, that the ultimate trust should be with the people, not the legislature; and that the provision constituted a means of proving to Alaskans that their rights would be enhanced under statehood. Opponents of direct legislation provisions argued that the two systems are

> cumbersome, costly, and totally unnecessary when the legislature is truly representative of the people as under the Alaska Constitution, and that the powers of initiative and referendum are outmoded systems instituted fifty years before when legislatures functioned differently. . . . Some also viewed these measures more as tools of organized special interests than as a democratic device of the people.[87]

The final version of Article XI represents a compromise, which provides for the initiative, referendum, and recall but puts limits on their use. The article takes most of its provisions from the revised (1945) constitution of Missouri. Speaking to its defense, delegate Irwin Metcalf said: "Another reason that makes me strongly in favor of the initiative and referendum is the fact . . . that you are having a strongly, centralized executive department. . . . [T]he people ought to have it in black and white, just what the rights are and not leave it to guesswork" (*PACC*, 963).

The constitution hedges all three forms of "direct democracy" with restrictions. The initiative, for example, cannot be used to amend the constitution. The legislature may amend an initiative once passed or enact a similar version before it is voted upon. Furthermore, the recall may not be used to remove judges.

The initiative has been a popular form of direct legislation, with over twenty appearing on ballots since statehood. A large number of propositions analogous to initiatives have appeared on the ballot—advisory votes, ratifications of legislative decisions, and policy questions such as moving the state capital. Only one bona fide referendum has gone to the voters, however.

SECTION 1

> **Initiative and referendum.** The people may propose and enact laws by the initiative, and approve or reject acts of the legislature by the referendum.

Section 1 establishes the basic right of the people to the initiative and referendum. It is not, however, an absolute right, as section 7 significantly qualifies both the initiative and referendum.

In commenting on section 1, the supreme court has said that the initiative and referendum are powers reserved to the people by the constitution and the laws of the state. Further, "the constitutional and statutory provisions under which they proceed should be liberally construed." To that end: "All doubts as to technical deficiencies or failure to comply with the exact letter of procedure will be resolved in favor of the accomplishment of that purpose" (*Boucher v. Engs-trom*, 1974, p. 462).

However, the court has held that the subject of the initiative must be legislation that the legislative body to which it is directed has the power to enact.

---

[87] Fischer, *Alaska's Constitutional Convention*, 79–80.

For this reason, the supreme court rejected an initiative concerning selection of apportionment plans for the unified municipality of Anchorage. It reasoned that prior to unification with the city of Anchorage, the greater Anchorage area borough assembly had no power to bind the subsequently created municipality of Anchorage. Thus, the people also could not accomplish such a result through the initiative process (*Municipality of Anchorage v. Frohne*, 1977).

The supreme court has also held that the subject of the initiative must be law, following other constitutional requirements of legislation, such as the single-subject rule (Article II, section 13). In *Yute Air Alaska, Inc. v. McAlpine* (1985), the court upheld an initiative proposition on "Reducing Government Regulation of Transportation." It found that the proposal on the initiative to seek the repeal of the Jones Act was indeed in the form of "law," and that covering both federal and state deregulation adhered to the single-subject rule.

Attorneys general have further qualified the initiative. An advisory opinion in 1975 said that the initiative could be used to repeal a law if the deadline for filing a referendum had passed or if voters wanted to overturn a law passed through an initiative. In 1982, the attorney general opined that the "Tundra Rebellion" initiative (which challenged federal ownership of unappropriated federal land in Alaska) was unconstitutional and should be ignored by the executive.[88]

SECTION 2

Application. An initiative or referendum is proposed by an application containing the bill to be initiated or the act to be referred. The application shall be signed by not less than one hundred qualified voters as sponsors, and shall be filed with the lieutenant governor. If he finds it in proper form he shall so certify. Details of certification shall be subject to judicial review.

Section 2 sets out the initial procedures to be followed in attempting to exercise the initiative and referendum. The application must contain the bill or act and signatures of at least 100 qualified voters (in order to limit frivolous attempts). The application is filed with the lieutenant governor, who determines whether the application follows the correct form (meeting the requirements of Article XI and statute). If the lieutenant governor declines to certify the application, review is permitted through the courts.

The supreme court has clarified the lieutenant governor's role in certifying petitions. It has held that anyone may challenge the lieutenant governor's certification of a petition (whether denied or approved) and that there is no time limit for judicial review (*Boucher v. Engstrom*, 1974).

---

[88] Harrison, *Alaska's Constitution*, 209.

The judicial review of certification has been challenged in several cases. In *Starr v. Hagglund* (1962), *Walters v. Cease* (1964), and *Boucher v. Engstrom* (1974), the high court held that courts could review an initiative to ascertain its compliance with particular constitutional and statutory provisions, notwithstanding the general limitation that only enacted legislation is subject to judicial review.

SECTION 3

> **Petition.** After certification of the application, a petition containing a summary of the subject matter shall be prepared by the lieutenant governor for circulation by the sponsors. If signed by qualified voters, equal in number to ten percent of those who voted in at least two-thirds of the election districts of the State, it may be filed with the lieutenant governor.

Section 3 continues the outline of procedures needed to bring an initiative or referendum before the voters. It is the lieutenant governor's responsibility to prepare a summary of the subject for circulation. At least 10 percent of the total voting in the preceding general election must sign petitions for them to be filed (a number designed to discourage frivolous initiatives and referenda). Moreover, those signing must represent at least two-thirds of the election districts in the state in order to ensure that there is general statewide support for the effort.

The delegates to the constitutional convention discussed at length the number of signatures required to move an initiative or referendum to the ballot. Proposals ranged from 8 through 15 to as high as 25 percent. This exchange between delegates Douglas Gray and Maurice Johnson conveys the flavor of the discussion:

> [Gray:] I would like to ask the mover how he arrived at the figure "fifteen." I had in mind "twenty five" but I don't know what the difference is between eight, ten or fifteen percent.
>
> [Johnson:] I suppose I arrived at my fifteen like you arrived at your twenty five. It was simply an estimate of what I thought would be a far better percentage of the electorate needed to initiate a proposal under this act. It seemed to me that eight percent was a little bit low. (*PACC*, 977)

The delegates finally voted 27 to 23 (with 5 absent) to set the percentage of signatures at 10 percent.

On one occasion in 1982, proponents of an initiative petition on "personal consumption of fish and game" challenged the lieutenant governor's crafting of the summary as misleading and biased. The initiative's objective was the repeal of the state's subsistence law, which gave preference to rural residents when a scarcity of fish and game resources made limits necessary. The lieutenant governor's summary said that the proposed initiative would eliminate all subsistence-hunting preferences in Alaska, while it would not eliminate federal subsistence preferences.

The supreme court held that the burden of proof rested with the challengers, the summary was not partial, and the lieutenant governor was not obliged to assume that every reader of the petition would take the wording of the summary at precisely its dictionary value. He or she could, said the court, assume that readers would understand that state initiatives are intended to change only state law (*Burgess v. Alaska Lieutenant Governor*, 1982).

SECTION 4

Initiative election. An initiative petition may be filed at any time. The lieutenant governor shall prepare a ballot title and proposition summarizing the proposed law, and shall place them on the ballot for the first statewide election held more than one hundred-twenty days after adjournment of the legislative session following the filing. If, before the election, substantially the same measure has been enacted, the petition is void.

Section 4 completes the outline of procedures for moving an initiative onto the election ballot. It places no time restrictions on the filing of a petition, and it entrusts the lieutenant governor with preparing the ballot title and summary. The initiative is then placed on the ballot of the next statewide election that occurs more than 120 days after the adjournment of the legislative session following the filing. This period of time gives the legislature the opportunity to gauge whether it will preempt the initiative process by passing similar legislation. If it does, then the petition is canceled.

A large area of concern during constitutional convention deliberations on Article XI concerned the potential drafting problems or cost of initiatives. Delegate Jack Hinckel noted that if the legislature acted on the subject of a petition, negating the need for it, there would be no need to hold the election (*PACC*, 1050). This was accomplished in the last sentence of section 4. The delegates also adopted an amendment eliminating special elections for referenda and initiatives, which accounts for the common requirement that they be voted on in statewide elections, whether primary, general, or a special election called for some other purpose.

The supreme court has interpreted the time period required before the initiative is placed on the ballot, the lieutenant governor's role in placing the initiative on the ballot, and the ability of the legislature to preempt petitions.

In *Starr v. Hagglund* (1962), the court held that the time requirement for initiative elections was a minimum. It was not the *only* time during which the initiative could be voted on.

In objecting to an initiative proposition that would deregulate air travel, Yute Air Alaska contended that the constitution required that signatures in support of the initiative be verified before the legislature both convened and adjourned in order for the initiative to be submitted to voters. The verification process done by the lieutenant governor, said the court, did not toll the time in which the initiative was to be considered by the legislature and proceed onto the ballot (or be voided by legislative enactment of substantially the same measure). The high court reasoned that it sufficed that a facially valid initiative be filed (*Yute Air Alaska, Inc. v. McAlpine*, 1985).

The supreme court dealt directly with the process and conditions by which enactments of the legislature could operate to prevent an initiative from appearing on the ballot in *Warren v. Boucher* (1975). In that case, the legislature adopted an act on election campaigns that the lieutenant governor, as advised by the attorney general, found was substantially the same as an initiative on campaign contributions and expenditures. The court noted that section 4 did not confer on any agency the power to determine whether acts and initiatives were "substantially the same" (p. 733). However, it found that the legislature had the power to determine a method and that the legislature's delegation of this power to the lieutenant governor (who supervises elections in Alaska), with review by the courts, was satisfactory. The court concluded that the legislature should have reasonably broad discretion in deciding how far the legislative act should differ from the provisions of the initiative.

As noted in the commentary on section 3, the court has not required the lieutenant governor, in crafting the initiative title and summary, to ensure that each reader will take the wording at its precise dictionary value (*Burgess v. Alaska Lieutenant Governor*, 1982).

Reforming Alaska's campaign finance laws provided a textbook example of what the framers had in mind for section 4. The legislature had balked at tightening campaign contribution limits, which gave disproportionate influence in the Alaska political process to corporations, unions, special interest groups, and Outside interests. Pressure for change began with Democratic governor Steve Cowper, who made campaign finance reform an agenda item during his administration (1986–1990), and pressure increased in the 1990s. In the absence of legislative action, a reform group led by Anchorage attorney Mike Frank collected over 32,000 signatures (well above the minimum) to place on the 1996 ballot an initiative limiting contributions from individuals to $500 and banning corporation, union, and other interest group donations.

Certification of the petition caused legislative leaders to take the issue seriously, hold hearings, and pass a comparable measure in 1996. During the legislative process, however, changes were made to the initiative's text: contributions from outside Alaska and Alaska political parties were limited, but not prohibited. This reflected deliberation in the legislature on first amendment rights of campaigners and the fear of a court challenge if the stricter limits were enacted. Also, the legislature added a ban on fundraising outside of election years. Most reformers, including Frank, were satisfied with the legislative compromise, and the lieutenant governor voided the initiative. The state's leading newspaper opined: "Without pressure from the citizen petition, campaign reform would have gone where it always goes—nowhere. With the initiative as a fallback, reform forces dealt from a position of strength."[89]

SECTION 5

Referendum election. A referendum petition may be filed only within ninety days after adjournment of the legislative session at which the act was passed. The lieutenant governor shall prepare a ballot title and proposition summarizing the act and shall place them on the ballot for the first statewide election held more than one hundred-eighty days after adjournment of that session.

Section 5 is the companion of section 4 and completes the outline of procedures for moving referenda onto the ballot. It does specify a time period for filing, limiting this to 90 days after the end of the legislative session. The lieutenant governor is responsible for preparing the title and summary of the act, which may not be voted on sooner than 180 days after the end of the legislative session. This time requirement is intended, as is that in section 4, to discourage frivolous filing of petitions while permitting sufficient public debate.

Section 5 was invoked by individuals objecting to the implementation of the Mandatory Borough Act in 1963. They argued that the filing of a petition for a referendum postponed the effective date of legislation pending the outcome of the referendum election. However, the supreme court, in *Walters v. Cease* (1964), disagreed. It pointed out that the referendum provisions of the Alaska Constitution were unique in that they do not specifically state whether the referral of an act of the legislature suspends the effective date of the act. However, based on the discussions of the constitutional convention as well as reference to analogous provisions (sections 17 and 18 of Article II), the court held that the act would remain in full force until the contrary had been established by the completed referendum process.

SECTION 6

Enactment. If a majority of the votes cast on the proposition favor its adoption, the initiated measure is enacted. If a majority of the votes cast on the proposition favor the rejection of an act referred, it is rejected. The lieutenant governor shall certify the election returns. An initiated law becomes effective ninety days after certification, is not subject to veto, and may not be repealed by the legislature within two years of its effective date. It may be amended at any time. An act rejected by referendum is void

---

[89] *Anchorage Daily News*, May 12, 1996.

thirty days after certification. Additional procedures for the initiative and referendum may be prescribed by law.

For either an initiative or a referendum to be adopted, only a simple majority of votes is required, and the lieutenant governor is made responsible for certification of the election. If an initiative proposition attracts a majority vote, it becomes effective 90 days following certification. Unlike ordinary legislation, it may not be vetoed by the governor or repealed within two years of becoming effective. However, it is like ordinary legislation in that the legislature may amend it at any time. If a majority votes for the referendum, the legislative act referred becomes void 30 days following certification. (The constitution does not prohibit the legislature from readopting a law overturned by a referendum.) The last sentence of section 6 gives the legislature the authority to craft additional procedures for both initiatives and referenda.

Several court cases have compared initiatives to ordinary legislation with respect to the amendment provision. In *Warren v. Boucher* (1975), the high court held that section 6 gave broad authority to the legislature to alter the terms of an initiated law through the process of amendment:

> This power amounts to a check or balance against the initiative process. No doubt the legislature was given this power to assure that initiatives which were ill-advised, which might seriously cripple or frustrate the sound workings of government, or which might be impracticable, could be altered or corrected rapidly by the legislature. It was obviously intended by the framers that the initiative process should not be permitted to disrupt vital governmental functions or to impose intolerable burdens upon established administrative systems. To this end the legislature was given the ability to substitute its judgment for that of the proponents of an initiative, (p. 737)

In *Warren v. Thomas* (1977), the supreme court similarly held that the legislature's amendment of a conflict of interest law, enacted by initiative, was constitutional. It ruled that the legislature had broad powers to amend laws enacted by initiative; in this particular case, it found that the amendment did not effect a "repeal" of the initiated law, which would have violated section 6. This case, said the court in *Yute Air Alaska, Inc. v. McAlpine* (1985), like the situation tested in the 1975 case, *Warren v. Boucher* (where the legislature preempted an initiative on campaign disclosures), established that provisions of section 6 vested the legislature "with broad powers to protect the state against the untoward effects of initiatives" (p. 1179).

SECTION 7

Restrictions. The initiative shall not be used to dedicate revenues, make or repeal appropriations, create courts, define the jurisdiction of courts or prescribe their rules, or enact local or special legislation. The referendum shall not be applied to dedications of revenue, to appropriations, to local or special legislation, or to laws necessary for the immediate preservation of the public peace, health, or safety.

Section 7 is the most controversial section of this article, in that it limits the range of initiatives and referenda, thus narrowing the power of the people to directly alter laws. Neither initiatives nor referenda may dedicate or eliminate dedications of revenues, make or alter appropriations, or enact or alter local or special legislation. Additionally, initiatives may not be used to change the judiciary's operations through such means as creating courts, changing court rules or the jurisdiction of the courts. Finally, referenda may not be applied to laws needed for protection of the public peace, health, or safety.

Delegates to the constitutional convention were influenced by the experience of other states whose constitutions placed no restrictions on the subject matter of initiatives. They adopted the appropriations restriction to avoid negative experiences of those states, which posed dangers of "rash, discriminatory, and irresponsible acts."[90] Delegate Warren Taylor explained the particular concern they had with give-away programs, which had an inherent popular appeal (*PACC*, 931).

The supreme court has reviewed—and often rejected—initiatives based on the criteria of section 7. When, in 1963, the legislature passed the Mandatory Borough Act, which incorporated organized boroughs in eight areas of the state, opponents sought to refer the act to the people in a statewide election. The supreme court ruled that the act was local and special legislation within the meaning of section 7, and thus a referendum could not be applied to it (*Walters v. Cease*, 1964).

When supporters of relocating the capital from Juneau to some other part of the state except Anchorage or Fairbanks prepared an initiative, opponents of moving the capital sought to keep the issue off the ballot by invoking the section 7 restriction against enacting local or special legislation. The supreme court found that the initiative did not fit into the classification of local or special legislation (*Boucher v. Engstrom*, 1974). The court observed that the question of where Alaska's capital should be located had obvious statewide interest and impact. Then it clarified the meanings of special and local by stating: "Legislation, whether enacted by the legislature or by the initiative, need not operate evenly on all parts of the state to avoid being classified as local or special. The critical element is whether there is a rational basis for the particular classification" (p. 463).

The supreme court has interpreted the meaning of the restrictions on making or repealing appropriations in several cases. In *Thomas v. Bailey* (1979), the court invalidated the Beirne initiative (Alaska Homestead Act), which made available 30 million acres of state land to residents for homesteading. It determined that

[90] Fischer, *Alaska's Constitutional Convention*, 80–81.

section 7 prohibited an initiative whose primary object was to require the outflow of state assets in the form of land as well as money: "[T]he Alaska Homestead Act would substantially deplete the state government of valuable assets just as surely as an initiative allowing to residents of unspecified years large sums of money" (p. 7).

In 1987, the supreme court invalidated the initiative of a political action committee, which sought to sell the municipally owned electric utility (valued at over $30 million) to a private, nonprofit, cooperative for $1. This, too, the court observed was unconstitutionally making an "appropriation" (*Alaska Conservative Political Action Committee v. Municipality of Anchorage*, 1987, p. 938).

The following year, the supreme court invalidated one section of an initiative, which sought to establish a separate community college system within the state government and require the university to transfer property to the new system. The court found that the proposed initiative made an impermissible appropriation to the extent it specified the amount of property to be transferred, even though it did not spell out exactly what property would be transferred (*McAlpine v. University of Alaska*, 1988).

The supreme court also invalidated a proposed initiative which would have set limits on attorneys' contingent fee recoveries (*Citizens Coalition for Tort Reform v. McAlpine*, 1991). The court held that this was an attempt to prescribe a rule of court, which was precluded by section 7.

SECTION 8

Recall. All elected public officials in the State, except judicial officers, are subject to recall by the voters of the State or political subdivision from which elected. Procedures and grounds for recall shall be prescribed by the legislature.

Section 8 on recall is more general than the provisions on direct legislation. It simply announces that all public officials, state and local (except judges), may be recalled and gives the legislature authority to establish detailed procedures and criteria. This section has not been subject to judicial interpretation.

Delegates to the constitutional convention debated recall procedures for some time. Victor Fischer proposed an amendment that would have required 20 percent of the electorate to sign a recall petition. The petition would be limited to 200 words and a special election would be held within 60 to 90 days after certification of the petition (*PACC*, 1233). This and several other amendments were defeated, and the delegates finally voted to allow the legislature to establish procedures. It has established grounds for recall (incompetence, lack of fitness, corruption, or neglect of duties) in statute—AS 15.45.470–720 provides for state officials and AS 29.26.240–350 for local officials—and procedures for reaching the ballot.

Article XII

General Provisions

Delegates to the constitutional convention called this the "miscellaneous article" because it covers a number of different topics that do not fit well in the other parts of the constitution. In addition to such provisions as defining phrases used throughout the constitution, setting up a merit and retirement system for state employment, in sections 12 and 13 it agreed in advance to conditions for admission to the Union.

SECTION 1

State boundaries. The State of Alaska shall consist of all the territory, together with the territorial waters, appurtenant thereto, included in the Territory of Alaska upon the date of ratification of this constitution by the people of Alaska.

This section identifies the territory and boundaries of the new state as those of the Territory of Alaska, following the description given in statehood legislation then before the Congress.

SECTION 2

Intergovernmental relations. The State and its political subdivisions may cooperate with the United States and its territories, and with other states and their political subdivisions on matters of common interest. The respective legislative bodies may make appropriations for this purpose.

Section 2 authorizes cooperative ties between the state and local governments and any other governmental entity in the United States. It is analogous to section 13 of Article X. The section is a recommendation of the *Model State Constitution*,[91] which facilitates the formation of interstate compacts and relationships of local government units with federal agencies.

SECTION 3

Office of profit. Service in the armed forces of the United States or of the State is not an office or position of profit as the term is used in this constitution.

Section 3 permits members of the U.S. military or national guard to serve as legislators, executives, or even judges of Alaska. Section 3 is one of two exceptions to the disqualification section of Article II, section 5. The second excludes from the definition of office of profit "employment by or election to a constitutional convention." Section 3 is read together with Article II, section 5; Article III, section 6; and Article IV, section 14. These articles prohibit members of the legislative, executive, and judicial branches from holding "positions of profit" (customarily defined as salaried, nontemporary employment) under the United States or the state. In the words of the supreme court in *Begich v. Jefferson* (1968), this reflects the intent "to guard against conflicts of interest, self-aggrandizement, concentration of power, and dilution of the separation of powers in regard to the exercise by these governmental officials of the executive, judicial, and legislative functions of our state government" (p. 35).

SECTION 4

Disqualification for disloyalty. No person who advocates, or who aids or belongs to any party or organization or association which advocates, the overthrow by force or violence of the government of the United States or of the State shall be qualified to hold any public office of trust or profit under this constitution.

Section 4 provides for the disqualification from any public office of those who are disloyal to the United States or the state. The section was taken from statehood bills before Congress during the constitutional convention.

---

[91] National Municipal League, *Model State Constitution*, 19, 49–50.

SECTION 5

Oath of office. All public officers, before entering upon the duties of their offices, shall take and subscribe to the following oath or affirmation: "I do solemnly swear (or affirm) that I will support and defend the Constitution of the United States and the Constitution of the State of Alaska, and that I will faithfully discharge my duties as to the best of my ability." The legislature may prescribe further oaths or affirmations.

The oath of office described in section 5 resembles that found in most state constitutions; it, too, was included in statehood legislation before the Congress.

SECTION 6

Merit system. The legislature shall establish a system under which the merit principle will govern the employment of persons by the state.

Section 6 requires, as a matter of constitutional mandate, that the state civil service system operate following the merit principle. It was a recommendation of the *Model State Constitution*.[92] The legislature has established the personnel system of Alaska following this mandate in Title 39 of the Alaska Statutes.

SECTION 7

Retirement systems. Membership in employee retirement systems of the State or its political subdivisions shall constitute a contractual relationship. Accrued benefits of these systems shall not be diminished or impaired.

By making the state and local government retirement systems contractual relationships between employees and the state and its political subdivisions, the state assumes obligations to protect these systems. This is specified further in the second sentence, which requires the state to insure that benefits for employees are not reduced.

Section 7 has been interpreted by the supreme court in two cases. When voters in 1976 repealed the short-lived Elected Public Officers' Retirement System, the court was asked whether those covered by the retirement system (including those participating in it for only a few months) would be entitled to benefits under that system upon retirement. The court held that section 7 covered all persons holding salaried positions with the state, including elected public officers, who would be eligible for the schedule of benefits upon retirement (*State v. Allen*, 1981).

---

[92] Ibid., 17, 48.

In *Hammond v. Hoffbeck* (1981), the supreme court considered action brought against the state by the public safety employees' association, which contended that reductions in the state's public employee retirement system were unconstitutional. The high court held that employees' rights to benefits vested on employment and enrollment in the system, and not when employees become eligible, as spelled out in the state's revision to the retirement system. Moreover, 1976 amendments that reduced disability and death benefits affected adversely those employed, and thus were unconstitutional.

SECTION 8

Residual power. The enumeration of specified powers in this constitution shall not be construed as limiting the powers of the State.

Section 8 recognizes that the state has residual powers in addition to the express and specified powers described throughout the constitution, and that its powers should be broadly construed. This section has not been subject to judicial interpretation.

SECTION 9

Provisions self-executing. The provisions of this constitution shall be construed to be self-executing whenever possible.

The Alaska Constitution has a number of provisions which take effect without legislation or other action of the legislature, such as the procedure for initiating and referring laws to the people in Article XL This provision indicates that other sections should receive the implementation by the legislature that they require.

SECTION 10

Interpretation. Titles and subtitles shall not be used in construing this constitution. Personal pronouns used in this constitution shall be construed as including either sex.

The first sentence of section 10 means that the language of constitutional sections is the basis for interpretation, and not the titles or subtitles. The second section refers to personal pronouns used throughout the constitution, which are male exclusively; they can imply either males or females.

SECTION 11

Law-making power. As used in this constitution, the terms "by law" and "by the legislature," or variations of these terms, are used interchangeably when related to law-making powers. Unless clearly inapplicable, the lawmaking powers assigned to the legislature may be exercised by the people through the initiative, subject to the limitations of Article XI.

The first sentence of section 11 clarifies the language used throughout the constitution to describe law-making powers. Whether the term is "by law" or "by the legislature" or some variation such as "according to law," the meaning is "the law-making power of the legislature." The second sentence equates the law-making power of the legislature with the people's power through the initiative process unless inapplicable or restricted, as in Article XI, section 7.

This section has been subject to several high court interpretations. In *Starr v. Hagglund* (1962), the supreme court ruled that to amend the section of the constitution providing that the state capital shall be at Juneau (section 20 of Article XV, Schedule of Transitional Measures) did not require a constitutional amendment. It could be done "by law," either through the legislature or through popular initiative.

The high court applied section 11 to resolve the issue of whether the lieutenant governor had legally declared an initiative proposal void. It held that section 11 gave the legislature the power to enact a method of determining whether two provisions were "substantially the same," and this power could be delegated to the lieutenant governor (*Warren v. Boucher*, 1975, p. 733).

When the state included University of Alaska land within a state park, the university complained that the state had violated a trust relationship and should have obtained university approval before transferring the lands. The supreme court held that the constitutional statement that university property was to be "administered and disposed of according to law" allowed the legislature to dispose of university land without obtaining the university's approval (*State v. University of Alaska*, 1981, p. 808).

Finally, the high court has interpreted the second sentence of section 11 to mean that the requirements (such as the one-subject rule) for initiative propositions cannot be more restrictive than those for legislative action (*Yute Air Alaska, Inc. v. McAlpine*, 1985).

SECTION 12

Disclaimer and agreement. The State of Alaska and its people forever disclaim all right and title in or to any property belonging to the United States or subject to its disposition, and not granted or confirmed to the State or its political subdivisions, by or under the act admitting Alaska to the Union. The State and its people further disclaim all right or title in or to any property, including fishing rights, the right or title to which may be held by or for any Indian, Eskimo, or Aleut, or community thereof, as that right or title is defined in the act of admission. The State and its people agree that, unless otherwise provided by Congress, the property, as described in this section, shall remain subject to the absolute disposition of the United States. They further agree that no taxes will be imposed upon any such property, until otherwise provided by the Congress. This tax exemption shall not apply to property held by individuals in fee without restrictions on alienation.

Section 12, along with section 13, states the conditions under which Alaska entered the federal union. The five sentences disclaim rights and titles to U.S. property, including fishing rights, by the state of Alaska, its political subdivisions, and its people. The section acknowledges that U.S. property and property subject to U.S. disposition will continue to remain under federal control. The section provides that no taxes will be imposed on U.S. property, but allows taxes on private property that is held by individuals and has free title.

Delegates to the constitutional convention understood the necessity for including the disclaimer clauses in order to avoid land disputes between the federal government and the new state, but they were uncomfortable about disclaiming interests when the enabling act had not yet been written. (Federal enabling acts were written prior to the constitutions of almost all new states.) Moreover, the delegates did not trust Congress to write an act acceptable to Alaskans (*PACC*, 3060). As it happened, the Alaska Statehood Act passed by Congress contained comparable language in section 8.

Section 12 was interpreted by the supreme court shortly after statehood. The Metlakatla Indian community and the villages of Kake and Angoon sought to halt enforcement of the law prohibiting the use of fish traps, making specific reference to the second sentence of section 12, which disclaimed title to Native fishing rights. The high court held that no act of Congress had established any right or title in fishing rights for Alaska Natives at the time the compact between the United States and Alaska for admission to statehood was made (*Metlakatla Indian Community, Annette Island Reserve v. Egan*, 1961). Thus, the Alaska law prohibiting the operation of fish traps was applicable to Natives.

However, the reference to Native rights in the second sentence is one of the bases to the resolution of Native claims to land in the Alaska Native Claims Settlements Act of 1971.

SECTION 13

Consent to act of admission. All provisions of the act admitting Alaska to the Union which reserve rights or powers to the United States, as well as those prescribing the terms or conditions of the grants of lands or other property, are consented to fully by the State and its people.

Section 13 is read together with section 12. It pledges the state and its people to observe the conditions of the enabling act as they pertained to U.S. rights and powers and to conditions of the transfer of lands and other property to Alaska.

This, too, was a controversial section at the constitutional convention. Reluctantly, it was agreed to because it was obvious that Alaska would be required to consent to a statehood bill and the conditions largely had been specified in pending legislation before Congress.

Section 13 was invoked in a three-way exchange of land between the state of Alaska, the United States, and the Cook Inlet Region, Inc., a Native regional corporation. The issue brought to the supreme court was whether the exchange violated state constitutional prohibitions against alienation of mineral rights in state lands. The supreme court held that there were no specific limitations to mineral alienation in section 13, nor were any terms or conditions incorporated by reference to an existing statute or code since the Statehood Act had not yet been enacted by Congress (*State v. Lewis,* 1977). While section 13 expressed advance consent to terms or conditions that might be required by Congress as a condition to admission to the Union, the court ruled that it did not embed any particular restrictions into the state constitution.

Article XIII

Amendment and Revision

Article XIII describes the processes through which the constitution can be amended. There are two ways to propose constitutional amendments. First, the legislature by a two-thirds vote may propose constitutional change, and second, a convention may discuss revision of the constitution and propose changes in it. The convention may be called by the legislature at any time or by the people through the initiative process. A third method of calling a convention is innovative—the automatic placing of the convention call on the ballot every ten years. The legislative route is the only one that had been followed in proposals to amend the constitution as of 1996. There is only one way to adopt an amendment—through a ratification by a majority of voters in a general election. The constitution may not be amended via the initiative process.

Delegates to the constitutional convention wanted the amendment process to reflect a happy medium: it should not be so easy as to encourage frivolous amendments or the passion of the moment, but it should not be so difficult as to discourage needed change. That is why they called for an extraordinary majority in the legislature but also placed the issue on the ballot every decade. They insisted on a process involving discussion, debate, and deliberation, and one in which the people had the final say.

The Alaska Constitution has been amended only 24 times in the 40 years since its adoption in 1956, which is below the postwar average for the amendment of state constitutions. This is at least partly attributable to the lack of heavily detailed provisions and the assignment of so many matters to the legislature.

SECTION 1

Amendments. Amendments to this constitution may be proposed by a two-thirds vote of each house of the legislature. The lieutenant governor shall prepare a ballot title and proposition summarizing each proposed amendment, and shall place them on the ballot for the next general election. If a majority of the votes cast on the proposition favor the amendment, it shall be adopted. Unless otherwise provided in the amendment, it becomes effective thirty days after the certification of the election returns by the lieutenant governor.

Section 1 sets forth the primary means through which the Alaska Constitution may be amended. A two-thirds vote in each house of the state legislature is required to bring the proposed amendment to the voters. The proposed amendment is in the form of a resolution; it may not be vetoed by the governor, whose role in the revision process is limited to proposing amendments to the legislature. The lieutenant governor prepares the ballot title and summary for each proposed amendment and orders their placement on the next general election ballot. He or she also certifies the results of the balloting, which requires a majority of votes cast for adoption. Such amendments take effect in 30 days from the certification.

The framers did not allow the people to amend the constitution through use of the initiative, for that would have circumvented the deliberative process; and as of 1996, there has been no effort to authorize amendment through initiative. As a result, the Alaska Constitution is somewhat more difficult to amend than those of other states. On the other hand, there also are no limits on the number of amendments the legislature may submit to the voters.

Two changes have been made to the second sentence of section 1. It was amended in 1974 by replacing the word *statewide with general* (toward the end of the sentence), for more citizens vote in general elections than in primaries, which are the first statewide elections following the close of the legislative sessions. (Note the higher vote totals on proposed amendments after 1974, shown in the Appendix.) Second, the legislature set up a process for review of the wording of the ballot title and proposition prepared by the lieutenant governor, because it questioned the objectivity of wording for a 1976 proposal.[93]

What may or may not be amended was interpreted by the supreme court in a 1962 decision (*Starr v. Hagglund*). A divided court agreed that a change of the provision in the constitution designating Juneau as the capital could be made by initiative or statute instead of by constitutional amendment. The court explained its decision by observing that the provision was in an article of the constitution titled "Schedule of Transition Measures." Although the capital provision appeared in the body of the constitution, it was permitted to be changed without the necessity of a constitutional amendment.

---

[93] Harrison, *Alaska's Constitution*, 231–232.

A second interpretation of the need for constitutional amendment is found in the supreme court's decision in *State v. Lewis* (1977). A large issue in that case concerned whether the constitution contained prohibitions of alienation of mineral rights that would preclude a land exchange between the state, a Native corporation, and the federal government. Section 13 of Article 12 pledged the consent of the state and its people to "all provisions of the act admitting Alaska to the Union which reserve rights or powers to the United States." Moreover, section 6(i) of the Statehood Act (Alaska Statehood Act, Public Law 85-508, 1958) contained restrictions on alienability of mineral rights, which appeared to embed in the constitution a prohibition on transfer of mineral rights, such as would occur in a land exchange.

The supreme court argued, however, that Article XIII, section 13, and a similar provision in Article VIII, section 9, were not specific restrictions on alienation, but merely a consent to be bound by such reservations as would be required by the U.S. Congress. All that was required to release the restrictions, the court held, was congressional consent. Once it was secured, the Alaska legislature, in agreeing to the disposition of the land and mineral rights, was not violating any specific provision of the Alaska Constitution. For these reasons, then, the high court concluded that a constitutional amendment was not mandated.

SECTION 2

Convention. The legislature may call constitutional conventions at any time.

A constitutional convention is the second means in Alaska through which the constitution may be amended, and it is addressed in this and the following sections. The section appears to allow only the legislature to call a convention at will, but voters may do so also. Article XI, section 7, does not bar the use of the initiative to call a convention. As of 1996, neither the legislature nor the people, via the initiative process, had called a constitutional convention.

SECTION 3

Call by referendum. If during any ten-year period a constitutional convention has not been held, the lieutenant governor shall place on the ballot for the next general election the question: "Shall there be a Constitutional Convention?" If a majority of the votes cast on the question are in the negative, the question need not be placed on the ballot until the end of the next ten-year period. If a majority of the votes cast on the question are in the affirmative, delegates to the convention shall be chosen at the next regular statewide election, unless the legislature provides for the election of the delegates at a special election. The lieutenant governor shall issue the call for the convention. Unless other provisions have been made by law, the call shall conform as nearly as possible to the act calling the Alaska Constitutional Convention of 1955, including, but not limited to, number of members, districts, election and certification of delegates, and submission and ratification of revisions and ordinances. The appropriation provisions of the call shall be self-executing and shall constitute a first claim on the state treasury.

Section 3 presents an innovative part of the Alaska Constitution—its decennial call for a referendum on holding a constitutional convention. It spells out the procedure in some detail, making the process nearly automatic so that nothing will interfere with the expression of the people's preferences. The call must be made at least once in ten years if a constitutional convention has not been held. The lieutenant governor is charged with placing the question on the ballot, but section 3 gives the exact words of the question. If a majority of the voters disapprove, the question need not appear on the ballot for another ten years. This sentence was the result of an amendment at the constitutional convention, and was intended to ensure that if the people voted "no" at the end of a ten-year period, the question would not be on the ballot each election until they voted "yes" (*PACC*, 3436).

If, however, a majority agrees, the lieutenant governor is instructed to issue a call for the convention. Delegates are to be selected at the next statewide election unless the legislature calls a special election for this purpose. The convention call is to be based on the act calling the constitutional convention in 1955.

Alaska has not had a constitutional convention, either one called by the legislature, by the voters through the initiative process, or under the terms of section 3. However, the question has been placed on the ballot four times, and in a 1970 election, the proposition to call a constitutional convention received an affirmative vote of 34,911 to 34,472. This election was challenged, which brought the meaning of section 3 to the supreme court.

The issue concerned the language of the constitutional referendum ballot. Despite the explicit requirement of section 3, the ballot proposition was worded to read: "REFERENDUM As required by the Constitution of the State of Alaska, Art. XIII, Section 3: Shall there be a constitutional convention?" The high court ruled that this wording suggested that the constitution required that a convention be held when all the constitution required was that a referendum be held. An expert witness testified that the prefatory phrase had introduced a "significant bias" toward an affirmative vote on the proposition, and the bias infringed on the electorate's right to vote on the question (*Boucher v. Bomhoff*, 1972, p. 80). The court invalidated the election results, and called for a new vote at the next general election (where it was defeated).

SECTION 4

Powers. Constitutional conventions shall have plenary power to amend or revise the constitution, subject only to ratification by the people. No call for a constitutional convention shall limit these powers of the convention.

Section 4 gives a free grant to the convention to amend, revise, and even substitute a new for the existing constitution. All changes to the constitution, however, must be approved by the people. The unlimited nature of the constitutional convention is used by supporters of the existing constitution to oppose any call for a constitutional convention.

Article XIV

Apportionment Schedule

The original provisions of the apportionment article are obsolete. They have been replaced by current reapportionment under Article VI as detailed in the April 20, 1993, *Report and Proposed Permanent Plan of the Governor's Advisory Reapportionment Board,* and May 27, 1993, *Proclamation of Permanent Reapportionment and Redistricting and Accompanying Statement* (State of Alaska, Office of Lieutenant Governor, Juneau).

Article XV

Schedule of Transitional Measures

Article XV originally contained 25 sections, which were designed to provide an orderly transition from territorial rule to state government. Three sections were added in 1982 to implement the appropriation limit (Article IX, section 16).

The only controversial section of the article is section 20, on the location of the state capital in Juneau. Initially, it was proposed to make the section part of the constitution itself. After discussion, the delegates agreed to include it in the schedule appended to the constitution. When asked whether the capital could be changed, the chair of the Committee on Ordinances and Transitional Measures replied: "After the state became a government, under the ordinance here it would be possible to change the capital by method of the legislature or it would even be open to the initiative and referendum" (*PACC*, 87).

When sponsors of an initiative petitioned to move the capital from Juneau to some place in western Alaska, the superior court enjoined the secretary of state from placing the proposition on the ballot, arguing that section 20 could only be altered through a constitutional amendment. The supreme court held that section 20 (and inferentially, all of Article XV) was not intended to be a permanent and abiding part of the fundamental law of the state. The court said that the section could be changed by law, as enacted either by the legislature or by the people through the initiative (*Starr v. Hagglund*, 1962).

Section 24 of Article XV called for the placement of three ordinances on the ballot. The first was the ratification of the constitution. Ordinance 2 provided for the adoption of the "Alaska-Tennessee Plan." This plan would place on the ballot the election of two U.S. senators and one U.S. representative. Upon election, they would lobby Congress for Alaska statehood, following the example of Tennessee representatives, who used this method to gain statehood.

Ordinance 3 provided for the abolition of fish traps. The traps, which were of log-pole construction, were a very effective means of harvesting salmon for use by canneries. They also were a symbol of the absentee control of Alaska's fisheries resources, because they excluded the resident fishermen of southeast Alaska from much of the salmon harvest. The proposed ordinance was extensively discussed at the constitutional convention. Delegate Bob Robertson made a strong statement against the fish trap ordinance: "This schedule is penal in nature; it is legislative in nature . . . [and] it violates the first policy resolution adopted by the Convention, that our Constitution should consist of a framework of government and not of legislative law" (*PACC*, 3771). However, most delegates supported the proposed ordinance, and it was included as ordinance 3. All three ordinances passed by large margins in the 1956 election.

The transitional schedule is included—without substantive commentary—because it remains part of the Alaska Constitution. However, it is not a functional part of the state's basic law, and at some future modernization of the constitution it will likely be eliminated.

■ SCHEDULE OF TRANSITIONAL MEASURES

To provide an orderly transition from a territorial to a state form of government, it is declared and ordained:

SECTION 1

Continuance of laws. All laws in force in the Territory of Alaska on the effective date of this constitution and consistent therewith shall continue in force until they expire by their own limitation, are amended, or repealed.

SECTION 2

Saving of existing rights and liabilities. Except as otherwise provided in this constitution, all rights, titles, actions, suits, contracts, and liabilities and all civil, criminal, or administrative proceedings shall continue unaffected by the change from territorial to state government, and the State shall be the legal successor to the Territory in these matters.

SECTION 3

Local government. Cities, school districts, health districts, public utility districts, and other local subdivisions of government existing on the effective date of this constitution shall continue to exercise their powers and functions under existing law, pending enactment of legislation to carry out the provisions of this constitution. New local subdivisions of government shall be created only in accordance with this constitution.

SECTION 4

Continuance of office. All officers of the Territory, or under its laws, on the effective date of this constitution shall continue to perform the duties of their offices in a manner consistent with this constitution until they are superseded by officers of the State.

SECTION 5

Corresponding qualifications. Residence, citizenship, or other qualifications under the Territory may be used toward the fulfillment of corresponding qualifications required by this constitution.

SECTION 6

Governor to proclaim election. When the people of the Territory ratify this constitution and it is approved by the duly constituted authority of the United States, the governor of the Territory shall, within thirty days after receipt of the official notification of such approval, issue a proclamation and take necessary measures to hold primary and general elections for all state elective offices provided for by this constitution.

SECTION 7

First state elections. The primary election shall take place not less than forty nor more than ninety days after the proclamation by the governor of the Territory. The general election shall take place not less than ninety days after the primary election. The elections shall be governed by this constitution and by applicable territorial laws.

SECTION 8

United States senators and representatives. The officers to be elected at the first general election shall include two senators and one representative to serve in the Congress of the United States, unless senators and a representative have been previously elected and seated. One senator shall be elected for the long term and one senator for the short term, each term to expire on the third day of January in an odd-numbered year to be determined by authority of the United States. The term of the representative shall expire on the third day of January in the odd-numbered year immediately following his assuming office. If the first representative is elected in an even-numbered year to take office in that year, a representative shall be elected at the same time to fill the full term commencing on the third day of January of the following year, and the same person may be elected for both terms.

SECTION 9

Terms of first governor and lieutenant governor. The First Governor and Lieutenant Governor shall hold office for a term beginning with the day on which they assume office, and ending at noon on the first Monday in December of the even-numbered year following the next presidential election. This term shall count as a full term for purposes of determining eligibility for reelection only if it is four years or more in duration. [The secretary of state title was changed to "lieutenant governor" by constitutional amendment in 1970.]

SECTION 10

Election of first senators. At the first State general election, one senator shall be chosen for a two-year term from each of the following senate districts, described in Section 2 of Article XIV: A, B, D, E, G, I, J, L, N, and O. At the same election, one senator shall be chosen for a four-year term from each of the following senate districts described in Section 2 of Article XIV: A, C, E, F, H, J, K, M, N, and P. [These senate districts no longer exist.]

SECTION 11

Terms of first state legislators. The first State legislators shall hold office for a term beginning with the day on which they assume office and ending at noon on the fourth Monday in January after the next general election, except that senators elected for four-year terms shall serve an additional two years thereafter. If the first general election is held in an even-numbered year, it shall be deemed to be the general election for that year.

SECTION 12

Election returns. The returns of the first general election shall be made, canvassed, and certified in the manner prescribed by law. The governor of the Territory shall certify the results to the President of the United States.

SECTION 13

Assumption of office. When the President of the United State issues a proclamation announcing the results of the election, and the State has been admitted into the Union, the officers elected and qualified shall assume office.

SECTION 14

First session of legislature. The governor shall call a special session of the first state legislature within thirty days after the presidential proclamation unless a regular session of the legislature falls within that period. The special session shall not be limited as to duration.

SECTION 15

Office holding by first legislators. The provisions of Section 5 of Article II shall not prohibit any member of the first State legislature from holding any office or position created during his first term.

SECTION 16

First judicial council. The first members of the judicial council shall, notwithstanding Section 8 of Article IV, be appointed for terms as follows: three attorney members for one, three, and five years respectively; three non-attorney members for two, four, and six years respectively. The six members so appointed shall, in accordance with Section 5 of Article IV, submit to the governor nominations to fill the initial vacancies on the superior court and the supreme court, including the office of chief justice. After the initial vacancies on the superior and supreme courts are filled, the chief justice shall assume his seat on the judicial council.

SECTION 17

Transfer of court jurisdiction. Until the courts provided for in Article IV are organized, the courts, their jurisdiction, and the judicial system shall remain as constituted on the date of admission unless otherwise provided by law. When the State courts are organized, new actions shall be commenced and filed therein, and all causes, other than those under the jurisdiction of the United States, pending in the courts existing on the date of admission, shall be transferred to the proper state court as though commenced, filed, or lodged in those courts in the first instance, except as otherwise provided by law.

SECTION 18

Territorial assets and liabilities. The debts and liabilities of the Territory of Alaska shall be assumed and paid by the State, and debts owed to the Territory shall be collected by the State. Assets and records of the Territory shall become the property of the State.

SECTION 19

First reapportionment. The first reapportionment of the house of representatives shall be made immediately following the official reporting of the 1960 decennial census, or after the first regular legislative session if the session occurs thereafter, notwithstanding the provision as to time contained in Section 5 of Article VI. All other provisions of Article VI shall apply in the first reapportionment.

SECTION 20

State capital. The capital of the State of Alaska shall be at Juneau.

SECTION 21

Seal. The seal of the Territory, substituting the word "State" for "Territory," shall be the seal of the State.

SECTION 22

Flag. The flag of the Territory shall be the flag of the State.

SECTION 23

Special voting provision. Citizens who legally voted in the general election of November 4, 1924, and who meet the residence requirements for voting, shall be entitled to vote notwithstanding the provisions of Section 1 of Article V.

SECTION 24

Ordinances. Ordinance No. 1 on ratification of the constitution, Ordinance No. 2 on the Alaska-Tennessee Plan, and Ordinance No. 3 on the abolition of fish traps, adopted by the Alaska Constitutional Convention and appended to this constitution, shall be submitted to the voters and if ratified shall become effective as provided in each ordinance.

SECTION 25

Effective date. This constitution shall take effect immediately upon the admission of Alaska into the Union as a state.

SECTION 26

Appropriations for relocation of the capital. If a majority of those voting on the question at the general election in 1982 approve the ballot proposition for the total cost to the State of providing for relocation of the capital, no additional voter approval of appropriations for that purpose within the cost approved by the voters is required under the 1982 amendment limiting increases in appropriation (art. IX, sec. 16). [Approved in 1982.]

SECTION 27

Reconsideration of amendment limiting increases in appropriations. If the 1982 amendment limiting appropriation increases (art. IX, sec. 16) is adopted, the lieutenant governor shall cause the ballot title and proposition for the amendment to be placed on the ballot again at the general election in 1986. If the majority of those voting on the proposition in 1986 rejects the amendment, it shall be repealed. [Approved in 1982.]

SECTION 28

Application of amendment. The 1982 amendment limiting appropriation increases (art. IX, sec. 16) applies to appropriations made for fiscal year 1984 and thereafter.

Agreed upon by the delegates in Constitutional Convention assembled at the University of Alaska, the fifth day of February, in the year of our Lord one thousand nine hundred and fifty-six, and of the Independence of the United States the one hundred and eightieth.

Wm. A. Egan
President of the Convention

R. Rolland Armstrong
Dorothy J. Awes
Frank Barr
John C. Boswell
Seaborn J. Buckalew, Jr.
John B. Coghill
E. B. Collins
George D. Cooper
John M. Cross
Edward V. Davis
James P. Doogan
Truman C. Emberg
Helen Fischer
Victor Fischer
Douglas Gray
Thomas C. Harris
John S. Hellenthal
Mildred R. Hermann
Herb Hilscher
Jack Hinckel
James Hurley
Maurice T. Johnson
Yule F. Kilcher
Leonard H. King
William W. Knight
W. W. Laws
Eldor R. Lee
Maynard D. Londborg
Steve McCutcheon
George M. McLaughlin
Robert J. McNealy
John A. McNees
M. R. Marston
Irwin L. Metcalf
Leslie Nerland
James Nolan
Katherine D. Nordale
Frank Peratrovich
Chris Poulsen
Peter L. Reader
Burke Riley
Ralph J. Rivers
Victor C. Rivers
John H. Rosswog
B. D. Stewart
W. O. Smith
George Sundborg
Dora M. Sweeney
Warren A. Taylor
H. R. Vanderleest
M. J. Walsh
Barrie M. White
Ada B. Wien

ATTEST:
Thomas B. Stewart
Secretary of the Convention[94]

[94] Delegate Bob Robertson was the only delegate who did not sign the constitution.

Ordinance No. 1: Ratification of the Constitution

SECTION 1

Election. The Constitution for the State of Alaska agreed upon by the delegates to the Alaska Constitutional Convention on February 5, 1956, shall be submitted to the voters of Alaska for ratification or rejection at the territorial primary election to be held on April 24, 1956. The election shall be conducted according to existing laws regulating primary elections so far as applicable.

SECTION 2

Ballot. Each elector who offers to vote upon the constitution shall be given a ballot by the election judges which will be separate from the ballot on which candidates in the primary election are listed. Each of the propositions offered by the Alaska Constitutional Convention shall be set forth separately, but on the same ballot form. The first proposition shall be as follows: " Shall the Constitution for the State of Alaska prepared and agreed upon by the Alaska Constitutional Convention be adopted?"

Yes____ No____

SECTION 3

Canvass. The returns of this election shall be made to the governor of the Territory of Alaska, and shall be canvassed in substantially the manner provided by law for territorial elections.

SECTION 4

Acceptance and approval. If a majority of the votes cast on the proposition favor the constitution, then the constitution, shall be deemed to be ratified by the people of Alaska to become effective as provided in the constitution.

SECTION 5

Submission of constitution. Upon ratification of the constitution, the governor of the Territory shall forthwith transmit a certified copy of the constitution to the President of the United States for submission to the Congress, together with a statement of the votes cast for and against ratification.

Ordinance No. 2: Alaska-Tennessee Plan

SECTION 1

Statement of purpose. The election of senators and a representative to serve in the Congress of the United States being necessary and proper to prepare for the admission of Alaska as a state of the Union, the following sections are hereby ordained, pursuant to Chapter 46, SLA [Session Laws of Alaska] 1955.

SECTION 2

Ballot. Each elector who offers to vote upon the ratification of the constitution may, upon the same ballot, vote on a second proposition, which shall be as follows:

> "Shall Ordinance Number Two (Alaska-Tennessee Plan) of the Alaska Constitutional Convention, calling for the immediate election of two United States Senators and one United States Representative, be adopted?"
>
> Yes___No___

SECTION 3

Approval. Upon ratification of the constitution by the people of Alaska and separate approval of this ordinance by a majority of all votes cast for and against it, the remainder of this ordinance shall become effective.

SECTION 4

Election of senators and representative. Two United States senators and one United States representative shall be chosen at the 1956 general election.

SECTION 5

Terms. One senator shall be chosen for the regular term expiring on January 3, 1963, and the other for an initial short term expiring on January 3, 1961, unless when they are seated the Senate prescribes other expiration dates. The representative shall be chosen for the regular term of two years expiring January 3, 1959.

SECTION 6

Qualifications. Candidates for senators and representative shall have the qualifications prescribed in the Constitution of the United States and shall be qualified voters of Alaska.

SECTION 7

Other office holding. Until the admission of Alaska as a state, the senators and representative may also hold or be nominated and elected to other offices of the United States or of the Territory of Alaska, provided that no person may receive compensation for more than one office.

SECTION 8

Election procedure. Except as provided herein, the laws of the Territory governing elections to the office of Delegate to Congress shall, to the extent applicable, govern the election of the senators and representative. Territorial and other officials shall perform their duties with reference to this election accordingly.

SECTION 9

Independent candidates. Persons not representing any political party may become independent candidates for the offices of senator or representative by filing applications in the manner provided in Section 38-5-10, ACLA [Alaska Compiled Laws Annotated] 1949, insofar as applicable. Applications must be filed in the office of the director of finance of the Territory on or before June 30, 1956.

SECTION 10

Party nominations. Party nominations for senators and representative shall, for this election only, be made by party conventions in the manner prescribed in Section 38-4-11, ACLA 1949, for filling a vacancy in a party nomination occurring after a primary election. The names of the candidates nominated shall be certified by the chairman and secretary of the central committee of each political party to the director of finance of the Territory on or before June 30, 1956.

SECTION 11

Certification. The director of finance shall certify the names of all candidates for senators and representatives to the clerks of court by July 15, 1956. The clerks of court shall cause the names to be printed on the official ballot for the general election. Independent candidates shall be identified as provided in Section 38-5-10, ACLA 1949. Candidates nominated at party conventions shall be identified with appropriate party designations as is provided by law for nominations at primary elections.

SECTION 12

Ballot form; who is elected. The ballot form shall group separately the candidates seeking the regular senate term, those seeking the short senate term, and candidates for representative. The candidate for each office receiving the largest number of votes cast for that office shall be elected.

SECTION 13

Duties and emoluments. The duties and emoluments of the offices of senator and representative shall be as prescribed by law.

SECTION 14

Convention assistance. The president of the Alaska Constitutional Convention, or a person designated by him, may assist in carrying out the purposes of this ordinance. The unexpended and unobligated funds appropriated to the Alaska Constitutional Convention by Chapter 46, SLA 1955, may be used to defray expenses attributable to the referendum and the election required by this ordinance.

SECTION 15

Alternate effective dates. If the Congress of the United States seats the senators and representative elected pursuant to this ordinance and approves the constitution before the first election of state officers, then Section 25 of Article XV shall be void and shall be replaced by the following:

> "The provisions of the constitution applicable to the first election of state officers shall take effect immediately upon the admission of Alaska into the Union as a State. The remainder of the constitution shall take effect when the elected governor takes office."

Ordinance No. 3: Abolition of Fish Traps

SECTION 1

Ballot. Each elector who offers to vote upon the ratification of the constitution may, upon the same ballot, vote on a third proposition, which shall be as follows:

"Shall Ordinance Number Three of the Alaska Constitutional Convention, prohibiting the use of fish traps for the taking of salmon for commercial purposes in the coastal waters of the State, be adopted?"

Yes____ No____

SECTION 2

Effect of referendum. If the constitution shall be adopted by the electors and if a majority of all the votes cast for and against this ordinance favor its adoption, then the following shall become operative upon the effective date of the constitution:

"As a matter of immediate public necessity, to relieve economic distress among individual fishermen and those dependent upon them for a livelihood, to conserve the rapidly dwindling supply of salmon in Alaska, to insure fair competition among those engaged in commercial fishing, and to make manifest the will of the people of Alaska, the use of fish traps for the taking of salmon for commercial purposes is hereby prohibited in all the coastal waters of the State."

■ APPENDIX

Proposals to Amend the Alaska Constitution

Election Date	Subject of Amendment	Provisions Affected	Vote Totals	
			For	Against
8/23/66	Residency requirement to vote for president	art. V, sec. 1	36,667	12,383
8/27/68	Commission on judicial qualifications	art. IV, sec. 10	32,481	12,823
8/27/68	Compensation of judicial qualification commission	art. IV, sec. 13	27,156	17,467
8/25/70	English eliminated as requisite for voting	art. V, sec. 1	34,079	32,578
8/25/70	Secretary of state designated as lieutenant governor	art. III, secs. 7–11, 13–15, 25; art. XI, secs. 2–6; art. XIII, sees. 1, 3; art. XV, sec. 9	46,102	18,781
8/25/70	Chief justice election by supreme court	art. IV, sec. 2	44,055	19,583
8/25/70	Term of office for judicial system administrator	art. IV, sec. 16	43,462	18,651
8/22/72	Residency requirement for voting	art. V, sec. 1	31,130	20,745
8/22/72	Prohibition of sexual discrimination	art. 1, sec. 3	43,281	10,278
8/22/72	Right of privacy	art. 1, sec. 22	45,539	7,303
8/22/72	Eliminate city representation on borough assemblies	art. X, sec. 4	30,132	19,354
8/22/72	Limited-entry fisheries	art. VIE, sec. 15	39,837	10,761
8/27/74	Voting on constitutional amendments at general election	art. XIII, sec. 1	56,017	20,403
11/2/76	Action on veto of bills	art. II, secs. 9,16	71,829	39,980
11/2/76	Permanent fund from non-renewable resource revenue	art. DC, sees. 7,15	75,588	38,518
11/2/76	*Administration and review of state land disposals*	art. VIII, sec. 10	46,652	64,744
11/2/76	*Direct financial aid to students*	art. VII, sec. 1	54,636	64,211
11/7/78	*Powers of legislative interim committees*	art. II, sec. 11	48,078	68,403
11/4/80	*Legislative annulment of regulations*	art. II (new section)	58,808	82,010
11/4/80	*Disqualifications of legislators*	art. II, sec. 25	47,054	99,705
11/4/80	*Interim and special legislative committees*	art. II, sec. 11	41,868	102,270
11/4/80	*Appointment and confirmation of members*	art. II, sec. 26	56,316	90,056
11/2/82	Veterans' housing bond authority	art. IX, sec. 8	111,460	69,497

(Continued)

Election Date	Subject of Amendment	Provisions Affected	Vote Totals	
			For	Against
11/2/82	Changes in commission on judicial qualification	art. IV, sec. 10	123,172	53,424
11/2/82	Limiting increases in appropriation	art. IX, sec. 16; art. XV, sees. 26, 27, 28	110,669	71,531
11/6/84	*Legislative annulment of administrative regulations*	art. II (new section)	91,171	98,855
11/6/84	Limiting length of regular legislative sessions	art. II, sec. 8	150,999	46,099
11/4/86	*Legislative annulment of administrative regulations*	art. II (new section)	65,176	94,299
11/8/88	Resident hiring preference	art. I, sec. 23	162,997	30,650
11/6/90	Budget reserve fund	art. IX, sec. 17	124,280	63,307
11/8/94	Rights of crime victims and criminal administration	art. I, secs. 12, 24	78,858	27,641
11/8/94	Right to keep and bear arms	art. 1, sec. 19	153,300	57,636

Note: Proposals in italics were rejected by the voters.
Source: State of Alaska Legislative Research Agency, September 1992; Division of Elections, 1996.

BIBLIOGRAPHIC ESSAY

Although Alaska's Constitution is the second youngest, being only 40 years old in 1996, one can find a good body of materials on its development and interpretation. The following sections highlight the major sources of information.

ALASKA CONSTITUTIONAL ANTECEDENTS

A large number of studies describe and explain Alaska's development under Russian and American rule. Most comprehensive in its coverage of Alaska's history is Claus-M. Naske and Herman Slotnick's *Alaska: A History of the Forty-Ninth State*,2d ed. (Norman: University of Oklahoma Press, 1987). Examining the early years of American rule in Alaska are Ronald Jensen, *The Alaska Purchase and Russian-American Relations* (Seattle: University of Washington Press, 1975); Ted C. Hinckley, *The Americanization of Alaska*, 1867–1897 (Palo Alto, CA: Pacific Books, 1972); Jeannette Paddock Nichols, *Alaska: A History of Its Administration, Exploitation, and Industrial Development during Its First Half Century under the Rule of the United States* (New York: Russell and Russell, 1963); and William R. Hunt, *Distant Justice: Policing the Alaskan Frontier* (Norman: University of Oklahoma Press, 1987).

Several good studies describe the development and dynamics of the statehood movement after World War II. Ernest Gruening, territorial governor of Alaska, wrote *The State of Alaska* (New York: Random House, 1954) and an account entitled *The Battle for Alaska Statehood* (College: University of Alaska Press, 1967). The most thorough account of the statehood movement is found in Claus-M. Naske's *An Interpretative History of Alaska Statehood* (Anchorage: Alaska Northwest Publishing Company, 1973). Naske is also the author of biographies of the state's first two senators, who were strongly involved in the statehood movement: "Ernest Gruening: Alaska's Territorial Governor, 1939 to 1953" (unpublished 1990), and *Edward Lewis Bob Bartlett of Alaska . . . A Life in Politics* (Fairbanks: University of Alaska Press, 1973).

ALASKA CONSTITUTIONAL CONVENTION

A second source of information on the Alaska Constitution is especially rich: background materials prepared for the convention delegates, minutes of the proceedings, and reflections by participants, either soon after the convention or at anniversaries and other milestone events.

Preparatory research for the convention was done by staff of the Public Administration Service (PAS), a nonprofit government consulting organization of Chicago. PAS consultants prepared a series of papers for the use of convention delegates. The papers were mailed to all delegates before the convention convened and were available for use, and often referred to, in the proceedings. They are found in a three-volume set entitled *Constitutional Studies* (Chicago: PAS, 1955). In addition, George Rogers prepared *A Handbook on Alaska Regionalism* for the use of delegates to the convention (Juneau: Office of the Governor, November 21, 1955).

The best single documentary source on the Alaska Constitution remains the *Minutes of the Daily Proceedings of the Alaska Constitutional Convention* (Juneau: Alaska Legislative Council, 1965), in six volumes. In addition, convention committees produced reports, and the Style and Drafting Committee produced commentaries on the constitution, which are found as appendices to the proceedings.

Extensive newspaper coverage of the convention, particularly by the *Fairbanks Daily News-Miner,* provided a good contemporary record. Participants, too, reported their observations in monographs. Most comprehensive and informative is Victor Fischer's *Alaska's Constitutional Convention* (Fairbanks: University of Alaska Press, 1975). Fischer was a delegate to the convention, and at the time of the writing of his observations, he was director of the university's Institute of Social, Economic, and Government Research. Gerald E. Bowkett reported the human story to the convention in his *Reaching for a Star: The Final Campaign for Alaska Statehood* (Fairbanks: Epicenter Press, 1989).

Examples of other reflections on the convention and constitution from participants include George Sundborg's speech, "Who We Were: A Tribute to My Fellow Delegates," at the 35th reunion of the Alaska Constitutional Convention, April 26, 1991, Juneau (author's files); Judge Thomas Stewart's interview on the convention and constitution, March 16, 1990, Juneau (author's files); and the comments of participants reported in Claus-M. Naske, John S. Whitehead, and William Schneider's *Alaska Statehood: The Memory of the Battle and the Evaluation of the Present by Those Who Lived It* (Fairbanks: Alaska Statehood Commission, 1981).

In 1979–1980, the Alaska State Legislature established a joint committee to consider whether a new constitutional convention should be convened in Alaska. The committee commissioned constitutional convention delegate Victor Fischer to report his observations on the Hawaii constitutional convention, held in 1978, which revised that state's constitution. Fischer's report, "A New Constitutional Convention for Alaska? The Lesson of Hawaii," presents critical observations on the process of revising state constitutions. The joint committee also held hearings on whether Alaska should convene a convention to revise the state convention. Both the hearings transcript (March 10, 1980) and

Fischer's report are available from the Alaska Legislature, interim Committee on the Constitutional Convention, Juneau, Alaska.

ALASKA CONSTITUTIONAL INTERPRETATION

Primary interpretations of Alaska's constitution are found in cases of the Alaska Supreme Court, the court of appeals, superior courts, and, for cases of federal-state controversy, the U.S. Supreme Court.

Briefly, from 1963 to 1971, the *Alaska Law Journal* followed developments in Alaska law. More comprehensive and thorough interpretations of Alaska constitutional law, however, are found in the *Alaska Law Review*. Because Alaska has no law school, the review was initially (starting in 1972) published jointly with the University of California at Los Angeles (UCLA) as the *UCLA-Alaska Law Review*. Since 1984, the *Alaska Law Review* has been published by the Duke University School of Law.

Gerald Sharp's interpretations of the home rule provisions of the Alaska Constitution appeared in 1973 ("Home Rule in Alaska: Clash between the Constitution and the Court," *UCLA-Alaska Law Review* 3, no. 1 [1973]: 1–54). Attorney Jeffrey Feldman wrote two articles for the review on constitutional developments in criminal procedure: "Search and Seizure in Alaska: A Comprehensive Review," *UCLA-Alaska Law Review* 7, no. 1 (1977): 75–122; and "Criminal Procedure in Alaska," *UCLA-Alaska Law Review* 9, no. 2 (1980): 109–142. John F. Grossbauer chronicled the development of the right to privacy in "Note: Alaska's Right to Privacy Ten Years after *Ravin v. State:* Developing a Jurisprudence of Privacy," *Alaska Law Review* 2, no. 1 (1985): 159–183. Professor Michael B. Wise surveyed equal protection developments in "Northern Lights—Equal Protection Analysis in Alaska," *Alaska Law Review* 3, no. 1 (1986): 1–48. Professor Stephen K. Green focused on freedom of religion in "Freedom of Religion in Alaska: Interpreting the Alaska Constitution," *Alaska Law Review* 5, no. 2 (1988): 237–262. Constitutional law scholar Ronald L. Nelson provides a fine summary of the Alaska Supreme Court's development of independent standards for the protection of individual rights in "Welcome to the 'Last Frontier' Professor Gardner: Alaska's Independent Approach to State Constitutional Interpretation," *Alaska Law Review* 12, no. 1 (1995): 1–41.

On occasion, other law reviews publish articles on Alaska constitutional law, for example, Peter J. Galie's "State Constitutional Guarantees and the Alaska Supreme Court: Criminal Procedural Rights and the New Federalism 1960–1981," *Gonzaga Law Review* 18, no. 3 (1982–1983): 193–228.

The single most authoritative and comprehensive interpretation of the constitution is Gordon S. Harrison's *Alaska's Constitution: A Citizen's Guide* (Juneau: Alaska Legislative Agency). The first and second editions of Harrison's study were published in 1982 and 1986, and the third, broadly expanded, version appeared in 1992. Harrison's academic background and experience working for both the executive and legislative branches in Juneau have allowed him to connect constitutional interpretations with their effect on state government policies.

Other, shorter academic analyses give readers different perspectives on the meaning and significance of the Alaska Constitution. Victor Fischer wrote the chapter "Alaska's Constitution" for *Alaska State Government and Politics,* edited by Gerald A. McBeath and Thomas A. Morehouse (Fairbanks: University of Alaska Press, 1987). Thomas A. Morehouse wrote the chapter entitled "A Model Constitution" in the most recent study of Alaska's political development, *Alaska Politics and Government,* by Gerald A. McBeath and Thomas A. Morehouse (Lincoln: University of Nebraska Press, 1994).

Despite the state's short history, Alaska's constitutional development has been reported in a variety of different sources and from a range of perspectives.

TABLE OF CASES

A

B

C

D

E

F

G

H

I

J

K

L

M

N

O

P

R

S

T

U

V

W

Y

Z

■ INDEX

About the Author

GERALD A. McBEATH is Professor of Political Science, University of Alaska Fairbanks.

www.ingramcontent.com/pod-product-compliance
Ingram Content Group UK Ltd.
Pitfield, Milton Keynes, MK11 3LW, UK
UKHW021135160926
475595UK00020B/71

9 780199 778294